Pope Francis

His Life and Thought

Mario I. Aguilar

The Lutterworth Press

*To Gabriela Benítez, Glenda Tello
and Sara Aguilar*

The Lutterworth Press
P.O. Box 60
Cambridge
CB1 2NT
United Kingdom

www.lutterworth.com
publishing@lutterworth.com

ISBN: 978 0 7188 9342 2

British Library Cataloguing in Publication Data
A record is available from the British Library

Contents

Acknowledgments

Every book is like an empty canvas, or a tapestry in which subject, colour, style and aesthetic narrative are the choice of the artist. However, during the time in which the artist works, he is influenced by people, beauty, suffering and the lives that surround him or her. Thus, my acknowledgements are to those who have made this process of filling this particular canvas fruitful, painful, and controversial.

My gratitude goes out to each one of a countless number of academics, journalists, Jesuits and researchers who took an interest in this biography and showered me with suggestions, citations and bibliographies, including Jonathan Ablard (Ithaca College), Martin Edwin Andersen, Diego Armus (Swarthmore College), Benjamin Bryce (University of Toronto), Barry Carr (La Trobe University), Larry Clayton (Alabama), Henry Flores (St Mary's University, Texas), Michael Goebel, Robert Austin Henry (University of Queensland), Ben Nobbs-Thiessen (Emory University), Pablo Palomino (University of California at Berkeley), Emilia Perassi, Albert Schorsch (University of Illinois at Chicago) and Peter Stern (University of Massachusetts).

I am particularly grateful to Diego Armus who sent me an electronic version of his 1983 edition of the *Manuale dello emigrante italiano all' Argentina*, originally prepared by Arrigo de Zettiry in Rome in 1913, to Fr Fernando Montes SJ, rector of the Universidad Alberto Hurtado, Santiago, Chile and to Fr Gero McLoughlin SJ (Edinburgh) for their memories of Jesuit formation and help with aspects of canon law.

Research in Buenos Aires and Santiago was made possible by a research grant from the Carnegie Trust for the Universities of Scotland and additional funding from the Deans' Fund of St Mary's College, University of St Andrews. I am also grateful to David Baird, who read through the manuscript and made suggestions of a literary nature.

I dedicate this biography to three Catholic women who have influenced my own understanding and practice of Catholicism as an Oblate of the Camaldolese Benedictines: Gabriela Benítez, Glenda Tello and Sara Aguilar.

St Andrews, December 2013

Introduction

In one of the most compelling and contentious biographies of the twentieth century, Shirley Du Boulay, writing about the Catholic monk Swami Abhishiktananda, argued that his history was 'a story of transformation': 'the monk became a *sanyasi*, and Dom Henri became Swami Abhishiktananda'.[1] Biographical writers often highlight continuities, personal consistency rather than personal contradiction. However, this work explores both the continuities and discontinuities in the personal history of the Argentinean Jorge Mario Bergoglio from his birth until his election as Pope Francis. On 13 March 2013 Bergoglio, born in Buenos Aires on 17 December 1936, was chosen as the 266th bishop of Rome, and the pope of the Roman Catholic community throughout the world. This history of Pope Francis is not primarily about the public figure, Pope Francis, but more about the Argentinean, Jorge Mario Bergoglio, who became a priest, archbishop of Buenos Aires, and later a cardinal in the Roman Catholic Church. Finally he left his Argentinean roots in order to live within an international pastoral and theological milieu, that of the globalised Roman Catholic Church.

This work explores and outlines the history of Bergoglio, an Argentinean son of Italian immigrants, who became a Jesuit and was a Jesuit provincial during the difficult time of the rule of the military junta in Argentina. The decisions he had to make at this time were very testing.[2] Bergoglio was not a liberation theologian, but a confessor and parish priest, who felt very close to the people to

---

1 Shirley Du Boulay, 'Introduction' to *Swami Abhishiktananda: Essential Writings*, Maryknoll, NY: Orbis, 2006, p. 19.

2 I share Monica Furlong's approach when writing the biography of Thomas Merton: 'I have avoided the reverential approach, have tried to see him as the normal man he was, with his fair share, perhaps more than his fair share, of human frailties', *Merton: A Biography*. San Francisco CA: Harper & Row, 1980, p. xx.

whom he ministered and who, because of his health, did not venture into missionary work in other countries and therefore did not gain the international experience of most Jesuits. He completed all his studies in Chile and Argentina, but did not complete his doctorate in theology or other related fields as most Jesuits do. His theology was traditional and conservative, but his pastoral openness to other people enormous, warm and empathic. As bishop, he was extremely close to the people of Buenos Aires. This closeness demonstrates his traditional spirituality and popular religiosity rather than political actions. He was able to move thousands of people, who saw in Bergoglio a shepherd who intentionally sought out all types and classes of persons from the different social spheres of Buenos Aires. In so doing Bergoglio brought the Catholic Church out of its self-centeredness, and in the periphery of society he found the centre of his concerns. He shared very similar experiences to Archbishop Óscar Romero of El Salvador, a traditional priest who was changed and educated by the people around him, and who wrestled with those challenges in prayer.[1]

There have been many biographies of Pope Francis in which history and myth have been mixed with personal opinion; good contributions, but some of them devoid of references to primary textual sources (the writings of Bergoglio).[2] This work, written by a Latin American theologian and historian of the Church in Latin America, explores the life and theological thought of Bergoglio through primary and secondary Spanish sources and in the context of the Latin American history that challenged Bergoglio and shaped his theological thought.

In the writing of any biography, the biographer, in the words of Monica Furlong, 'has to maintain equilibrium, like a tightrope walker, discovering a balance and a kind of truth between all

---

1   James R. Brockman SJ, 'Introduction' to *Archbishop Oscar Romero: A Shepherd's Diary*, London: Catholic Fund for Overseas Development (CAFOD) and Catholic Institute for International Relations (CIIR), 1993, p. 11.

2   Biographical contributions have been taken from the following works: Saverio Gaeta, *Papa Francisco: Su vida y sus desafíos*, Buenos Aires: San Pablo, 2013; Evangelina Himitian, *Francisco: El Papa de la gente*, Buenos Aires: Aguilar, 2013; José Medina, *Francisco: El Papa de todos*, Buenos Aires: Bonum, 2013; Sergio Rubin and Francesca Ambrogetti, *El Jesuita: La historia de Francisco, el Papa argentino*, Buenos Aires: Javier Vergara, 2010; Paul Vallely, *Pope Francis: Untying the Knots*, London: Bloomsbury, 2013; and Mariano de Vedia, *Francisco, el Papa del pueblo: La primera biografía del hombre que quiere cambiar la Iglesia*, Buenos Aires: Planeta, 2013.

extremes'.[1] However, Bergoglio consistently demonstrated his concern for the poor and the marginalised, for the fostering of a prophetic and servant church, and for a church in full dialogue with the world and with other faiths. Those without faith, and those with faith in material comfort and the fashions of a globalised world, are not excluded. Bergoglio fundamentally sees the world as good because it is made and nurtured by God, and human beings are co-pilgrims in the journeys of hope and sorrow. Humans must question the world of politics, of economics and particularly the world of social injustice, as Bergoglio did in twentieth-century Argentina.

Annuntio vobis gaudium magnum:
Habemus Papam!
Eminentissimum ac Reverendissimum Dominum
Dominum Georgium Marium Sanctae Romanae Ecclesiae
Cardinalem Bergoglio
Qui sibi nomen imposiut Franciscum.

These were the words read by Cardinal Jean-Louis Tauran, a 67-year-old man fighting to control his Parkinson's disease, who gave the good news to Rome, to the Catholic Church and to the world: a new pope had been elected and a new bishop of Rome was about to greet his diocesan flock. The news had begun to spread with the appearance of the white smoke coming out of the chimney of the Sistine Chapel, where the conclave had been in session for only two days.[2] On the evening of Tuesday 13 March 2013, the 115 cardinals elected Jorge Mario Bergoglio, a cardinal from Argentina and archbishop of Buenos Aires, as the 266th pope of the Catholic Church.[3] A moment of silence followed the public announcement. The name of Cardinal Bergoglio was not familiar to the general

---

1   Monica Furlong, *Merton: A Biography*. San Francisco: Harper & Row, 1980, p. xiv.
2   Pius XII was elected after 3 ballots, Juan XXIII after 11 ballots, Paul VI after 5 ballots, John Paul I after 4 ballots, John Paul II after 8 ballots, Benedict XVI after 4 ballots and Francis after 5 ballots.
3   For a history of the other 265 popes, their controversies and their elections, see Eamon Duffy, *Saints and Sinners: A History of the Popes*, Yale University Press, 2006; P.G. Maxwell-Stuart, *Chronicles of the Popes: The Reign by Reign Record of the Papacy from St Peter to the Present (Chronicles)*, Thames & Hudson, 1997; John Julius Norwich, *Absolute Monarchs; A History of the Papacy*, Random House Trade Paperbacks, 2012; John W. O'Malley SJ, *The History of the Popes: From Peter to the Present*, Sheed & Ward, 2011; and Claudio Rendina, *The Popes: Histories and Secrets*, Seven Locks Press, 2002.

public; he was not in the list of frontrunners expected to succeed Benedict XVI as the leader of 1.2 billion Catholics.[1] Later, the fact of his low public profile became a point of ongoing discussion and surprise because, during the ballots to elect Benedict XVI in 2005, Bergoglio had come second in one ballot with forty votes. At that time Bergoglio had implored his supporters among the cardinals to vote for Cardinal Ratzinger in order to provide continuity to the long years served by John Paul II as Supreme Pontiff. Bergoglio's election as Pope Francis followed the resignation of Benedict XVI in February 2013 when he surprised Catholics all over the world by stepping down on account of his frailty and age. Arrangements for a conclave in March 2013 were quickly made after his announcement, as well as arrangements for the residency of two popes in Rome.

Jubilation and great emotion met the customary appearance on the balcony by the new pope to greet the Catholic world and give his first papal blessing. Benedict XVI's resignation had only just been accepted, and the new pope had been quickly elected. The new successor of Peter the Apostle was an Argentinean cardinal who had chosen the papal name Francis for St Francis of Assisi, the saint of the poor and friend of animals. Days after his election, Pope Francis told the media at the Vatican that the name had entered his head after he was given a two-thirds majority of the vote and a round of applause from the cardinals. At that moment, Cardinal Claudio Hummes, Emeritus Archbishop of Sao Paulo and Emeritus Prefect of the Sacred Congregation for the Clergy, embraced and kissed him, saying: 'do not forget the poor'. Cardinal Bergoglio thought of St Francis because of his relation to the world of the poor and because St Francis was as a man of peace, a value that had been stressed by Bergoglio in his previous messages to the Argentinean nation.[2] Cardinal Bergoglio was not only an Argentinean but a Jesuit, and the Latin American press, expressing a general public sentiment, very quickly embraced him as a Latin American citizen, loved and accepted by Catholics of all nation states in Latin America.[3]

---

1   While the Vatican commentators very quickly searched their bibliographical notes they were all taken by surprise by Bergoglio's appointment and the investigation of Bergoglio's history started in earnest the following day.

2   Papa Francisco, Encuentro con los representantes de los Medios de Comunicación, Sala Pablo VI, Vatican City 16 March 2013, see also Cardenal Jorge Mario Bergoglio, Homilías, Te Deum, Catedral Metropolitana de Buenos Aires, 25 May 2010 and *En él solo la esperanza: Ejercicios Espirituales a los Obispos Españoles*, Madrid: Biblioteca de Autores Cristianos, 2013.

3   See for example 'El nuevo Papa es latinoamericano: El argentino Jorge

Born in Buenos Aires on 17 December 1936, Cardinal Bergoglio entered the Jesuit order on 11 March 1958 and was ordained a priest on 13 December 1969. On 31 July 1973, Bergoglio was appointed provincial of the Jesuits of Argentina, a role that he filled for six years. A novice master, parish priest, confessor and university professor, Bergoglio was ordained auxiliary bishop of Buenos Aires in 1992, became archbishop of Buenos Aires in 1998, and a cardinal of the Catholic Church in 2001.

After his election, Pope Francis greeted the crowds at St Peter's Square in the Italian language with the simple and warm sentiment of 'Good Evening'. The pope 'from far away', as he presented himself to the crowd, asked those present to pray for him; he observed a moment of silence for prayer and, after imparting his papal blessing, bid them good night and a good sleep. Pope Francis has said that, while he regularly sleeps only five hours or so, his greatest penance is to go to bed after midnight. There is no doubt that the first Latin American pope in the history of the Catholic Church left millions wanting to hear more.

Latin American heads of state stressed the fact that for the first time the pope was from the Americas, or, more broadly, from the southern hemisphere, where the majority of the world's Catholics live. Thus, on the day of the papal inauguration, 18 March 2013, the Argentinean president could not stop repeating that the pope was Argentinean. The Brazilian liberation theologian, Frei Betto, replied with the words of an old rivalry: while the pope is Argentinean God is Brazilian. The pope made his first visit outside Europe in July 2013 to Brazil for the Youth World Congress.[1] The Brazilian President Dilma Rouseff, representing the country with the most Catholics in the world (123 million), met Francis at the private library of the Apostolic Palace to discuss Francis' visit to Brazil, and she similarly joked with the press, suggesting that Argentina was very blessed for having a pope but that God was Brazilian.[2] President Piñera of Chile was quick to remark that Francis had spent some years in Chile, and had accepted an invitation to visit Chile in the near future.

The evening before Francis' inauguration in Rome, there was a vigil at the Plaza de Mayo in Buenos Aires – the very square where

---

Mario Bergoglio', *La Nación* (Chile), 13 March 2013.

1 'Elección del Papa Francisco despierta vieja rivalidad Argentina-Brasil', AFP, 14 March 2013.

2 'Dilma: "El papa es argentino pero Dios es brasileño"', *La Nación* (Argentina), 20 March 2013.

Francis lived for a few years – in which an atmosphere charged with the prayers and the songs of thousands was broadcast worldwide by Argentinean television. Among those present for the occasion were young people from the shanty towns where Pope Francis worked and served every weekend while archbishop, as well as priests, known as 'curas villeros', who live a humble and dedicated life among the poor of Buenos Aires.[1] One of them, Fr José María Di Paola (el 'Padre Pepe'), reflected on the occasion, saying: 'One of the teachings that the new pope left us was that this place is not the centre. The Plaza de Mayo is not the centre. Pope Francis taught us that the centre is the periphery, the villas (shanty towns), where people are excluded. We hope that the wonderful things he did here will start to happen in the Catholic Church all over the world'.[2]

There is no doubt that the pope from Latin American fuelled the imagination of the world, and that the spirit of change – full of Francis' hope, happiness, closeness, warmth and affection – was associated with Latin America. Pope Francis spent most of his life in Argentina, and therefore it would be difficult to understand his religious experience without understanding the changes and developments that took place in Latin America after the Second Vatican Council. Also important for understanding him is a knowledge of the Latin American Bishops' conferences of Medellin (1968), Puebla (1979), Santo Domingo (1992) and Aparecida (2007), as well as the political developments in Argentina since the 1970s, particularly the Argentinean 'dirty war' that took place during the time of the military junta rule of Argentina (from 1976 to 1983). Pope Francis, as a Latin American and as a pope, can be best understood, personally, intellectually and theologically, by considering his role in changing the Catholic Church in Latin America over the past fifty years, and the social and religious history of this period in Latin America that affected and changed him. In the words of the Brazilian president, it is

1   Silvina Premat, *Curas villeros: De Mugica al padre Pepe*. Buenos Aires: Editorial Sudamericana, 2010 and Jorge Vernazza, *Para comprender una vida con los pobres: los curas villeros*. Buenos Aires: Editorial Guadalupe, 1989.

2   'La emoción del padre Pepe y los curas villeros en la Plaza de Mayo', *La Nación* (Argentina), 20 March 2013. Fr Di Paola has received the recognition of many for his work with the poor, for example, he received a donation from the profits of the sale of each copy of Sergio Rubin and Francesca Ambrogetti, *El Jesuita: La historia de Francisco, el Papa argentino*, Buenos Aires: Ediciones B Argentina, 2010. For a biography of Fr Di Paola see Silvina Premat, *Pepe: El cura de la villa*, Buenos Aires: Editorial Sudamericana, 2013.

clear that Pope Francis is a person 'with a significant option for the poor'.[1] It is this theme of the poor, and the enormous concern for the poor shown by the Church in Latin America, that one must study in order to understand the pastoral outlook of Bergoglio. However, a word of warning: he was not strongly influenced by the so-called 'liberation theologies'; he preferred the currents of popular religion, and, as a Jesuit provincial, did not go as far as other Jesuits, such as those of El Salvador, in the reform of schools, universities and Jesuit communities in Argentina.

Vatican II and Latin America

In 1956 the Latin American bishops, led by Chilean Bishop Manuel Larraín of Talca, created an organisation called the Latin American Episcopal Conference (CELAM). This organisation would allow all Latin American bishops to exchange views on the pastoral issues of their related countries, and would also provide some pastoral and biblical support in the form of further education for their clergy and a select number of lay people. The first meeting of CELAM took place in Brazil, pioneering a pastoral change that would embrace the whole of the Catholic Church when, in 1959, Pope John XXIII called for a council (Vatican II). Vatican II would foster the formation of local bishops' conferences in every country as well as in Africa, Asia and Latin America.[2]

These events coincided with the start of the period of novitiate of the future Pope Francis, which commenced on 11 March 1958 in the Jesuit novitiate of Villa Devoto. In the following years, Bergoglio studied within the Jesuit community in Chile, returning to Buenos Aires in 1963 to complete his licentiate in philosophy at the Colegio San José in San Miguel. By the time Bergoglio had completed his studies in philosophy and had become a teacher at the Colegio de la Inmaculada Concepción in Santa Fe (1964-1965), the Second Vatican Council had already made significant changes to the outlook and self-understanding of the Catholic Church. These changes, triggering an openness to the world and to other faiths, strongly influenced the early years of the young Jesuit Bergoglio's ministry, and later were to be manifested in his pastoral role as archbishop of Buenos Aires.

1 'Papa Francisco se reunió por media hora con la presidenta de Brasil', *La Nación* (Chile), 20 March 2013.
2 For a reflection on this moment fifty years later see Joseph A. Komonchak, 'Convening Vatican II: John XXIII Calls for a Council', *Commonweal,* 12 February 1999.

Two issues became central at Vatican II: conscience and human dignity. Without reflection on those two theological issues – the freedom of conscience given by God to all human beings, and the assertion of the dignity of each human being made in the image of God – further discussion about an inclusive church would have been extremely difficult. Those two concepts created a clear link between the Vatican II document on other religions, *In Our Age (Nostra Aetate)*, the *Constitution on the Church (Lumen Gentium)*, the *Pastoral Constitution on the Church in the Modern World (Gaudium et Spes)*, and the *Declaration on Religious Liberty (Dignitatis Humanae)*. They were central to the development of the order of the Jesuits in Argentina at a time when such communities were still somewhat inward-looking. This was due to an educational model of pastoral work that primarily served the Argentinean elites, and the fact of the close alignment of the Church with the Argentinean state. Minority organisations of the Argentinean Church such as the Jesuits put the developments of Vatican II into action with great enthusiasm.

The opening of the Catholic Church to the world – and particularly towards other Christian churches and other faiths – was signalled by *Dignitatis Humanae* (7 December 1965), a document partly prepared by the American theologian John Courtney Murray SJ. It safeguarded the religious freedoms of the individual by making them part of official Church teaching.[1] This was a complete reversal of Pius IX's policy: he had included all religious or political pluralism in his so-called *Syllabus of Errors*.[2] It was a change that was particularly needed by Catholics living in mostly Protestant societies such as the United States. *Dignitatis Humanae* argued that a state is not able to recognise the Church's authority, which flows from individual freedom rather than the establishment.[3] The platform for this change in doctrine, breaking with tradition from the time of Constantine, Justinian and Charlemagne, was the examination of the dignity of the human individual.[4] The right to individual freedom extends to all groups of believers and includes freedom of enquiry, association,

---

1   *Dignitatis Humanae* § 1-2; cf. John Paul II, *Essays on Religious Freedom*, Milwaukee: Catholic League on Religious and Civil Rights, 1984.

2   For a fuller commentary on *Dignitatis Humanae* see James Tunstead Burtchaell CSC, 'Religious Freedom (*Dignitatis Humanae*)' in Adrian Hastings, ed. *Modern Catholicism: Vatican II and After*, London: SPCK and NY: Oxford University Press, 1991, pp. 118-125.

3   *Dignitatis Humanae* § 6.

4   Owen Chadwick, *Catholicism and History: The Opening of the Vatican Archives*. Cambridge: Cambridge University Press, 1978.

communication, finance, public testimony, worship and common moral endeavour.[1] *Dignitatis Humanae* put a new, strong emphasis on individual conscience, stating that 'it is through this conscience that man sees and recognises the demands of the divine law'.[2]

Vatican II also established a magisterial principle of inclusion for the world religions that was based on a return to an inclusivist understanding of church, and a refreshed sense of the spirit of dialogue. Both concepts were outlined by Paul VI in the encyclical letter 'On the Church' (*Ecclesiam Suam*), promulgated on 6 August 1964.[3] The encyclical manifested a new openness, necessary to enhance the work of the Church. According to Cardinal F. König, President of the Secretariat for Nonbelievers, in an interview given to Vatican Radio before *Ecclesiam Suam* was approved by the council fathers, 'the Church was called to dialogue, but only in order to carry out its proper task, namely the saving proclamation of Christ'.[4]

The first of Paul VI's encyclicals, *Ecclesiam Suam* is divided into three parts dealing with self-awareness, renewal and dialogue, and it describes the Church's role as being 'to serve society'.[5] The Church must reflect 'on its own nature, the better to appreciate the divine plan which it is the Church's task to implement'.[6] The Church, according to Paul VI, belongs to the world, 'even though distinguished from it by its own altogether unique characteristics'.[7] Further, 'the Church is deeply rooted in the world'; 'it exists in the world and draws its members from the world'.[8] However, because it exists in the world it is bound to feel worldly tensions and pressures.[9] Thus it is necessary, according to Paul VI, to frequently revisit the Church's own existence in the scriptures and the apostolic tradition.[10]

---

1 *Dignitatis Humanae* § 4-7.
2 *Dignitatis Humanae* § 3.
3 Text available at http://www.vatican.va/holy_father/paul_vi/encyclicals/ documents/hf_p-vi_enc_06081964_ecclesiam_en.html
4 Ricardo Burigana and Giovanni Turbanti, 'The Intersession: Preparing the Conclusion of the Council' in Giuseppe Alberigo, ed. *History of Vatican II*, vol. IV *Church as Communion: Third Period and Intercession September 1964 – September 1965*, pp. 453-615 at p. 610, Maryknoll, NY: Orbis and Leuven: Peeters, 2003.
5 *Ecclesiam Suam* § 5.
6 *Ecclesiam Suam* § 18.
7 *Ecclesiam Suam* § 18.
8 *Ecclesiam Suam* § 26.
9 *Ecclesiam Suam* § 26.
10 *Ecclesiam Suam* § 26.

Paul VI considered two documents that had shed important light on the activities and the task of the Church in the past: the encyclical *Satis Cognitum* (Leo XIII, 1896) and the encyclical *Mystici Corporis* (Pius XII, 1943).[1] According to Paul VI, the strengthening of understanding of the Mystical Body of Christ, the Catholic Church, creates conditions in which a spiritual uplifting can come from a deep reflection on the nature of the union between Christ and his Church.[2] Further, this self-reflection can create a 'renewed discovery of its vital bond of union with Christ'.[3] However, for Paul VI, the nature of the Church is not a matter for speculative theology; it has to be lived, 'so that the faithful may have a kind of intuitive experience of it, even before they come to understand it clearly'.[4]

Time and again Paul VI stressed the importance of the conciliar deliberations on the nature of the Church, and reaffirmed that the foundational principle for a Church immersed in the world is 'in the world, but not of it'.[5] He reminded readers of John XXIII's word for the council – 'aggiornamento', 'a bringing up to date' – and his own adherence to the concept as it was still necessary for the Church to be immersed in the contemporary world and to look for the 'signs of the time'.[6] One of the important points mentioned by Paul VI for the renewal of the Church in general, and the renewal of ecclesiastical life in particular, was 'the spirit of poverty, or rather, the zeal for preserving this spirit'.[7] Such was the centrality that Paul VI gave the theme of the spirit of poverty that he asserted: 'it is a fundamental element of that divine plan by which we are destined to win the Kingdom of God, and yet it is greatly jeopardised by the modern trend to set so much store by wealth'.[8] The Pope recognised the difficulties that everyone has in maintaining a spirit of poverty, and announced particular canonical regulations and directives regarding poverty to highlight clearly that 'spiritual goods far outweigh economic goods, the possession and use of which should be regulated and subordinated to the conduct and advantage of our apostolic

1   *Ecclesiam Suam* § 30.
2   *Ecclesiam Suam* § 31.
3   *Ecclesiam Suam* § 35.
4   *Ecclesiam Suam* § 37.
5   *Ecclesiam Suam* § 49.
6   *Ecclesiam Suam* § 50.
7   *Ecclesiam Suam* § 54.
8   *Ecclesiam Suam* § 54.

mission'.[1] Regarding wealth, the pope also spoke on issues of technical economics and of the importance of helping those who are in need; thus wealth should be used 'justly and equitable for the good of all', and ultimately redistributed.[2] Together with the spirit of poverty, charity emerges as 'the very heart and centre of the plan of God's providence as revealed in both the Old and the New Testament'.[3] Paul VI, using the word charity rather than love, was inspired by Paul's hymn of love (1 Corinthians 13) to argue strongly that 'charity is the key to everything. It sets all to rights. There is nothing which charity cannot achieve and renew'.[4]

The third part of *Ecclesiam Suam* deals with the issue of dialogue, and particularly with dialogue with the world.[5] The world for Paul VI was defined as:

> Either those human beings who are opposed to the light of faith and the gift of grace, those whose naive optimism betrays them into thinking that their own energies suffice to win them complete, lasting, and gainful prosperity, or, finally, those who take refuge in an aggressively pessimistic outlook on life and maintain that their vices, weaknesses and moral ailments are inevitable, incurable, or perhaps even desirable as sure manifestations of personal freedom and sincerity.[6]

Paul VI reminded Catholics that Christians are different from people in 'the world' because that they have been justified, which, in Catholic terms, alludes to the theological understanding that they are participants in the Paschal Mystery through baptism, 'which is truly a rebirth'.[7] Christians differentiate themselves from the world without indifference, fear or contempt toward the world; on the contrary, the Church distinguishes herself from humanity in order to become closer to humanity, and to show

---

1   *Ecclesiam Suam* § 54.
2   *Ecclesiam Suam* § 55.
3   *Ecclesiam Suam* § 56.
4   *Ecclesiam Suam* § 56.
5   It is important to recall here that the Church and the world in Catholic theology are not opposed means of grace – as has been assumed by some Calvinist Protestant theology – but that God imparts grace on a world that is his creation and that is completely under his positive guidance; see Vatican II's Pastoral Constitution on the Church in the Modern World – *Gaudium et Spes* § 1.
6   *Ecclesiam Suam* § 59.
7   *Ecclesiam Suam* § 60.

more concern and more love for all.[1] Thus, the Church must enter into dialogue with the world because it has something to say, a message to give and an important communication to make.[2]

Paul VI acknowledged that issues of dialogue with the world are built upon a foundation laid by Leo XIII, Pius XI, Pius XII and John XXIII.[3] Those popes showed that if the Church is to bring people to Christ, she must engage in dialogue with the world.[4] Dialogue arises out of the experience of God in prayer and in spiritual discernment: God Himself is 'the noble origin of this dialogue'.[5] It is in the dialogue between Christ and human beings that He reveals how he wishes to be known: as pure love.[6] Paul VI stressed the paradigm of dialogue established by the Father who sent his Son, and who is in dialogue with us through the Church, a dialogue that should be established with the whole of humanity.[7] In his reflection, Paul VI stressed that God initiated this dialogue first in love, which should be an important characteristic of the Church's dialogue with others: it should be initiated by the Church without waiting for others, and in the spirit of love.[8] God's dialogue was conducted freely, without coercion, in a spirit of conversational openness. The same process of dialogue with others in 'human friendliness, interior persuasion, and ordinary conversation' is expected of the Church.[9]

Within Paul VI's teachings, the concept of dialogue is promoted as catholic and perseverant, with the Church taking the initiative; dialogue is therefore the advised method for creating closer relations between the Church and the world.[10] In order to respect a human being's freedom and dignity, Paul VI suggests that dialogue must have the following characteristics: (i) dialogue should be intelligible, (ii) it should be humble, truthful and peaceful, (iii) it should carry confidence in the power of words as well as in the goodwill of the other party, and (iv) it should be conducted with the prudence of a teacher.[11]

---

1   *Ecclesiam Suam* § 63.
2   *Ecclesiam Suam* § 65.
3   *Ecclesiam Suam* § 68.
4   *Ecclesiam Suam* § 69.
5   *Ecclesiam Suam* § 70.
6   *Ecclesiam Suam* § 70.
7   *Ecclesiam Suam* § 71.
8   *Ecclesiam Suam* § 72-73.
9   *Ecclesiam Suam* § 74-75.
10 *Ecclesiam Suam* § 76-78.
11 *Ecclesiam Suam* § 81 cf. § 79.

In the final part of *Ecclesiam Suam,* Paul VI provided a positive view of developments and changes in the world, stating that:

All things human are our concern. We share with the whole of the human race a common nature, a common life, with all its gifts and all its problems. We are ready to play our part in this primary, universal society, to acknowledge the insistent demands of its fundamental needs, and to applaud the new and often sublime expressions of its genius.[1]

Among the most difficult sectors of society with whom the Church might dialogue, Paul VI mentioned those who followed atheism and communism because of their non-adherence to a world ordered as communal by God.[2] Among positive partners in dialogue, Paul VI mentioned those who seek and work for peace, those who share a faith in the One God (Jewish and Muslim) and those who follow Afro-Asiatic religions.[3] Regarding those who follow non-Christian religions, Paul VI asserted:

We desire to join with them in promoting and defending common ideals in the spheres of religious liberty, human brotherhood, education, culture, social welfare, and civic order. Dialogue is possible in all these great projects, which are our concern as much as theirs and we will not fail to offer opportunities for discussion in the event of such an offer being favourably received in genuine, mutual respect.[4]

Finally, Paul VI referred to those who share a belief in Christ, stressing the commonalities between the Christian churches rather than the differences.[5] The fact that representatives of all the Christian churches were present at the Second Vatican Council (properly labelled 'ecumenical') was already a sign of the things to come.

As a result of all those reflections, dialogue was to be central to the life of the Church in a post-conciliar climate. In the case of Jewish-Christian relations, many groups started conversations and lives-in-dialogue via groups that took part in each other's rituals, an ecclesiological development that was to influence Bergoglio's active dialogue with Jews and Muslims in Buenos

---

1   *Ecclesiam Suam* § 97.
2   *Ecclesiam Suam* § 99-104.
3   *Ecclesiam Suam* § 106-107.
4   *Ecclesiam Suam* § 108.
5   *Ecclesiam Suam* § 109.

Aires.[1] As Donald Nicholl has argued, 'the depth of that change is probably hard for anyone to measure who was not personally acquainted with the situation before the Second Vatican Council'.[2]

Latin America after Vatican II

Following the completion of Vatican II in 1965, the Latin American Episcopal Conference, headed by the progressive Chilean Bishop Manuel Larraín, scheduled a general meeting of Latin American bishops at Medellin (Colombia) that took place in 1968. The meeting coincided with a period of soul-searching about the poverty and injustice in Latin America, and was the start of a period in which the rule of military regimes was the norm rather than the exception.[3] Preparations at local diocesan level for Medellin were intense. Those leading the deliberations at the continental level were not theologians but pastoral bishops, who, in the case of Brazil, had already witnessed systematic violations of human rights since the military had taken charge of the Brazilian government in 1964.

Within this difficult political context, the Latin American countries had responded to the implementation of Vatican II with enthusiasm, supported by a committed Catholic laity that had been heavily influenced by John XXIII's *Pacem in Terris* (1963) and Paul VI's *Populorum progressio* (1967). Both encyclicals spoke of the possibility of a just order in society, but an order that must consider development rather than armed struggle as its core value, and whose aim is an economic stability that provides the possibility of restoring dignity to all nations and to all human beings. It is worth remarking again that, within the Argentinean Church, the majority of persons chose to dwell more on the pragmatic importance of the Catholic Church to the building of the nation, rather than prioritising *Populorum Progressio*'s suggestions for development and economic justice.

1   According to Evangelina Himitian, Bergoglio had three obsessions: poverty, education and inter-religious dialogue. See Evangelina Himitian, *Francisco: El Papa de la gente*, Buenos Aires: Aguilar, 2013, p. 227.

2   Donald Nicholl, 'Other Religions (Nostra Aetate)' in Adrian Hastings, ed. *Modern Catholicism: Vatican II and After*, London: SPCK and New York: Oxford University Press, 1991, pp. 126-134 at p. 131.

3   For a detailed analysis of the relation between Church and State at the period and within different Latin American countries see Jeffrey Klaiber SJ, *The Church, Dictatorships, and Democracy in Latin America*, Maryknoll, NY: Orbis, 1998.

The genesis of Latin American liberation theology coincided with broader Christian reflections on development, and the Church's expanding involvement with the world, an involvement that extended to the search for a theology of inculturation in Africa, and of dialogue with world religions in Asia.[1] However, also during this time, a Peruvian priest, Gustavo Gutiérrez, became the face of liberation theology. Such priests were trying to develop a systematic framework of thought that connected the life of the Latin American poor, development theory, and a divine sense of history, under the umbrella of theological and material liberation.[2] Gutiérrez's *A Theology of Liberation* (1971) became the classic theological monograph on the subject, while many other theologians started concurrently working on Christology, ecclesiology, soteriology, the history of the Church and the role of the Basic Christian communities.[3] The final document of the general meeting at Medellin supported the theological program of engaging with the world by reiterating the

---

1 At the theological level African and Latin American theologians encountered each other through the Ecumenical Association of Third World Theologians (EATWOT) and the first period of their work was co-ordinated by Enrique Dussel and François Houtart, see a useful historical overview in Enrique Dussel, 'Theologies of the "Periphery" and the "Centre": Encounter or Confrontation?', in Claude Geffré, Gustavo Gutiérrez and Virgil Elizondo (eds.), *Different Theologies, Common Responsibility, Babel or Pentecost?*, *Concilium* 171, 1984/1, Edinburgh: T&T Clark, 87-97, see also EATWOT, *The Emergent Gospel*, Maryknoll, NY: Orbis Books, 1976. For a theological overview see Theo Witvliet, *A Place in the Sun: An Introduction to Liberation Theology in the Third World*, London: SCM Press, 1985. An Asian Christianity as a Christian project was more problematic; numbers of Christians in Asia, with the exception of the Philippines, remain small and the post-Vatican II discussions on salvation within the world religions created more than an impasse between those who adhered to a Christ centric option (exclusivists) and those who understood the world religions as places where God could save (inclusivists), see Paul F. Knitter, *No Other Name? A Critical Survey of Christian Attitudes towards the World Religions*, London: SCM Press, 1985.

2 For historical data on his life see Sergio Torres, 'Gustavo Gutiérrez: A historical sketch', in Marc H. Ellis and Otto Maduro (eds.), *The Future of Liberation Theology: Essays in Honor of Gustavo Gutiérrez*, Maryknoll NY: Orbis, 1989, 95-101.

3 Gustavo Gutiérrez, *Teología de la liberación: Perspectivas* (Salamanca: Ediciones Sígueme, 16th edition 1999 and Lima: Centro de Estudios y Publicaciones 1971); for a full review of the theological works of 18 Latin American theologians see Mario I. Aguilar, *The History and Politics of Latin American Theology*, vols. 1-2, London: SCM Press, 2007.

materiality and humanity of God's salvation and incarnation, and by encouraging ecclesial immersion in the life of the materially poor, the marginalised and those victimised by unjust social structures – included by the Latin American bishops under the term 'structural sin'.[1]

The development of Latin American theology is enormously complex, but it can in part be traced to the European training received by Gustavo Gutiérrez and Juan Luis Segundo SJ, who both studied in France when, in 1959, John XXIII called the Second Vatican Council and spoke of 'a church of the poor'.[2] Juan Luis Segundo SJ and Gustavo Gutiérrez had different pastoral experiences, however, and these experiences shaped what Segundo called 'two kinds of liberation theology'.[3] As a result of his life in the slums, Gutiérrez believed that the poor and the marginalised were at the centre of God's work. They represented the incarnation of God and the presence of God within society. Theology, within this social context is a reflection, a 'second act' in the social drama of God and his people. In Gutiérrez's opinion, Jesus expressed a real closeness to the poor, and so for him liberation theology arose from 'our better understanding of the depth and complexity of the poverty and oppression experienced by most of humanity; it is due to our perception of the economic, social, and cultural mechanisms that produce that poverty; and before all else, it is due to the new light which the word of the Lord sheds on that poverty'.[4] As a consequence, the 'option for the poor' assumed by the Latin American bishops came out of God's own option for the poor and the marginalised.

---

1 See Second General Conference of Latin American Bishops 1968, *The Church in the Present-Day Transformation of Latin America in the Light of the Council II Conclusions*, Washington, DC: United States Catholic Conference USCC, 1970.

2 For a comprehensive history of liberation theology and of some of the most prominent theologians of liberation see Mario I. Aguilar, *The History and Politics of Latin American Theology*, 3 volumes, London: SCM Press, 2007-2008.

3 Juan Luis Segundo SJ, 'Two Theologies of Liberation', Toronto 22 March 1983 in Alfred T. Hennelly (ed.), *Liberation Theology: A Documentary History*, Maryknoll, NY: Orbis, 1990, 353-66.

4 Gustavo Gutiérrez, 'Option for the Poor' in Ignacio Ellacuría SJ and Jon Sobrino SJ (eds.), *Mysterium Liberationis: Fundamental Concepts of Liberation Theology*, Maryknoll, NY: Orbis and North Blackburn, Victoria: Collins Dove, 1993, 235-250 at 250.

For Segundo, who had experienced pastoral work with the social sphere of the Uruguayan educated elites, liberation theology remained within the realm of educated theologians, whose primary pastoral ministry was to pass fresh ideas about the implementation of Vatican II to the laity and to the Catholic faithful in parishes. Segundo himself worked extensively with university students and young professionals, and was committed to a systematic investigation of theological themes in service of the Church.

There is no contradiction in the role of the theologian in Gutiérrez and Segundo's theological writings, but Gutiérrez's work certainly inspired numerous theological writings that used Marxism as a hermeneutical tool for exploring social realities. Within the Latin American context of the 1970s, Christians and Marxists encountered one another while involved in the same project of challenging unjust social structures. Christians followed the values of the Kingdom of God, Marxists the ideals of a movement which advocated for revolution to achieve equality. They were inspired by the Cuban Revolution of 1959. The radicalisation of Latin American theologians coincided with the ascent of Christians who equated the Gospel with the socialist political project, the so-called groups of Christians for Socialism that supported the election and the government of Salvador Allende in Chile.[1] These clergy and pastoral agents were persecuted by the military in Brazil, Chile, Argentina, Uruguay, Paraguay, El Salvador and Guatemala. Bergoglio was part of an educated elite that assumed the values of Vatican II, but he certainly did not agree with the involvement of Christians within radical political movements such as the Christians for Socialism in Chile. Nor did he believe Christians should play a leading political role, as the Christian communities in Brazil did when they challenged the private ownership of land (they held large demonstrations against this practice, supported by the Brazilian bishops).[2]

The optimism of the Council Fathers, and the rich documents that reincorporated the Church into the contemporary world, created

1   John Eagleson, ed. Christians and Socialism: Documentation of the Christians for Socialism Movement in Latin America, Maryknoll, NY: Orbis, 1975, and Gonzalo Arroyo, Golpe de estado en Chile, Salamanca: Ediciones Sígueme, 1974.

2   The ideological mover of the Brazilian Christian communities was the Brazilian theologian Leonardo Boff who challenged the clerical developments within the Catholic Church arguing for the centrality of the Basic Christian Communities (BCC), see Mario I. Aguilar, *The History and Politics of Latin American Theology*, vol. 1, London: SCM Press, 2007, 121-36.

an optimistic and exciting atmosphere in Latin America. However, there was no way that all the Catholic pastoral agents were going to act and think in the same way. There was a need to renew the Christian communities during this period, but also a need to outline a course of economic development in Latin America for a better distribution of wealth within society. The complexity of the bishops' task at Medellin was therefore enormous, and the dissemination of pastoral ideas was needed and greatly desired by religious sisters, lay people and particularly grass-roots communities.

The means to achieve this social and economic change were the concern of Christians and Marxists alike, and after the Cuban revolution some Christian communities and priests, following a more political stance on Vatican II's call to watch 'the signs of the time', felt called to join Latin American groups attempting to foster violent revolution. Such was the case for Fr Camilo Torres Restrepo, a Colombian priest who was to become a symbol of Christian commitment to Latin American revolutions. Already, at the time of the Council, Camilo Torres had developed the idea that the revolutionary struggle could be a Christian and a priestly activity. He held large influence in Colombian society because he came from a well-to-do family, but also because he was involved with students at the National University of Colombia. Cardinal Luis Concha moved him from the university to a suburban parish, where he started verbally attacking the hierarchy of the Church by suggesting that they were part of the Colombian oligarchy; a group that, according to him, impeded the formation of a more just society in Colombia. In June 1965, he asked to be relieved from his priestly duties, and in November 1965 he joined the Colombian guerrilla, the Ejército de Liberación Nacional. Torres was killed on 15 February 1966, and became an iconic revolutionary figure to many Christians in Latin America.

Within this context of ongoing change and political challenges, in 1968 Paul VI travelled to Bogotá, Colombia to open the thirty-ninth International Eucharistic Congress. The first visit by a pope to Latin America was seen as a great moment for the growing Church. Leading Latin American bishops, such as Cardinal Silva Henríquez of Chile, felt great excitement about the pope's visit to Latin America, seeing the visit as a service to all.[1] The 'continent of hope', according

---

1   Silva Henríquez gave the following thoughts in an interview with U.S. News & World Report: 'Este proceso, válido para toda la Iglesia, se singulariza y reviste de connotación particular en América Latina. Continente en vías de desarrollo, el servicio eclesial a América Latina

to Paul VI, was felt to be the best ground for the implementation of the changes of Vatican II. Finally the servant of the servants of God was arriving to visit the poor of Latin America. The meeting of the Latin American Episcopal Conference at Medellin in 1968 would set the guidelines for the implementation of Vatican II in Latin America. Protests against the papal visit took place in Bogota, orchestrated by radical Christians who thought the expenses of such a visit inappropriate when Latin America was immersed in levels of extreme poverty. It is possible to argue that without the arrival of Paul VI, the meeting of Latin American bishops at Medellin would not have had the same strength or impact on the pastoral life of the Church in Latin America as it did. The papal visit opened the meeting of bishops in which the Latin American Catholic Church opted for a more simple life of poverty and immersed herself in a ministry located in places where the materially poor lived.

On 21 August 1968, the Chilean cardinal Silva Henríquez travelled to Colombia to await the pope's arrival on the following day. During his visit to Colombia, Paul VI ratified the changes of Vatican II, including increased focus on the poor and a Church that would learn from the poor. He also condemned violent attempts to achieve a just society in Latin America and his visit coincided with the celebration of the International Eucharistic Congress in Bogotá between 18 and 25 August 1968. Unlike previous Eucharistic congresses in Buenos Aires and Sao Paulo, the Colombian one was a celebration of the Christian communities under the motto *Vinculum Caritatis (The Union of Love)*.[1] During the Eucharistic Congress, the pope, addressing peasants, stressed his commitment, and the commitment of the whole Church, to defending the poor, proclaiming human and Christian dignities, denouncing injustices and abuses against peasants and fostering initiatives and programs that supported impoverished peoples and their development.[2] In summary, the pope reaffirmed a strengthening ecclesial conviction in Latin America: that the poor are a sacramental presence of Christ

---

se concreta en un servicio al desarrollo, entendido en la acepción de Populorum Progressio: de condiciones menos humanas, hacia un humanismo integral, que incluye el don de la fe', *Memorias* II: 137.

1 Josep-Ignasi Saranyana, director and Carmen-José Alejos Grau, co-ordinator, *Teología en América Latina*, vol. III: *El siglo de las teologías latinoamericanistas 1899-2001*, Madrid: Iberoamericana and Frankfurt am Main: Vervuert, 2002, p. 124.

2 Ibid., vol. III, P. 124.

because Christ is in those who are the most vulnerable in society.[1] The pope warned those attending the celebrations about the danger of putting their trust in violence or revolution.[2] The importance of the first papal visit to Latin America cannot be overstated: this was the first time that a pope had visited Latin America to be physically present with the sick and orphans.[3]

Paul VI inaugurated the second general meeting of Latin American bishops at Medellin in the cathedral in Bogotá on 24 August, and then returned to Rome. Those in attendance at the Medellin conference were 137 bishops with right to vote, and 112 delegates and observers.[4] The Medellín conference was a fruitful opportunity for renewal, and many of the concepts outlined in the final document became additions to the social doctrine of the Church: for example, 'truly human economics', and the avoidance of 'institutionalised violence' and 'sinful structures'.

The Impact of Medellin

At Medellin, in 1968, a Latin American theological movement driven by lay unpublished theologians was born.[5] The Church in Latin America had had to consider their religious practice within difficult political circumstances, and, aided by the theological reflection of Gutiérrez, the bishops did not separate religion and politics. Their response included commitment to political change and the defence of human rights, a commitment that Paul VI would honour during his visit to the United Nations. Virgilio Elizondo has argued that the transformative impact of the Medellin Conference on the Church's pastoral practice and theology was far greater than that exercised by any other council of the Church. No particular dogmas or confessions of faith were questioned or challenged – Protestant or Catholic. Instead, the whole edifice of Constantinian Christian thought, imagery, and symbolism was radically challenged in the name of Christianity. Hallmarks of Constantinian practise included keeping the altar at a distance from the people, and an absence of

1   Ibid., vol. III, p. 125.
2   Ibid., vol. III, p. 126.
3   Ibid., vol. III, p. 126.
4   Ibid., vol. III, p. 126.
5   'Emergence of a World Church and the irruption of the poor', in Gregory Baum (ed.), *The Twentieth Century: A Theological Overview*, Maryknoll, NY: Orbis, 1999, p. 108.

churches at the margins of society. What was initiated was not a new academic or philosophical theology, but the transformation of the very structures and methods of the practice of theology. To be faithful and authentic, it was decided that Christian theology must spring from the spiritual experience of the believing community, grapple with its history and respond to its situation. The pastoral implementation of the conclusions of Medellin was very different in different Latin American countries, but, with the exception of Argentina and Colombia where the Catholic Church continued being conservative in doctrine and practice, allowed a renewed challenge to the state of oppression understood as 'structural sin'. In the case of Chile, for example, the bishops challenged the military regime of President Pinochet; by contrast, in neighbouring Argentina there was an avoidance of any denunciation of the government in the name of the Gospel.[1] The Argentinean Church supported the military for the most part, while the Jesuits – and Fr Jorge Bergoglio SJ, who was teaching and leading retreats there – followed the directives of their congregations to lead a more simple life and to embrace poverty in the spirit of St Ignatius of Loyola, their founder. While Bergoglio supported the persecuted, this was not a specific national pastoral guideline laid down by the Argentinean bishops, a fact that gives Bergoglio's actions for the protection of the persecuted much more weight: during this period the Argentinean Church did not protect those persecuted by the military regime. He did not follow the general trend among the clergy of ignoring the political realm and ignoring the violence that abounded in Argentina in the period before and during military rule.

Several religious groups particularly were experiencing spiritual renewal during the 1960s: what might even be called a Latin American reformation. Among them were the Jesuits. In 1968 they made a public declaration about their lifestyle and their pastoral work throughout Latin America, an announcement that preceded the conference at Medellin. When the provincials of all the Jesuit provinces of Latin America met in Rio de Janeiro, Brazil, 6-14 May 1968, they reflected on their view of mission and their positioning within Latin America. As a result of their deliberations, they decided to reiterate their involvement 'in the temporal life of humankind'.[2]

---

1   See Mario I. Aguilar, *A Social History of the Catholic Church in Chile*, vol. I, *The First Period of the Pinochet Government 1973-1980*, Lewiston, Queenston, and Lampeter: Edwin Mellen Press, 2004.

2   Provincials of the Society of Jesus, 'The Jesuits in Latin America', May

However, within the particular context of Latin America, their statement pushed for a greater involvement with social movements that challenged unjust structures. There was no high theology within the document, but a challenge to the individual and community lives of the Jesuits who had become attached to the elites and had strayed from their social and religious utopia. In a central passage of that document they asserted:

> In all our activities, our goal should be the liberation of humankind from every sort of servitude that oppresses it: the lack of life's necessities, illiteracy, and the weight of sociological structures which deprive it of personal responsibility over life itself, the materialistic conception of history. We want all our efforts to work together toward the construction of a society in which all persons will find their place, and in which they will enjoy political, economic, cultural, and religious equality and liberty.[1]

Within this document the Jesuits responded to a frequent criticism of their academic institutions, particularly their schools and universities: that Jesuit schools educated the children of the rich, and that their universities reinforced an elitist social system. The document argued that all Jesuit institutions should foster the social gospel, and that all students should be involved in practical activities that would expose them to different social realities: for example, working in soup kitchens, living in shanty towns, harvesting and visiting prisons.[2] The Jesuit provincials called for the formation of consciences among their students, and encouraged the use of media to foster such formation. A call was directed to all Jesuit superiors to implement these changes as soon as possible, even when some of those changes would take some time. Deep questions were asked of each individual Jesuit working in Latin America posing a real challenge towards a new religious conversion:

> Are we capable of responding to the world's expectations? Are our faith and charity equal to the anxiety-ridden appeals of the world around us? Do we practice self-denial sufficiently, so that God is able to flood us with light and energy? Does personal prayer have its proper place in our life, so that we

---

1968, in Alfred T. Hennelly (ed.), *Liberation Theology: A Documentary History*, Maryknoll, NY: Orbis, 1990, pp. 77-83.

1   Provincials of the Society of Jesus, 'The Jesuits in Latin America', § 3.
2   Provincials of the Society of Jesus, 'The Jesuits in Latin America', § 7.

are united with God in this great human task that cannot succeed without God? Can the Society keep within its ranks those members who do not want to pray or who do not have a real and personal prayer in life?[1]

The response to the tenets of Medellin by the Jesuit communities in Latin America was swift, and sometimes unsettling for parents and teachers of the students involved. Parents were told about the revised Jesuit aims within their schools and were asked to adhere to them, despite conservative parents' apprehension about the proposed formation of their children through extracurricular pastoral activities led by the Jesuits. Despite the fact that a large number of Jesuits left the Society of Jesus after Vatican II, Jesuit secondary schools maintained their academic excellence while instituting programmes of extra-curricular activities such as summer work in harvesting for students, or activities of a social nature in their last years of secondary school. Within universities it was easier for the Jesuits to implement social service programmes, as most university students were inspired by a climate of change, political awareness and political questioning to go out into the communities. Thus, the Jesuits not only affected the developments of theologies in Latin America, pastoral or otherwise, but also became practically involved in many activities related to the defence of indigenous minorities, political refugees and migrants.

In El Salvador, where the prominent theologian Jon Sobrino SJ worked, the Jesuits decided to build a university that was to be a reflection of the open spirit of Vatican II, and, at the same time, demonstrate a deep commitment to the poor and the marginalised. The Jesuit community in El Salvador felt assured that Medellin was not only a *kairos* (a time of grace), but also a movement that could not easily be stopped. A short outline of the influential educational Jesuit enterprise arising out of Medellin is in order here, particularly the contribution of the Jesuit University of Central America (UCA). The educational reform led by the Jesuits in El Salvador resulted in several assassinations of Jesuits by the Salvadorian Army and death squads paid by Salvadorian landowners. However, the new reforms had strong support among Jesuits, and they, together with Mgr Óscar Romero, were pivotal in applying its tenets to Central American society in general and El Salvador in particular.

---

1   Provincials of the Society of Jesus, 'The Jesuits in Latin America', § 10.

The UCA campus was built in the 1970s by loans from the Inter-American Development Bank (Banco Interamericano del Desarrollo – BID). The UCA, under the rectorship of Román Mayorga Quirós, quickly aligned with the progressive changes of the Jesuit order, and by 1976 Professor Ignacio Ellacuría SJ attracted the animosity of El Salvador's President Arturo Armando Molina by writing an editorial in the university's magazine that criticised the halting of Salvadorian agrarian reform. The government withdrew educational subsidies to the UCA, and attacks on the Jesuits started with the assassination of Rutilio Grande in March 1977. From that moment, the UCA supported all pastoral plans by Archbishop Romero through its department of theology, headed by Jon Sobrino. In 1979, Ignacio Ellacuría SJ became rector of the UCA, and oversaw a move towards research programs related to the national realities of El Salvador, while immersing students, staff and the university community into the social realities of the poor of El Salvador. As the Salvadorean Civil War continued, Ellacuría became prominent as the mediator of peace accords, and spoke out strongly against injustice and human rights abuses via television, UCA radio and the UCA publications.

Ellacuría, rector of the university at the time of his assassination, articulated the particular ministry of the university in the following words: 'the university should be present intellectually where it is needed: to provide science for those who have no science; to provide skills for the unskilled; to be a voice for those who have no voice; to give intellectual support for those who do not possess the academic qualifications to promote and legitimate their rights'.[1] Jon Sobrino SJ, by contrast, was less optimistic about the scope of the university, due to past experiences of Jesuit universities becoming top educational institutions but, in the process, compromising their ability to challenge unjust and sinful structures within society.

Sobrino advocated 'the option for the poor' within Christian universities by arguing that it was unrealistic to suggest that a university should be located in poor areas, but that all activities of a Christian university should be geared towards the poor. In his opinion, the central activities of the university must include the dialogue between faith and science, and the teaching and researching of theology as a reflection on the life of the poor and the marginalised. Sobrino's statement about theology within a university is central to understanding the challenges that the Jesuit

1   Ignacio Ellacuría SJ, 'The Task of a Christian University', in Jon Sobrino, Ignacio Ellacuría and Others, *Companions of Jesus*, p. 150.

Order posed to the powerful in El Salvador. The Jesuits provided many communities with their extra-mural courses (non-curricular courses that could be followed by those who were not reading for a degree) and training for leaders of Christian communities. Sobrino argued very strongly that 'theology must be turned, then, towards the people of God; it should be inserted effectively among them, draw its agenda from them and accompany them. In this sense, university theology should be a moment of theo-praxis for the whole people of God and should be considered as a theo-culture, a Christo-culture, an ecclesio-culture – that is, an instrument that cultivates and nurtures faith, hope, and love of God's people'.[1]

The impact of the 1968 conference of bishops on Latin America cannot be underestimated. The conclusions of the conference followed deep reflection on the role of the Catholic Church in Latin America, and triggered change both within the Church and within spheres of ecclesial influence in Latin America.

The Jesuit response to the Medellin conference – a response also embraced by Jorge Bergoglio – was crucial, because the Jesuits were in charge of the best schools and best universities of Latin America. They had a timely influence on Latin American intellectuals and professionals. The Jesuits responded to the Medellin document with communitarian acts of love, and a theological response to liberation that allowed the questioning the contemporary Jesuit way of life. Thus, the Jesuit reformed *themselves* while simultaneously triggering challenges and reform within the Latin American Catholic Church in which they played a central religious and political role. Other religious congregations followed their example, and undertook an exodus from well-to-do areas of ministry. Christian nuns and laywomen left their teaching positions in affluent public schools and moved to where the poor lived and worked: mainly in shanty towns and deprived areas of Latin American cities. Missionary orders staffed by foreigners also took the conclusions of Medellin very seriously, and opened new parishes in locations only accessed previously by Marxist activists and left-wing ideologists.

The role of religious communities has been generally under-played in the assessment of political changes that took place in 1968 and after in Latin America. It is important to remember that

1 Jon Sobrino SJ, 'The University's Christian Inspiration', in Jon Sobrino, Ignacio Ellacuría and Others, *Companions of Jesus*, pp. 170-1.

many Catholics, though expatriate missionaries (from Ireland, Spain, France and the United States), also expressed their own journey to follow the Gospel more closely in a movement away from their convents and religious houses toward the periphery, to the shanty towns and to places where they were most needed.

This movement towards the peripheries of society, and the involvement of Christians with movements of liberation more generally, amounted to a golden pastoral moment in Latin America which, by the 1970s and 1980s, could be called a true *kairos* arising from the events of 1968. The period marked the formation of a movement for liberation that would shape the pastoral development of the universal Catholic Church. In conclusion, the year 1968 marked the beginning of a new reformation in and for Latin America. The third meeting of Latin American bishops in Puebla (Mexico, 1979) re-emphasised the importance of this movement towards the poor in society, and proclaimed God's preferential option for the poor once more. The fourth meeting of Latin American bishops in Santo Domingo (1992) reflected on the 500 years since the arrival of Christianity in Latin America, and stressed the central role of indigenous populations in the decision-making for and future of the Church in Latin America. The fifth meeting of Latin American bishops in Aparecida (Brazil, 2007) reflected on the role of the Church in a secularising and increasingly democratic Latin American society, emphasising – under the guidance of Cardinal Bergoglio – the mission of the Church to the marginalised in society. Aparecida's final document was written with the help of Bergoglio's strong hand, a document that emphasises the service and mission of the Church and gives a secondary role to the expansion or self-reflection of the Church.

It is this Argentinean cardinal, Jorge M. Bergoglio, with his wide experience of focusing on the poor and the marginalised since 1968 in Latin America, who is elected as pope. He was born into an immigrant Italian family, and experienced violence and political tension under the Argentinean military regime, and laboured diligently for years as auxiliary bishop, archbishop and cardinal in Buenos Aires. From these experiences Bergoglio learned the importance of a simple life, and of a Catholic Church that reaches out to the marginalised, who need the support, grace and the comfort of God. The following chapters outline some crucial influences on Bergoglio from his childhood, and consider some of his main speeches, homilies and involvement with the social, ecclesial and political world of Argentina.

1. From Son of Immigrants to Jesuit
1936-1971

Pope Francis was born in Buenos Aires on 17 December 1936 and baptised Jorge Mario Bergoglio. His Italian grandparents and his father, at that time only twenty-four years of age, had landed in Buenos Aires in January 1929 in a wave of Italian immigrants escaping from poverty – mainly rural poverty, but also poverty stemming from the global economic crisis in the aftermath of the Wall Street Crash. They brought their own history to Argentina, and also the Catholicism that nurtured Bergoglio in his early years.[1]

There is no doubt that Italian immigration to Argentina provided the largest numbers from any European country, with an estimated six million Italians arriving in Argentina from 1814 to 1970.[2] There were more Italian immigrants to Argentina than Spanish immigrants: the latter amounted to four million during the nineteenth and twentieth centuries.[3] In *Sobre el océano* (1889), one of the first books to document the lives of Italians leaving for Argentina, Edmundo De Amicis recorded the testimony of a man who, when asked why he was leaving Italy when the government was giving subsidies to peasants and farmers, replied 'Mi emigro

---

1 Federico Finchelstein, *Transatlantic Fascism: Ideology, Violence and the Sacred in Argentina and Italy 1919-1945*, Durham, NC: Duke University Press, 2010.

2 For a general treatment of this immigration see Samuel L. Baily, *Immigrants in the Land of Promise: Italians in Buenos Aires and New York City 1870-1914*, Ithaca, NY: Cornell University Press, 2004; Fernando DeVoto, *Nacionalismo, tradicionalismo y fascismo en la Argentina moderna: Una historia*, Buenos Aires: Siglo XXI, 2002, and *Historia de la immigración en la Argentina*, Buenos Aires: Editorial Sudamericana, 2004. For some figures see *Resumen estadístico del movimiento migratorio en la República Argentina, años 1857-1924*, Buenos Aires: Talleres Gráficos del Ministerio de Agricultura de la Nación, 1925.

3 Jose C. Moya, *Cousins and Strangers: Spanish Immigrants in Buenos Aires 1850-1930*, Berkeley, CA: University of California Press, 1998.

per magnar' – 'I am emigrating in order to eat'. The land given to immigrants by the Argentinean government, with the sole stipulation that they must cultivate it, attracted large numbers of immigrants, who arrived to stay at hotels specially prepared for immigrants at Buenos Aires. Men and women were segregated for a period of five days in order to arrange their papers and to make sure that they didn't carry any deadly diseases. Their passage into Argentina had already been prepared in Italy, where the Italian government supplied printed materials for the Italian immigrants that included the *Manuale dello emigrante italiano all' Argentina*, originally prepared by Arrigo de Zettiry in Rome in 1913.[1] The manual for immigrants contained sections on legal requirements, passports and Argentinean work books, details on the purchasing of tickets for the journey, life in the boat, where to stay on arrival in Argentina, and life in Argentina.

The acquisition of new territories by Argentina after the War of the Triple Alliance (1860-1870) meant that people were needed to occupy these territories. Thus, subsequent Argentinean governments welcomed Italians to these lands; the state did not want to rely on the indigenous populations, who distrusted the centralised Argentinean state that, to them, was just a continuation of the colonial impositions made by the Spanish crown.[2] The first Italian immigrants had experienced the impoverished social conditions that followed the wars of unification of Italy in the late nineteenth century and a new Italian state unable provide for all its citizens. These early immigrants came from Piedmont – as Bergoglio's relatives did – from Liguria and from Lombardy, and they settled in the Pampas (Santa Fe, Córdoba and Mendoza) and Resistencia, the capital of the Chaco. However, later immigrants arrived from all regions of Italy, and by the late twentieth century it was estimated that 52% of the Argentinean population had direct connections with Italy, while 70% had some Italian descent. By the time the Bergoglio family arrived in Argentina, Italian immigrants

1   I am very thankful to Diego Armus, who sent me a copy of his Spanish edition of this Italian manual published as Diego Armus, ed. *Manual del Emigrante Italiano*, Buenos Aires: Centro Editor de América Latina, 1983. This edition of the *Manuale* was used as a teaching tool within Argentinean universities, Diego Armus to Mario I. Aguilar 25 April 2013.

2   Lilia Ana Bertoni, *Patriotas, cosmopolitas y nacionalistas: La construcción de la nacionalidad argentina a fines del siglo XIX*, Buenos Aires: Fondo de Cultura Económica, 2001 and Carl E. Solberg, *Immigration and Nationalism: Argentina and Chile 1890-1914*, Austin TX: University of Texas Press, 1970.

and their children were entitled to Argentinean nationality: a law was passed in 1910 under the presidency of Roque Sáenz Peña (1910-1914) that gave the vote to all Argentinean males, including European immigrants.[1] This government policy aimed to integrate Italian immigrants into a modern Argentinean nation; however, Italian immigrants continued belong to two nations, linked by family ties to Italy.[2]

When Bergoglio's grandparents arrived in Buenos Aires, his grandmother Rosa brought all the possessions she could carry and jewellery hidden in her coat's lining. Rosa Margherita Vasallo was born in Val Bormida in 1884, and married Giovanni Bergoglio in Turin. They travelled to Argentina in the ship *Giulio Cesare* from the port of Genoa, not to escape poverty, but because they wanted to live near their extended family. Bergoglio's three great-uncles had travelled to Argentina in 1922, leaving the Piedmont region of the north of Italy (capital Turin), specifically a small town called Portacomaro. They had initially booked to make the voyage on the ship *Principessa Mafalda*, a ship that sank near the northern coast of Brazil with the loss of hundreds of lives, but fortunately they had had to postpone their departure because of family circumstances.

Bergoglio's grandparents did not stay, as was customary, at the Hotel de los Inmigrantes on arrival, but, after clearing customs, proceeded to Paraná where they stayed with Bergoglio's great-uncles, who had started a company that repaired roads. The Hotel de los Inmigrantes was a large warehouse with shared rooms where immigrants were given daily rations of food as well as advice on how to establish themselves in Argentina. Nevertheless, it was a place best avoided by those who already had relatives in Argentina. In Paraná, the Bergoglios had built a beautiful house: a four-storey palace that was the first in town to have a lift installed. With a beautiful roof on top, and very similar in shape to the El Molino Confiteor of Buenos Aires, the house provided accommodation for each of the three brothers and their families on a separate floor. However, the financial crisis of 1932 in Argentina forced the closure of the company and the sale of all family assets to others. By that time the brother who acted as president of the company had died of cancer. After the closure

---

1 Felipe Barreda Laoz, *Roque Sáenz Peña*, Buenos Aires: Lombardi y Cie, 1954.
2 Samuel L. Baily and Franco Ramella, eds., *One Family, Two Worlds: An Italian Family Correspondence across the Atlantic 1901-1922*, New Brunswick, NJ: Rutgers University Press, 1988.

of the family business, one of his uncles re-started in business alone and did well, while the youngest of his uncles moved to Brazil. Bergoglio's grandfather borrowed 2,000 pesos and bought a grocery store – his father, who had already done administrative work in the previous family business, helped with the distribution of groceries, carrying them in a basket.

Bergoglio' parents met at Mass in 1934 at the Salesian oratory of San Antonio at the Almagro neighbourhood of Buenos Aires. They married in 1935 and had five children. His mother was the daughter of a woman from Piedmont, who had married an Argentinean man whose family had emigrated from Genoa. He taught the young Bergoglio many songs from Genoa that Bergoglio later realised were quite salacious and not very appropriate for family occasions. Bergoglio grew up very close to his grandparents, who lived nearby, partly to help his mother: Bergoglio's younger brother was only thirteen month younger than him. Thus, in order to alleviate Bergoglio's mother's burdens, his grandmother collected him every morning, looked after him during the day, and brought him back to his mother every evening. Bergoglio's grandmother taught him how to pray, and she influenced his faith by telling him stories about a wide variety of saints. With his grandparents Bergoglio also learned how to speak Piedmontese. Bergoglio's father did not like to speak Italian: he wanted a better future and did not want to be reminded of the impoverished country they had left. It is said that Buenos Aires was built by immigrants with similar attitudes: facing inland rather than towards the sea.

Bergoglio remembers his parents as a couple who were always playful and happy; he also remembers visiting the sport club of San Lorenzo, where his father played basketball. At the time, Club San Lorenzo was a small Italian sports association, and it was only later that it became well-known for its professional football team and large stadium. Football was very popular. The sport had arrived in Argentina in 1884, when 'Alejandro' Watson Hutton introduced it to the Buenos Aires English School. The English School, together with the British clubs of Quilmes, Lomas, Flores and the railway club of Buenos Aires-Rosario, later formed the Argentine Association Football League.[1] The young Bergoglio's affiliation with the San Lorenzo Club was to remain a life-long commitment: he is still a member.

1   Alberto Elguera and Carlos Boaglio, *La vida porteña en los años veinte*, Buenos Aires: Grupo Editor Latinoamericano, 1997, p. 219.

On Saturdays at 2.00 pm, Bergoglio and his mother listened to the weekly opera on the Radio del Estado. His mother would gather the children before the start of the opera and explain to them the complexities of the story, while at the start of an important aria she would tell them to listen very carefully because it was going to be very beautiful. He has described his fond memories of those moments shared with his two brothers, close in age to him, and his mother. Of course the children got distracted, but her mother was relentless in explaining the upcoming events of the opera. While his grandparents faded away in their old age, Bergoglio's mother cared for the children as best she could, giving them instruction on how to cook as she had been left temporarily immobilised after her fifth pregnancy. When the children arrived home from school she was usually sitting down peeling potatoes and preparing other ingredients, and she gave the children instructions on how to put them together to prepare the evening meal. Bergoglio remembers his parents as being fully present in the lives of their children. The young Bergoglio was a romantic. At the age of twelve he told his young girlfriend Amalia Damonte: 'if I don't marry you I shall become a priest'.

A Working Life

After completing his primary school education, Bergoglio was told by his father that, as well as pursuing his secondary education, it would be advantageous for him to take up a part-time job during the summer. He was thirteen, and was at first somewhat disconcerted by this development, since the family did not face any financial pressures. While they did not have a car or go on holidays, he wanted for nothing at home, and all expenses were covered by his father's job as an accountant. Nonetheless, he started to work in a stockings' factory linked to his father's accountancy firm, first as a cleaner (a job that lasted for two years), and later doing small administrative jobs. His father wanted him to start work at an early age to prepare him for a working life. During those years he studied at an industrial secondary school where he learned a trade rather than studying the humanities. This trade was the chemistry of food, and he started a part-time job at a laboratory at the age of sixteen in which he worked from 7 am to 1 pm. He had an hour for lunch, and then went to the technical school to study until 8 pm.

Bergoglio later valued this experience of hard work, because it was during his time at the laboratory that he learned that any human task has good and bad aspects.[1] His boss was a Paraguayan lady, Esther Balestrino de Careaga, a communist sympathiser whose son and daughter-in-law were kidnapped by the security forces during the time of the military regime in Argentina (1976-1983). On 8 December 1977, Mrs Balestrino was herself kidnapped by the military, together with the French nuns Alicia Domon and Léonie Duquet. After days of interrogation and torture they were thrown into the sea. The bodies of Mrs Balestrino and Sr Léonie Duquet were washed ashore with other dead bodies, and were buried at unknown graves in the cemetery of the town of General Lavalle. Years later, the bodies were identified and buried once more in the gardens of the Iglesia de Santa Cruz. Sr Alicia Domon remains among the 30,000 Argentineans arrested and killed and whose bodies were never recovered. Bergoglio remembered that Mrs Ballestrino used to question the speed with which he completed some of the chemical analyses she had asked him to carry out. The young Bergoglio had actually been guessing rather than properly carrying out the analyses, assuming that tests would produce similar results. Bergoglio later admitted that Mrs Balestrino had taught him how to do jobs well and thoroughly for the rest of his life.

Sickness and Vocation

At the age of twenty-one, Bergoglio became very ill with a high fever, and for some time the doctors were puzzled by the cause. They finally diagnosed him with severe pneumonia that had created three wounds on his right lung. Once he had recovered some strength, he had to have a tube inserted daily to circulate liquid for washing the wounds and the lung. The tube that sucked out the liquid was quite primitive, connected to a water-pipe that provided an exit point for the circulating liquid. As methods of medical liquid extraction were still embryonic, the process Bergoglio had to endure was painful and laborious.

---

1 'Le agradezco tanto a mi padre que me haya mandado a trabajar. El trabajo fue una de las cosas que mejor me hizo en la vida y, particularmente, en el laboratorio aprendí lo bueno y lo malo de toda tarea humana', in Sergio Rubin and Francesca Ambrogetti, *El Jesuita; La historia de Francisco, el Papa argentino*, Buenos Aires; Ediciones B Argentina, 2010, p. 34.

During his long convalescence a nun named Dolores, who had prepared him for his first Holy Communion, visited him daily and offered Bergoglio comforting words. She told him that in his suffering he was imitating Jesus. This episode built on a previous encounter Bergoglio had with God at the age of seventeen. On 21 September, the so-called 'Day of Students' in Argentina, he was preparing to celebrate with friends and classmates, a group that included a girl he was in love with. They had plans to spend the day together and to go dancing in the evening. A lover of the Argentinean tango, Bergoglio danced it well (his favourite tango singers were Carlos Gardel, Julio Sosa and Ada Falcón).

Before joining his friends he decided to visit a parish church, the Iglesia de San José de Flores of Buenos Aires. There is no doubt that his parents had successfully passed their Catholic faith on to him; he was a practising Catholic who related his daily activities to his faith and that of his Italian ancestors. When he entered the church he met a priest who inspired a confidence in him, and he asked him to hear his confession. During his confession, Bergoglio experienced a moment of grace in which God came to him, and after receiving absolution he knew that his vocation in life was to become a priest.[1] Thus, on that September day he did not join his friends, but went home instead. He completed his secondary education at the industrial secondary school E.N.E.T. No. 27 (today called E.T. No. 27) 'Hipólito Yrigoyen', and received the professional title of chemical technician. He continued working in the laboratory in a state of 'passive solitude', or inner solitary life, which he later differentiated from 'active solitude', a state of solitude triggered by an external event: God's call to the priesthood. Finally, at the age of twenty-one (1957), he decided to pursue his vocation for the priesthood, and entered the Diocesan Seminary of the archdiocese of Buenos Aires at Villa Devoto. However, he was there for only a few months before requesting entrance to the novitiate of the Jesuits.

The reasons for his choice to enter the Society of Jesus were various, but he saw in the Jesuits a force for progress within the Church and society, partly due to their soldierly obedience and

---

1 Fifty years later Bergoglio told his interviewers: 'En esa confesión me pasó algo raro, no sé qué fue, pero me cambió la vida; yo diría que me sorprendieron con la guardia baja' (Within that confession something strange happened to me, I don't know what it was; I guess I was surprised without defences [my translation]), see *El Jesuita*, p. 45.

discipline. Bergoglio was also attracted by the missionary work carried out by the Jesuits in the Far East, particularly Japan. He was later to ask to be sent to Japan, but because of his health problems he was unable to go. Bergoglio's testimonies suggest that he did not know what joining a religious order would be like; however, it is clear that he liked the idea of the well-prepared and militarily-organised religious congregation, which was very well-known in the Argentinean educational circles. The Jesuits also had a missionary pedigree, exemplified by St Francis Xavier and his missionary outreach to Asia during the sixteenth century.

The Jesuits first arrived in South America in 1550 and preached at San Salvador de Bahia in Brazil, in today's Paraguay. The first European settlements in Paraguay were founded in 1554 within the district of Guayrá, on the upper waters of the river Paraná. Above this cataract Don Ruy Díaz de Melgarejo founded the towns of Ontiveros, Ciudad Real and Villa Ríca.[1] Only a few years after their arrival in South America, the Jesuits in Chile, Peru, Argentina and Paraguay began to face challenges from the colonial authorities because they questioned the poor treatment of indigenous peoples by the conquistadors. The Jesuits appealed to King Philip III, requesting the protection of his indigenous subjects, a request that was granted by the king in 1608. The Jesuits were also granted a mission to convert the indigenous peoples located in the province of Guayrá. The Italian Jesuits Simon Maceta and José Cataldino arrived at the banks of the river Paranapané in February 1610 and founded the first *reducción* (mission enclosure) of Loreto among the Guaraní, who had already come into contact with the Jesuit Frs Fields and Ortega.[2] The contribution of the Jesuits was not just limited to the protection of the indigenous populations who, contrary to the beliefs of the slave traders, they deemed capable of Christian conversion, human beings with souls. They were committed to the development of communal farms, schools and communities based upon the values of the Gospel. The Jesuit missions represented an experience for the indigenous population that was very different from their experience of European colonial domination in their ancestral lands.

1   Robert Bontine Cunninghame Graham, *A Vanished Arcadia: Being Some Account of the Jesuits in Paraguay 1607-1767*, London: Century, 1988 (1901), pp. 47-48.
2   The Spanish word *reducción* (sometimes translated in English as reduction) was the name for a missionary establishment where indigenous populations lived and were under the protection of the Jesuits.

Due to the large number of indigenous peoples who began to trust the Jesuits, a second *reducción* was founded, that of San Ignacio, in memory of the Jesuit founder. The Jesuits provided an alternative to the *Paulistas*, Portuguese settlers of São Paulo, who enslaved Guaranís. The Jesuits took a policy of isolation from the European colonies, not only because the Jesuits had to show that they were not part of the colonial administration, but also because the life of the missionary settlements was different to that outside the Jesuit *reducciónes*. Many of the indigenous people living in the *reducciónes* left them because the orderly and semi-military life of the Jesuits was as hard as their own. Of the *reducciónes*, Voltaire wrote:

> When in 1768 the missions of Paraguay left the hands of the Jesuits, they had arrived at perhaps the highest degree of civilisation to which it is possible to conduct a young people, and certainly a far superior state than that which existed in the rest of the new hemisphere. The laws were respected there, morals were pure, a happy brotherhood united every heart, all the useful arts were in a flourishing state, and even some of the more agreeable sciences; plenty was universal.[1]

Thus, despite the facts that many of the indigenous peoples who were brought to the *reducciónes* left them, and that mainly women and children lived there – some of them compelled by violence and hunger to seek shelter there – the Jesuits gave their best efforts to the missions and to the education of the Guaraní. Once the *reducciónes* had become established within the colonial landscape, the Jesuits sent large numbers of priests and brothers there. On 9 July 1717, for example, three boats arrived from Cádiz at the port of Buenos Aires, carrying the largest Jesuit group ever to arrive: more than fifty Jesuits from Spain, Italy, Germany and Switzerland. Among them were some very capable Italian artists and musicians, such as the composer and organist Domenico Zipoli, and Gianbattista Primoli and Andrea Bianchi, both architects.[2]

---

1 Robert Bontine Cunninghame Graham, *A Vanished Arcadia*, pp. 51-2.
2 T. Frank Kennedy SJ, 'An Integrated Perspective: Music and Art in the Jesuit Reductions of Paraguay', in Christopher Chapple (ed.), *The Jesuit Tradition in Education and Missions: A 450-Year Perspective*, Scranton: University of Scranton Press, London and Toronto: Associated University Presses, 1993, pp. 215-25 at p. 215.

It was clear that the indigenous populations were very receptive to music; therefore every Jesuit settlement had a school of music, and many first-class European musicians visited the *reducciónes*, sent by the Jesuits in Europe. Music was composed within the *reducciónes*, with two European periods of music becoming central: the polyphonic music of the Renaissance and the music typical of the Baroque, introduced with the arrival of the Jesuit Antonius Sepp in 1691.[1]

The end of the *reducciónes* occurred when the kings of Portugal and Spain decided to negotiate land transfers. King Ferdinand VI gave the seven towns of the *reducciones* to Portugal. However, with his death in 1760, his heir Charles III listened to the plea of the Jesuits and reclaimed the *reducciónes* as possessions of Spain. The area covered by the Jesuits was important for Spain because it provided a Spanish presence above the falls, a natural boundary between the Portuguese territory of Brazil and the Spanish colonies to the south of the falls. However, animosity against the Jesuits grew alongside rumours: that they had great wealth which they intended to use to form a Jesuit territory independent of the kings of Spain and Portugal, and that they had 14,000 indigenous peoples as prisoners within their territories. As a result, the expulsion of the Jesuits was decreed by the Spanish King Charles III in 1767 and orders were given for groups of indigenous peoples to leave the *reducciónes* and move to the countryside. All Jesuits were to be arrested and sent back to Spain.[2] It is possible to argue that the Jesuits, who had arms to defend the *reducciónes* from the Portuguese, could have resisted the advances of the small Spanish army and most probably have defeated it, aided by indigenous allies. But this did not happen, and the Jesuits were banished from South America, and from all Spanish territories.

---

1   T. Frank Kennedy SJ, 'An Integrated Perspective', p. 216.
2   Charles III signed the Royal Decree at Pardo, Madrid on 5 April 1767 with the title 'Real cédula para que en los reinos de las Indias se cumpla y observe el Decreto relativo al extrañamiento y ocupación de temporalidades de los Religiosos de la Compañía de Jesús'. The Royal Decree was sent by the Count of Aranda to the Governor of Buenos Aires, General Bucareli y Ursúa, who ordered the arrest of the Jesuits, the confiscation of their lands and personnel and their repatriation to Spain. All Jesuits were immediately replaced by other clergy, see Silvio Palacios and Ena Zoffoli, *Gloria y tragedia de las misiones guaraníes: Historia de las Reducciónes Jesuíticas durante los siglos XVII y XVIII en el Río de la Plata*, Bilbao: Ediciones Mensajero, 1991, p. 165.

The expulsion of the Jesuits from the Spanish territories in 1767 had two main effects on the history of Latin America. On the one hand, the now expelled Jesuits had prepared the way for a further colonisation of the continent by establishing the *reducciónes* and the Jesuit lands; on the other, their dislike of Spain (many Jesuits were of mixed race, European and indigenous) resulted in the dissemination of the first ideas of emancipation in Europe that later on would influence the formation of nationalist movements fostering independence from Spain.[1]

Much later the Jesuits were dissolved by the papal edict of Clement XIV in 1773, although a few Jesuits survived in Poland and Russia under the protection of Empress Catherine II. By that time the Society of Jesus had grown enormously and 'it was operating more than eight hundred universities, seminaries, and especially secondary schools almost around the globe'.[2] The Jesuits were restored as a religious order in 1814. It is worth asking why the Society of Jesus expand so quickly, and what made the army of priests and religious so disciplined, then and now. The answer is twofold: the Jesuits were highly organised and intellectually prepared; and they had a clear personal commitment to God fostered by the *Spiritual Exercises*. The Exercises, as they are commonly known, are a set of spiritual practices, meditations and reflections written by St Ignatius, and undertaking them has become the spiritual norm for Jesuits all over the world to experience the presence of God and discern their vocation and calling at different stages of their religious life. These meditations are usually carried out in solitude through a continuous period of prayer and silence lasting for thirty days.

---

1 Edwin Williamson, *The Penguin History of Latin America*, London: Penguin, 1992, p. 162-4. Among them the Mexican Jesuit scholar Francisco Javier Alegre and the Jesuit Francisco Javier Clavijero, historian and anthropologist of ancient Mexico and of California, see Miguel Batlori, *La cultura hispano-italiana de los jesuitas expulsos*, Madrid: Editorial Gredos, 1966, Allan Figueroa Deck, *Francisco Javier Alegre: A Study in Mexican Literary Criticism*, Rome: Historical Institute of the Society of Jesus, 1976, and 'Jesuit Contributions to the Culture of Modernity in Latin America: An Essay Toward a Critical Understanding', in Christopher Chapple (ed.), *The Jesuit Tradition in Education and Missions: A 450-Year Perspective*, Scranton: University of Scranton Press, London and Toronto: Associated University Presses, 1993, pp. 169-81, and Bernabé Navarro, *Cultura mexicana moderna*, Mexico, DF: UNAM, 1964.
2 John W. O'Malley, *The First Jesuits*, p. 16.

A Latin American Jesuit

When Bergoglio told his parents about his decision to become a priest, they reacted in different ways. His father he was very happy and only asked him if he was sure that he really wanted to become a priest. His mother, however, asked him many questions and did not take well to the idea. She reminded him that he was the eldest son, traditionally the one who took over the family business; that he was doing well at work; that he could study further. She even suggested that he should wait before joining the seminary. His mother felt the loss of a dear son when he began his training, and for years she didn't visit the seminary. Whenever he returned home his mother was happy. They didn't quarrel about his decision to join the Seminary, but she did not play an active part in his life as a seminarian. Bergoglio's mother was a very religious person but she kept her distance from the seminary. When she visited him in the Jesuit Novitiate of Córdoba, after his priestly ordination, she knelt for his blessing; but she always expressed the belief that he had rushed into a decision that required a longer period of consideration. Bergoglio's grandmother was happy for him, and told him 'If God calls you, blessed be Him'. Those words were followed by her assurance that if he wanted to return at any point, he would be welcome at home – a warm sentiment at a time in which failed seminarians were stigmatised and ostracised by Latin American society because of the pedestal on which they placed those who answered God's call to the priesthood. For many devout Catholics at that time, if the person found, while studying for the priesthood, that his vocation lay elsewhere, he was considered at fault for not persevering or praying enough.

In the four years of youthful life between Bergoglio's confession at the church of San José de Flores and the actual day when he joined the seminary at twenty-one, he not only pursued spiritual goals, but also became intellectually immersed in the politics of the time. He read *Nuestra Palabra* and *Propósitos* avidly. *Propósitos* was a publication of the Argentinean Communist Party, in which several writers took turns addressing the aspirations and problems of the Argentinean proletariat. Bergoglio was particularly fond of the writings of Leonidas Barletta, a writer who influenced his political thought. However, as Bergoglio clarified several times when asked, he was never a member of the Argentinean Communist Party.

Bergoglio entered the novitiate of the Jesuits on 11 March 1958, and, during his first year of spiritual learning and community life, he undertook the *Spiritual Exercises*. At that time the Exercises were preached through a series of public conferences given to a group, rather than experienced in solitude with the help of a single director, as they are often experienced today. The Jesuits were only beginning to recover the source of Ignatian spirituality that would later be known as the thirty-day retreat. During those thirty days, a director guides a person taking the *Exercises* by arranging several periods of one-hour prayer during the day – including a period of prayer in the middle of the night – aided by biblical passages, which the person making the *Exercises* uses as a guide for meditation and prayer. John O'Malley, referring to the unique identity of the first group of Jesuits, has argued that 'with the hindsight of over four hundred years, we see more clearly than they did that the *Spiritual Exercises* and the schools were the two most important institutional factors that, when taken in their full implications, shaped the distinctive character of the Society of Jesus'.[1] Others, such as Paul Crowley SJ, have argued that the Jesuit emphasis on education must necessarily have theology as its central discipline, and that the *Spiritual Exercises* are a properly Jesuit approach to theology.[2]

There is no doubt that the *Spiritual Exercises* are central to the formation and the spiritual growth of a Jesuit, not only because the *Exercises* were given by Ignatius to all his companions and followers, but because the spiritual 'movement' within the *Exercises* makes a Jesuit who he is as much now as they did in the past. A striking reality in the life of a Jesuit is that all Jesuits throughout the ages have had the experience of the *Exercises,* and, from the experience of spending thirty days in prayer with the help of a director, they are encouraged to continue searching for Christ and for his will throughout every period of their lives. In my own experience, having made the *Exercises* at Loyola Hall in Liverpool in the summer of 1985, the solitude of a whole month meditating on the Scriptures and listening to God empties oneself of any intellectual constraint, and brings about a personal crisis of self-expressed faith that reveals itself as a need for God's consolation. Thus, David Fleming SJ has argued that: 'What appears to be a rigidly structured approach,

---

1   John W. O'Malley, *The First Jesuits*, p. 372.
2   Paul G. Crowley SJ, 'Theology in the Jesuit University: Reassessing the Ignatian Vision', in Christopher Chapple (ed.), *The Jesuit Tradition in Education and Missions: A 450-Year Perspective*, Scranton: University of Scranton Press, London and Toronto: Associated University Presses, 1993, pp. 155-68.

so meticulously ordered in hours of prayer and examination, in positions of prayer, in the use of food, sleep, penances, and so on, can only be studied with comprehension by someone who has had the experience of making the Exercises.'[1]

The *Exercises* were written by Ignatius during his experience of deep spiritual conversion at Manresa, and these drafts were finalised and edited while he was a student in Paris. His reflections were not intended to be a pious book read by others for personal inspiration, but a guide for spiritual directors who are leading others in search of God and personal conversion. During his arrests and interrogation by the Inquisition, Ignatius maintained that he was guiding others towards God, not towards himself, and that the *Exercises* guided his own spiritual structuring of a deep reflection on his own experience of conversion.

Ignatius and the Exercises

Ignatius, born in 1491 to a Basque family, enlisted in the army of the Duke of Najera, the rich and powerful viceroy of Navarre. In May 1521 the French Army attacked Navarre, and the viceroy fled, leaving behind a small garrison; Ignatius was among these soldiers. On 20 May 1521, a cannon ball smashed his right leg and damaged his left, leaving him useless for battle; the French did not kill him but sent him home to Azpeitia, fifty kilometres away.[2] It was during the long period of physical healing that Ignatius underwent a personal conversion and decided that, when he was well enough, he would go to Jerusalem, sell his possessions, and take up the life of a penitent and of a man of prayer. Ignatius departed for the Benedictine monastery of Montserrat in Catalonia, the first step of his journey to Jerusalem. At Montserrat he spent a night in prayer before the statue of the Black Madonna, and laid down his sword and dagger, changing them for a pilgrim's staff and a beggar's clothing. He followed the Benedictine practice of the time, taking three days to write down his sins, make his confession and break completely with his former life.

Ignatius stopped in Manresa, a small town near Barcelona,

---

1   David L. Fleming SJ, 'The Ignatian Spiritual Exercises: Understanding a Dynamic', in David L. Fleming SJ, *Notes on the Spiritual Exercises of St Ignatius of Loyola*, St Louis, MO: Review for Religious, 1983, p. 3.

2   Michael Floss, *The Founding of the Jesuits 1540*, London: Hamish Hamilton, 1969, pp. 61-7.

and for many reasons – including an outbreak of the plague – remained there for almost a year. During those months he searched for God, and the experiences of this time were recorded and became a large part of the *Spiritual Exercises*: a text that, in the eye of Ignatius, might be helpful to those who wanted to guide Christians searching for conversion and deeper prayer, as he had guided some of the people of Manresa.[1]

The *Exercises* became a path to inner conversion, but at the same time a marker of identity. Anyone wishing to become a Jesuit must pass through a rite of passage: the experience of God through the *Exercises*. Thus, over the centuries, Jesuit novices and seasoned Jesuits have undertaken the Exercises, not only once, but several times during their lifetime. In the contemporary life of the Jesuits, novices make the *Exercises* during the first spiritual steps of their Jesuit life, and once again during their tertiary period, a period of discernment and renewed apostolic zeal before their final religious profession as a Jesuit for life, some fifteen years or so after their first profession following their novitiate.[2] The original text of the *Exercises* was edited and revised by Ignatius while he was a student in Paris in order to direct his first Jesuit companions through the same experience of prayer and conversion, even before any of them took any religious vows, or the canonical existence of the Society of Jesus was approved by the papacy.

The person making the *Exercises* usually retreats to a quiet place – in contemporary terms a Jesuit retreat house – where he is assigned a director, and where he remains in silence throughout the four weeks of prayer proposed in the *Exercises*.[3] The director acts as a

1   John W. O'Malley, *The First Jesuits*, p. 25.
2   These norms and practices were revised by the Thirty-Fourth General Congregation of the Jesuits in 1995; Gero McLoughlin SJ writes: 'The requirement that novices make the *Exercises* appears in the General Examen that is shown to candidates. The General Examen is part of the Constitutions (almost a preamble). The reference is cited like this: Examen, c.4, § 9-10. The requirement also appears in the Complementary Norms and is cited CN 46 § 2. As regards the tertianship, making the Spiritual Exercises is not specifically required either by the Constitutions or by the Complementary Norms [. . .] The Complementary Norms also speak of the Spiritual Exercises as the 'source and centre of our vocation', Gero McLoughlin SJ to Mario I. Aguilar, Edinburgh, 13 March 2007.
3   Herbert F. Smith SJ, 'The Nature and Value of a Directed Retreat', and William A. Barry SJ, 'Silence and the Directed Retreat', in David L. Fleming SJ, *Notes on the Spiritual Exercises of St Ignatius of Loyola*, St Louis, MO: Review for Religious, 1983, pp. 20-6, 68-71.

spiritual catalyst, an aide to the one making the *Exercises*; he suggests biblical texts for periods of prayer and meditation and 'listens' for the movements of the soul, the feelings and the experiences of the one going through these weeks of God's presence.[1] It is understood by the participants that God directs the person towards his purpose and goal, not the retreat director; however, the retreat director should have the spiritual maturity as to be able to speak of God freely, and not to be afraid of travelling with someone through 'a spiritual labyrinth'.[2] According to Barry, 'the work of the spiritual director now becomes one of helping the person praying to discern, that is, to figure out what is going on, what is God's voice, what not'.[3] The director faces as much challenge as the person making a retreat, and all Jesuits, by the fact that they have made the *Exercises*, can be potential retreat directors.[4] The challenges faced by the directors during the *Exercises* are the same of those of a teacher or a theologian, inasmuch as they must allow freedom for the people they are guiding to explore God's path freely and to move according to their experiences of God. William Connolly SJ, in summarising the dangers faced by a controlling director of the *Exercises*, has outlined the characteristics of a person who is probably not an educated and discerning Jesuit:

> The director of a personalised retreat must combat within himself five major enemies of the other person's freedom: the director's own desire to have others dependent on him; his fear that he may lose control of the retreat if the retreatant exercises freedom; the worry that he may not know what to do if the retreatant takes a path that he himself is not accustomed to; his desire to achieve results in the retreat; inflexibility in his own spiritual life, with the tendency to feel his personal spirituality threatened when the retreatant goes his own way.[5]

1   Paul J. Bernadicou SJ, 'The Retreat Director in the Spiritual Exercises', in David L. Fleming SJ, *Notes on the Spiritual Exercises of St Ignatius of Loyola*, pp. 27-38.

2   George P. Leach SJ, 'Growing Freedom in the Spiritual Director', and William J. Connolly SJ, 'Appealing to Strength in Spiritual Direction', in David L. Fleming SJ, *Notes on the Spiritual Exercises of St Ignatius of Loyola*, pp. 39-47, 48-51.

3   William A. Barry SJ, 'The Contemplative Attitude in Spiritual Direction', in David L. Fleming SJ, *Notes on the Spiritual Exercises of St Ignatius of Loyola*, pp. 52-60 at p. 57.

4   Judith Roemer OSF, 'Discernment in the Director', in David L. Fleming SJ, *Notes on the Spiritual Exercises of St Ignatius of Loyola*, pp. 249-256.

5   William J. Connolly SJ, 'Freedom and Prayer in Directed Retreats', in

One of the aims outlined by Ignatius in the *Exercises* is the attainment of freedom, the freedom to experience a deep conversion, the centrality of God in all things and a detachment and indifference to other things. This feeling flows from a deep experience of God.[1] Each day of the four-week retreat is structured by four or even five periods of prayer.[2] At the end of the *Exercises* the person involved starts his 'fifth week', a long week that will last the rest of his life, or until he undertakes the *Exercises* again.

The text of the *Exercises* starts with the *Principle and Foundation*, a set of presuppositions written by Ignatius that are very important as foundations for a general understanding of Ignatius' view of 'the truth about human existence'.[3] The *Principle and Foundation* outline the basic principles of a Christian life lived to the full, within the Jesuit order in particular. The practising of the *Exercises* partially explains the indifferent reaction shown by Jesuits when they are criticised for their political involvement in modern societies that do not recognise priests as part of the socio-political order within a 'secular world'. Ignatius wrote:

Man was created to praise, reverence, and serve God our Lord, and by this means to save his soul; and the other things on the face of the earth were created for man's sake, and in order to aid him in the prosecution of the end for which he was created [. . .] It is therefore necessary that we should make ourselves indifferent to all created things, in all that is left to the liberty of our free will, and is not forbidden.[4]

David L. Fleming SJ, *Notes on the Spiritual Exercises of St Ignatius of Loyola,* pp. 61-67 at p. 63.

1 William A. Barry SJ, 'On Asking God To Reveal Himself in Retreat', in David L. Fleming SJ, *Notes on the Spiritual Exercises of St Ignatius of Loyola,* p. 72-77.

2 Prayer within the *Exercises* is understood as listening, seeing, responding and acting, see John R. Sheets SJ, 'The Four Moments of Prayer', in David L. Fleming SJ, *Notes on the Spiritual Exercises of St Ignatius of Loyola,* pp. 163-174.

3 David L. Fleming SJ, 'The Ignatian Spiritual Exercises: Understanding a Dynamic', in David L. Fleming SJ, *Notes on the Spiritual Exercises of St Ignatius of Loyola,* p. 5.

4 W.H. Longridge, *The Spiritual Exercises of Saint Ignatius of Loyola,* translated from the Spanish with a commentary and a translation of the *Directorium in Exercitia,* London: Robert Scott, 1919, p. 26.

The emphasis in the *Exercises* is on movement: the Spirit moves the
retreatant towards God through a structured series of meditations
from the Gospels. By this means, the retreatant is able to discern
God leading him into a life more oriented towards Him, or towards
a different path in life within the same *Principle and Foundation*.[1]
During the First Week the retreatant expands from an intellectual
knowledge of the *Principle and Foundation* towards a more reflexive
dialogue with God, in which he meditates on sin and on his own
past life, so as to prepare for 'a movement of the senses' in which
he can experience the mercy and love of God.[2] During the Second
Week, the retreatants listen for the call of God the King to work
with Him and to serve in His army, thus, making a conscious
choice between the two standards (flags in battle). In doing so, the
retreatant hopes to acquire, by the mercy of God, the humility to
serve and to centre one's life on the values of the King and of his
Kingdom.[3] During the Third Week, the movement and emphasis is
on staying with God, in a contemplative sense; of requesting small
experiences of the divine presence which kindle the sentiments and
the senses with an intimation of God as the centre of all. It is during
the Third week that retreatants are encouraged to pray during the
night, and when they awake without setting an alarm, because they
are called by God to do so. By the Third Week the retreatants have
become accustomed to the routine of prayer, and desperately seek
consolation when 'the standards of the Kingdom' seem high and
the body is tired from the interrupted nights.[4] The Fourth Week
concentrates the senses on the love of God through contemplation

1   Charles J. Healey SJ, 'Prayer: The Context of Discernment', David T. Asselin
    SJ, 'Christian Maturity and Spiritual Discernment', John R. Sheets SJ, 'Profile
    of the Spirit: A Theology of Discernment of Spirits', and Herbert F. Smith
    SJ, 'Discernment of Spirits', in David L. Fleming SJ, *Notes on the Spiritual
    Exercises of St Ignatius of Loyola*, pp. 195-200, 201-213, 214-225, 226-248.
2   See as an example of the possible texts and reflections generated by the
    topic and experience of conversion Carolyn Osiek RSCJ, 'The First Week
    of the *Spiritual Exercises* and the Conversion of St Paul', and William A.
    Barry SJ, 'The Experience of the First and Second Weeks of the *Spiritual
    Exercises*', in David L. Fleming SJ, *Notes on the Spiritual Exercises of St
    Ignatius of Loyola*, pp. 86-94, 95-102.
3   William Connolly SJ, 'Story of the Pilgrim King and the Dynamics
    of Prayer', in David L. Fleming SJ, *Notes on the Spiritual Exercises of St
    Ignatius of Loyola*, pp. 103-107.
4   William J. Connolly SJ, 'Experiences of Darkness in Directed Retreats', in
    David L. Fleming SJ, *Notes on the Spiritual Exercises of St Ignatius of Loyola*,
    pp. 108-114.

of the Resurrection.[1] At the end of the *Exercises* the retreatant starts the Fifth Week, in which all practices of contemplation and prayer that were acquired during the four weeks in solitude will be carried forward into the rest of the person's life, with time especially set aside for prayer, and a sense of intensity that comes from a full month's solitude away from ordinary life and work.[2]

It is possible to argue, following this short exploration of the spiritual foundations of Jesuit life, that through the *Exercises* the Jesuits have developed a tremendous sense of the ultimate centrality of God in the happenings of regular life, and thus a heightened sense of mission, as well as a diminished fear of personal danger and discomfort. As it was during the time of the first 'soldiers' of the Company of Jesus, the *Exercises* help develop a strong and orderly sense of reflection and discernment that, together with a challenging academic program, makes Jesuits able to discern important social and political changes within society, and consequently to act in the world to create space for God's Kingdom, rather than the agendas of other peoples' kingdoms, governments or dominations.[3]

Junior Years in Chile

After completing the period of his Novitiate and taking his first vows, Bergoglio joined a remarkable group of young Jesuits at the Jesuit house located in Marruecos (later known as Padre Hurtado) in the outskirts of Santiago, Chile. It was a property that hosted Jesuit novices and juniors. Residing there were the Chilean novices, as well as junior Jesuits from Chile and Argentina; these countries were still co-operating with one another even after Chile became an independent Vice-Province of the Jesuits in 1936.[4] By the time of Bergoglio's arrival, the novice master was

---

1 Dominic Maruca SJ, 'The Graces of the Third and Fourth Week', in David L. Fleming SJ, *Notes on the Spiritual Exercises of St Ignatius of Loyola*, pp. 134-143.

2 Charles C. Murphy SJ, 'On Leaving Retreat: To Go Out Can Be To Go In', in David L. Fleming SJ, *Notes on the Spiritual Exercises of St Ignatius of Loyola*, pp. 144-155 and William O'Malley SJ, *The Fifth Week*, Chicago: Loyola University Press, 1976.

3 William J. Connolly SJ, 'Social Action and the Directed Retreat', in David L. Fleming SJ, *Notes on the Spiritual Exercises of St Ignatius of Loyola*, pp. 286-290.

4 The first vice-provincial of Chile was Fr Pedro Alvarado SJ aided by a group of Chilean Jesuits who had been sent to study in Europe including Fr Alvaro Lavín SJ and Fr Alberto Hurtado SJ, see José Aldunate Lyon SJ, *Un peregrino cuenta su historia*, Santiago: Ediciones Ignacianas, 2003, p. 31.

Fr José Aldunate, who served in that capacity from 1952 to 1962. The community was large, considering that Fr Aldunate had an average of eighteen novices in his charge in each of his ten years as novice master.[1] The house had been bought by the Chilean Jesuit Fr Alberto Hurtado (later St Alberto Hurtado) in 1940, in order to house the destitute of society, and later it was re-assigned for the formation of young Jesuits.[2] There Bergoglio followed the normative course of humanities and classical sciences that included history, literature, Latin and Greek.

One of the residents of the house at that time was the young Jesuit scholastic Fernando Montes, later to become novice master, provincial and rector at the Jesuit Alberto Hurtado University of Santiago. Fr Montes' recollection of those years were of a Jesuit community that spent most of its time in silence, studying and praying, set apart from the worries of the world.[3] However, they were also living together in a community where Fr Alberto Hurtado's concern for the poor and the workers within society had already been felt. Jesuits took their goal of acquiring a basic knowledge of the arts and humanities seriously, as it was necessary for Jesuits who were going to be immersed in educational establishments, and would interact with the elites of Chile and Argentina, to be well-educated. The two countries were members of the same Jesuit province, and the Argentinean province sent

---

1   José Aldunate Lyon SJ, *Un peregrino cuenta su historia*, pp. 68-73.
2   Fr Alberto Hurtado, a Chilean Jesuit who died in 1952, was canonized on 23 October 2005. He joined the Jesuits in 1923 and after studies in Chile and, Europe, he became chaplain to university students all over Chile. His concern was to support the development of the whole person, and under his guidance the chaplaincies grew rapidly - from 1,500 students in 50 centres in 1941 to 12,000 students in 500 centres in 1944. In 1944 he met a sick and starving beggar who made such an impression in his life that he was strengthened in his dedicated apostolate towards the poor, the unemployed and those without a home who lived under the Santiago bridges. He founded the Home of Christ, despairing that in a country where the majority were Christians there were people who were ill, without a home and had to spend the cold winter nights without shelter begging and waiting for others to help them. Fr Hurtado helped with the training of those youth and was hated by traditional Catholics when he started asking questions about the reasons for poverty in society. By the time of his death in 1952 he had started an organization for workers at a time when workers belonged to the Chilean Communist Party and didn't find a place within a very traditional Chilean Catholic Church.
3   Conversation with Fr Fernando Montes SJ at the Universidad Alberto Hurtado, Santiago, 23 May 2013.

their young students, known as scholastics, to Chile to be trained. Latin was used for the liturgy, in class, and for study. While Bergoglio resided there the announcement came of John XXIII's calling of the Second Vatican Council, which inspired Jesuits to engage with the contemporary world after their intellectual training.

In letters to his family from Chile, Bergoglio didn't talk very much about the daily life of the Jesuit community, but dialogued in his own personal style about reality, particularly Christian reality, with those with whom he corresponded. Thus, in a letter of May 1960 to his sister Maria Elena, he confided that he was teaching religious studies to local children who were very poor: they didn't have shoes or enough food and they suffered in the cold winters in Santiago. He also confided to her the fact that a lady who had talked to him had expressed the simple dream of having enough money to buy a blanket. However, before outlining his own personal concerns about social realities, he told his sister 'I would like you to be a saint', and, as he would throughout life, he asked her to pray for him.[1]

Bergoglio returned to Argentina in 1963. He studied theology from 1967 to 1970 at the Colegio San José in San Miguel and graduated with a licentiate in theology. He was ordained as a priest on 13 December 1969 by Archbishop José Ramón Castellano. On the occasion of Bergoglio's ordination to the priesthood, he recalled that his grandmother had advised him while he was a seminarian that the most important function of a priest was to celebrate every Mass as if it were the first and the last to be celebrated. His classmates and students of the 1960s remember Bergoglio, the teacher of philosophy and psychology, as severe and respected, with a deep spirituality, a personal charisma and strong negotiating skills.

Between 1964 and 1965 Bergoglio taught literature and psychology at a secondary school, the Colegio de la Inmaculada

---

1 At the head of the paper Bergoglio's letter has the letters 'J.H.S.', used by the Jesuits since the time of their founder St Ignatius of Loyola and later used by Bergoglio within his episcopal coat of arms. Bergoglio wrote in the letter: 'Yo doy clases de religión en una escuela a tercero y cuarto grado. Los chicos y chicas son muy pobres; algunos hasta vienen descalzos al colegio. Muchas veces no tienen nada que comer, y en invierno sienten el frío en toda su crudeza. Tú no sabes lo que es eso, pues nunca te faltó comida, y cuando sientes frío te acercas a la estufa', Letter from Jorge Bergoglio to María Elena Bergoglio, Padre Hurtado, 5 May 1960.

Concepción de Santa Fe, and in 1966 he taught the same subjects at the Universidad del Salvador in Buenos Aires. During those years, traditional Catholic families from Santa Fe, from other Argentinean provinces and even from abroad sent their children to this well-known Jesuit school. Bergoglio had himself studied industrial chemistry, but was asked to teach psychology, a subject he had studied during his philosophical studies in preparation for the priesthood, and literature – a subject for which he had to prepare the preceding summer. A former student, Jorge Milia, wrote about his experience in the Jesuit school in the book *De la edad feliz,* and remembered Bergoglio as a teacher who taught him attitudes that remained with him for the rest of his life. When Milia was being examined by a committee, Bergoglio requested that, instead of choosing only a single part of the subject of study, Milia should expand upon the whole subject in front of his examiners. Milia did well and Bergoglio suggested granting him not the top mark (10), but the next highest (9). He hoped Milia would remember that the most important thing in life is daily effort, and that transitory markers of achievement can seduce people into accomplishing less in the long run.[1]

Bergoglio tried to make his lectures varied and flexible, and if one of his students preferred a particular period in the history of literature or a particular author within that period, he would cater to that student's inclination. Bergoglio remembers that when he taught the seminal work *El Cid,* a student asked him if he could study Machado's poem about *El Cid.* Bergoglio agreed, knowing that Machado was one of his students' favourite authors. His former student Milia suggested that Bergoglio was capable of bringing his pupils to the most difficult tasks in a militant spirit, as if they were charging great wind mills like the characters in *Don Quixote.* Bergoglio asked his students to write short stories, and once, on a trip to Buenos Aires, he showed a collection of the stories to the well-known Argentinean writer Jorge Luis Borges. Borges liked them so much that he encouraged their publication in a volume named *Cuentos Originales* and wrote the prologue himself. Milia remembered this publication with emotion, as well as the occasion on which Borges came and gave a lecture to them. To Milia, Bergoglio was a kind of Jesuit commando. He wanted to get the best out of his students, and, after they completed their

---

1   *El Jesuita,* pp. 55-56.

education, continued meeting them as a confessor, friend and supporter. In the prologue to another book, this time Milia's own, Bergoglio confessed that he loved his students, that they made him into a better person and taught him how to be a brother rather than a religious father.

A Jesuit post-Medellin, 1968

Following a long Jesuit spiritual formation, Bergoglio spent the years of 1970 and 1971 in Spain, where he undertook his third period of spiritual exercises at the Jesuit house in the Spanish city of Alcalá de Henares. On 22 April 1971, he made his solemn profession to be a Jesuit for life. He is remembered fondly in Spain for his kindness and his personal warmth. He returned to Argentina, where he became Novice Master in Villa Barilari, San Miguel (1972-1973), a lecturer at the Faculty of Theology, a member of the Jesuit provincial council, and rector of the Colegio Máximo. It was during these years, before he became provincial, that Bergoglio was linked with the youth organisation of the Peronistas, youth followers of President Perón. They were known as the Guardia de Hierro, an organisation that was in turn member of the Organización Única de Trasvasamiento Generacional (OUTG), an association of groups that was dissolved in 1974. This link with the Guardia de Hierro, even as a chaplain, has suggested over the years that Bergoglio supported the Peronistas within the national politics of Argentina (Peronistas advocated for greater social equality in the country).

It is clear that throughout Latin America the Jesuits had embraced the 1968 directives on simplicity of life and poverty as signs of the Kingdom in their communities. This poverty was also a way of life connected to the *Exercises,* and embodied their lessons and values. The *Exercises,* once again, provide an explanation as to why the Jesuits shaped their work in 1968 on behalf of the Church and of Christ into a movement oriented towards the poor and the marginalised. During the Second Week of the *Exercises,* the main emphasis is on the two standards (the two flags carried by armies facing one another in battle). It is expected that the retreatant will choose to follow the standard of Christ's army and the service of the heavenly King. Three degrees of humility are also considered. The third degree of humility requires that the retreatant contemplate the choice of being with the poor, not because of an exultation of poverty, but because Christ chose to be with the poor and the marginalised. At that moment of the *Exercises,* the choice of work or location in society is not the main issue: a full personal commitment to the person of Christ, and therefore a commitment to the poor, becomes preferable because that was the choice of Christ himself. William J. Byron has argued in very personal terms that the Second Week is crucial for internalising this option for Christ – and therefore for an option the poor – in the following words:

> I regard the meditation on the Two Standards as a personal exercise in conscientisation, the process of consciousness-raising, written about by Paulo Freire and concerned essentially with the dawning awareness of dominant values which can, in fact, be the oppressive forces. Once aware of the dominant values of Satan and of their oppressive, destructive force in my life and my world, I pray for the courage to choose and be chosen for the dominant values of Christ. I elect identifiable membership in a counterculture.[1]

On 31 July 1973, Bergoglio was elected provincial superior for all Jesuits in Argentina, a role that he was to fill for six years in total – he was re-elected in 1976. During this period, Bergoglio lived through a period of increasing violence and social turmoil that ended with the formation of the government of Isabel Perón. The military takeover was to have deep consequences for Bergoglio in particular and Argentinean society in general.

---

1   William J. Byron SJ, 'Social Consciousness in the Ignatian Exercises', in David L. Fleming SJ, *Notes on the Spiritual Exercises of St Ignatius of Loyola,* pp. 272-285 at p. 279.

2. The Military and the 'Dirty War'

In 1973 Bergoglio was elected provincial superior of the Jesuits in Argentina and inevitably became immersed in the complex Argentinean political world. Bergoglio was elected Jesuit provincial in 1973 and served for two terms, an indication that he was well-liked by his fellow Jesuits, and the military was in power from 1976 until 1983.[1] The military government of those years was headed by a junta of three senior officers appointed from the Army, the Navy and the Air Force. They were known as 'the gentlemen', and were President General Jorge Rafael Videla,[2] Admiral Emilio

1 For the history of the Argentina during this period see Marta Castiglione, *La militarización del estado en Argentina 1976-1981*, Buenos Aires: Centro Editor de América Latina, 1992, Andrés Fontana, 'Political Decisionmaking by a Military Corporation: Argentina, 1976-1983', Ph.D. Thesis, University of Texas, 1987, Donald Hodges, *Argentina's Dirty War: An Intellectual Biography*, Austin TX: University of Texas Press, 1991 and *Argentina 1943-1987: The National Revolution and Resistance*, Albuquerque: University of New Mexico Press, 1988, and Paul H. Lewis, *Guerrillas and Generals: The Dirty War in Argentina*, Westport, CT: Praeger, 2002.

2 *General Jorge Rafael Videla* was born in Mercedes, Buenos Aires on 2 August 1925 and died at the Marcos Paz Prison in Buenos Aires on 17 May 2013 having been found dead at 8.30 am while serving a life sentence for crimes against humanity. After the military coup of 24 March 1976 he was declared president of Argentina by the military junta that took power under the name Proceso de Reorganización Nacional and served as president until 1981. Videla was also head of the Argentinean military from 1975 and 1978. In 1983 Videla was tried, convicted and sentenced to life in prison for crimes of lesser humanity during the government of President Raúl Alfonsín. He was also stripped of his military rank. In 1990 President Carlos Menem pardoned him together with other high ranking officers. However, in 1998 he was again imprisoned, accused of stealing hundreds of newborn babies born in captivity during his term as head of the country. After a short spell in prison, Videla was allowed to serve his sentence at home until 2008 when new crimes were heard by the courts and Videla was moved to the military base of Campo de Mayo.

Eduardo Massera,[1] and Brigadier General Orlando R. Agosti. In 1981, after Videla completed his term in office, he was replaced by General Roberto Viola, Army Chief of Staff. Viola started talks with still-illegal political parties, and was replaced in late 1981 by General Leopoldo Galtieri. In 1982, another change was made in order to prepare Argentina for a return to democracy, and General Reynaldo Bignone was inaugurated as head of the last Argentinean military junta.[2]

By the 1970s the Jesuits in Argentina were powerful educators involved in seminaries, theological faculties, schools and universities, all sites of social tension between the military government and the opposition. Similar tensions had surrounded Jesuit missions in northern Argentina during colonial times.[3] Most

---

Videla was at the military base from October 2008 until June 2012 when he was convicted of stealing babies born in captivity, sentenced to life in prison and transported to the Marcos Paz Prison, where he died.

1   *Admiral Eduardo Emilio Massera* was born in Paraná, Entre Rios, on 19 October 1925 and died on 8 November 2010 at the Pedro Mallo Naval Hospital where he had been kept since 2002 since being admitted for suffering a stroke. Massera joined the Argentinean Navy in 1942 and served in the naval intelligence unit; he was promoted to admiral by President Juan Domingo Perón, the youngest navy officer to have been promoted to admiral in the history of the Argentinean Navy. Massera only served two years in the first military junta, having he left this office in order to start a political party, the Partido para la Democracia Social. Massera was tried for multiple crimes committed at the Naval Academy of Buenos Aires (Escuela de Mecanica Superior de la Armada – ESMA) and for the disappearance of babies born in captivity. In 1990 he was pardoned alongside other military men by President Carlos Menem, and later in 1988 he was once again convicted and sentenced to home arrest at his farm of El Talar de Pacheco. Later he was moved to the military unit of Campo de Mayo because of irregularities in his house arrest, until 2002 when he had a stroke and was moved to a naval hospital. In 2005 he was deemed incapable of facing trial and in 2009 he was deemed insane and unable to face trials, including extradition procedures incited by the governments of Italy and Germany.

2   For a general overview of the historical complexities of this period of Argentinean history involving a systematic abuse of human rights, see Marguerite Feitlowitz, *A Lexicon of Terror: Argentina and the Legacies of Torture*, NY: Oxford University Press, revised edition 2011, 'Introduction', pp. 3-20.

3   T. Frank Kennedy SJ, 'An Integrated Perspective: Music and Art in the Jesuit Reductions of Paraguay', in Christopher Chapple, ed., *The Jesuit Tradition in Education and Missions: A 450-Year Perspective*, Scranton: University of Scranton Press, London and Toronto: Associated University Presses, 1993, pp. 215-225.

members of the colonial Argentinean elite had been educated at the University of Córdoba, founded by the Jesuits in 1622, and at the San Ignacio School, founded in 1661.[1]

The Jesuits in the 1970s

During the 1970s the Jesuits of Argentina did not have the same level of involvement in protecting human rights as the Chilean Jesuits, probably because the public role of the Catholic Church was perceived in different ways in the two countries.[2] Only a few Jesuits in Argentina were involved with the working classes, Argentina being exceptional among the Latin American countries, and they paid the price of arrest and torture as a result. In Chile, not only was the leader of the movement Christians for Socialism a Jesuit (Gonzalo Arroyo SJ), but in their formation Chilean Jesuits were strongly influenced by the memory of St Alberto Hurtado, a Chilean Jesuit who had dedicated himself to the poor and workers.[3] After the 1973 military coup in Chile, the Chilean Cardinal Raúl Silva Henríquez had requested that some young Jesuits – for example Patricio Cariola SJ and Patricio Salas SJ – become directly involved in the archdiocesan structures defending human rights through the Pro Paz Committee, and later through the Vicariate

1 In a letter written in German, Fr Strobel SJ wrote: 'one has to believe that God must take special pleasure in these thirty settlements that the company has built and maintains along the Uruguay and Paraná Rivers and that the entire community of Indians, with few exceptions, is inscribed in the Book of Life', Fr Strobel, 'The Jesuit Mission' in Gabriela Nouzeilles and Graciela Montaldo, eds. *The Argentina Reader: History, Culture, Politics*, Durham and London: Duke University Press, 2002, pp. 34-37 at p. 36; see also Robert Bontine Cunninghame Graham, *A Vanished Arcadia: Being Some Account of the Jesuits in Paraguay 1607-1767*, London: Century, 1988 (1901).

2 For a theological and historical analysis of the involvement of the Jesuits in Latin America during the 1970s, see Mario I. Aguilar, *The History and Politics of Latin American Theology*, vol. 2: Theology and Civil Society, London: SCM Press, 2008, chapter 4 'The Jesuits', pp. 79-96.

3 St Alberto Hurtado died in 1952 and was canonized by John Paul II in his visit to Chile in 1981. Hurtado founded the Hogar de Cristo in Santiago, despairing that in a country where the majority were Christians there were people who were ill, homeless, and had to spend the cold winter nights without shelter, begging and waiting for others to help them. He helped in the training of those poor and was hated by the well-to-do whenever he asked questions about the real causes of poverty in Chile.

of Solidarity.[1] By the time the military was in power in both Chile and Argentina, and particularly during 1976, the security forces of both countries were co-operating in handing over and arresting prisoners who were wanted in both countries. As a result, the Jesuits of both countries shared a similar experience of the military even while belonging two very different episcopal conferences and having two very different ecclesial experiences.

The political conservatism of most of the Catholic Church in Argentina prevented there being any diocesan structures that could deal with violations of human rights and challenge the military regime; Christian charity to the populace and concern for the suffering of catechists and clergy were shown, but neither the bishops nor the provincial of the Jesuits had the public authority to challenge the military junta. There was a lack of ecclesial structures to help those suffering from violence and persecution, structures that were very common in other Latin American countries, particularly in Brazil and El Salvador, where Archbishop Romero publicly spoke against human rights abuses and was backed by the Jesuits of the University of Central America. Bergoglio, regardless of his intellectual and pastoral qualities, was younger than other civic or military leaders in Argentina – he was forty years of age at the time of the military coup – and had no real means of challenging the authorities without the support of the Argentinean bishops, particularly without the support of Cardinal Juan Carlos Aramburu, archbishop of Buenos Aires at the time of the military takeover. Aramburu repeatedly denied the reality of government-ordered disappearances, and even the possibility that the military might be violating human rights. As archbishop of Buenos Aires, he was the first person relatives of victims of this political repression approached, but he ignored their complaints.

One of the most convincing explanations for the conservatism of the Catholic Church in Argentina – and the close alliance between bishops and clergy and the Argentinean military – has been offered by Jeffrey Klaiber SJ, who summarised the diverse possible explanations into one: 'as a consequence of the extraordinary influence that the tradition of national Catholicism, forged in the

---

1   For the biography of Cardinal Silva Henríquez see Mario I. Aguilar, *A Social History of the Catholic Church in Chile*, vol. 2: *The Pinochet Government and Cardinal Silva Henríquez*, Lewinston, Queenston and Lampeter: Edwin Mellen Press, 2006.

Eucharistic Congress of 1934, had over it, the Argentine church lost vital contact with large sectors of the population' and 'that same tradition impeded the church from becoming a symbol of national unity under Videla and the other military, much less a symbol of democracy and human rights'.[1]

The foundations for conservatism and traditionalism in Argentinean Catholicism were laid in the decades after Argentina gained independence from Spain. By the second half of the nineteenth century, Argentina experienced an economic boom as it became the main international exporter of beef, wheat and wool to the world markets, particularly those associated with the British Empire, and hubs of the industrial revolution such as Manchester. Within this climate 'two Argentinas' started to emerge. The first Argentina was that of landowners, managers of meat-processing plants and banks, who started to adopt European – and particularly British – manners, and who lived mainly around or near Buenos Aires. A second Argentina was that of the provinces – where life was slower and the colonial organisation of society around agriculture was still intact. This sector of society was emerging as a challenge to Buenos Aires. With the arrival of large numbers of European immigrants, the voices of working-class people, associated later with the Peronistas (followers of the Argentinean President Juan Domingo Perón), also became louder; a third strand, distinct from the landowners and the immigrants. These three were politicised when, in 1910, Argentinean law allowed all males, including immigrants, to vote. By the start of the twentieth century, the Catholic Church in Argentina had lost its societal centrality, and some priests attempted to connect the social doctrine of the Church with the actions of many religious orders who ran hospitals, dispensaries and worked closely with the poor. Many also worked with those who were disenchanted with an Argentinean society that did not give a voice to the working class. The rise of Argentinean Catholic Action in the 1920s, and the founding of the magazine *Criterio* in 1928 (criticised by President Yrigoyen in 1930, perhaps contributing to his overthrow) show a Catholic Church attempting to unify the three visions of the Argentinean nation. Unity was also desired by the Argentinean military, which had lost much of its political influence to the sway of emerging business and private enterprise.

---

1   Jeffrey Klaiber SJ, *The Church, Dictatorships, and Democracy in Latin America*, Maryknoll, NY: Orbis, 1998, chapter 4 'Argentina (1976-1983): "The Dirty War"', pp. 66-91 at p. 90.

The Thirty-Second International Eucharistic Congress was held in Argentina on 14 October 1934, and was organised by Archbishop Santiago Luis Copello, who would shortly thereafter be created a cardinal (in 1936). Eugenio Pacelli, later to become Pius XII, was the Vatican envoy for the occasion. The Argentinean Church, having just witnessed the collapse of the liberal project for Argentina, used the occasion to publicly advocate for the social doctrine of the Church, the centrality of the progressive movement Catholic Action, and Christian political ideas that were later linked to the international Christian Democrats of Europe, Chile and Venezuela. The ceremonies of the Congress attracted 200,000 people, and caused the Argentinean Armed Forces to consecrate themselves to the Virgin of Luján. President Justo consecrated Argentina to the Blessed Sacrament. The model of a Catholic society that included the Church, the military and civilian groups, who all rejected socialism and liberalism, was forged during the 1934 Eucharistic Congress; and throughout the twentieth century in Argentina the Catholic Church was allied with the military, both seen as jointly protecting the Argentinean nation.[1] All the Argentinean presidents elected after 1934, including Perón, were constrained therefore to seek authority and legitimation from the Church, and could not seek to implement a national project for a liberal society without the Church's approval.

The roots of Argentinean conservatism did not arise only from the alliance between Church and military, however, but also from the formation and nature of the Argentinean clergy and the nature and ancestry of the Argentinean bishops. An understanding of this formation will help understand the different public responses of Chilean and Argentinean bishops to military rule. While most of the Chilean bishops came from land-owning and aristocratic families, most of the Argentinean bishops came from lower-status immigrant groups who were seduced by the prospect of social mobility, and consequently keen to win the respect of Argentinean elites and mix in upper-class circles. The Second Vatican Council made very little impact in Argentina, and the Argentinean seminaries were in general very traditional and conservative, advancing a clericalist model of social order in which the priest was dominant in society. This meant that in

---

1   I am grateful to Jeffrey Klaiber SJ for his clear analysis of 1934 as foundational to understanding the 'Dirty War' and the (non-)response of the Argentinean bishops; see also Klaiber, *The Church, Dictatorships, and Democracy in Latin America*, p. 69-70.

practice some bishops, such as Bishop Tortolo of Paraná, who was president of the Argentinean Episcopal Conference at the time of the military takeover, kept their dioceses completely removed from any implementation of Vatican II.

Argentinean Political Continuity

When Bergoglio was a provincial superior of the Jesuits, Argentinean politics had been dominated for years by the figure of Juan Domingo Perón. Perón, and later his followers, mostly working class men and women, made a consistent effort to exclude the middle classes from the ongoing running of the nation by advocating for total social and financial equality for all Argentineans.[1] Mid-twentieth century Argentinean politics were dominated by the Peronist/anti-Peronist dichotomy, with trade unions forming the base of the Peronist movement (*sindicalismo peronista*), and the Argentinean Armed Forces and their associates pushing an anti-Peronist agenda as a rationale for political action.[2] This political and social dichotomy, suppressed for years, re-emerged with the return of Perón and his new wife, María ('Isabel') Estela Martínez de Perón, to Argentina on 20 June 1973, after eighteen years of exile. Subsequently, on 23 September 1973, Perón was elected president of Argentina; but critically he failed to reach an understanding with the trade unions and influential business organisations because he could not prevent a major economic crisis in the country. Argentina became extremely violent as an economic crisis unfolded. Inflation rocketed, and, by 1974, the European Common Market had closed down meat imports from Argentina. The financial crisis had already become a political crisis by this point.

The primary political crisis took place amongst the Peronistas. Some revolutionary factions were unhappy with his economic practices or with Isabel Perón's (Juan Perón's third wife), alliance with private businesses that took place after Perón's death in July 1974. In 1975 the displaced left-wing groups among the followers of Perón – i.e. the revolutionary wing of the Peronist Party, *Montoneros*, and the Marxist *Ejército Revolucionario del Pueblo* (ERP) – continued

1   Daniel James, *Resistance and Integration: Peronism and the Argentine Working Class, 1946-1976*, Cambridge University Press, 1988, pp. 7-30.

2   This dichotomy is elegantly explained by Laura Tedesco, *Democracy in Argentina: Hope and Disillusion*, London: Frank Cass, 1999, pp. xix-xx, see also D. James, *Resistance and Integration: Peronism and the Argentine Working Class 1946-1976*, Cambridge: Cambridge University Press, 1988.

an armed struggle against the establishment with attacks on military barracks, kidnappings of well-to-do people, and frequent assassinations.[1] In response to these events, right-wing military groups organised by the *Alianza Anticomunista Argentina* (AAA) targeted their opponents, particularly supporters of left-wing organisations who did not go into hiding because of their positions, i.e. teachers, lawyers, university professors, medical doctors and other middle-class professionals. In previous years, the Minister for Social Welfare, José López Rega, had organised 'the Triple A' (AAA), a neo-fascist group whose aim was to cleanse the Peronist Party of Marxist elements and their supporters, and to restore a peaceful state of affairs to Argentina.

As a result of this political chaos and political violence, and encouraged by the example of the Chilean military, the Argentinean Armed Forces deposed Isabel Perón and took over the government. Argentinean lay pastoral agents suffered heavy casualties as a result of political persecution of 'subversives', while the Argentinean bishops did not speak openly about the gross human rights violations by the military junta, which was led by Jorge Videla, President of Argentina from March 1976 to 1981.[2] Other civil organisations, such as 'the mothers of the disappeared' (*Madres de la Plaza de Mayo*), took a public stand against these human rights violations, and every Thursday they paraded in silence in Buenos Aires' May Square, requesting information about their loved ones.[3] The military regime supported an anti-communist, pro-American crusade throughout Latin America, and remained in power until the war for the Malvinas/Falklands Islands challenged the authority of the military and their ability to lead the Argentinean nation into the future.[4] On 30 October 1983, the Radical Party won 51.75% of the total vote, and on 10 December 1983 Raúl Alfonsín became the new, democratically-elected president of Argentina.[5]

---

1   See for example Richard Gillespie, *Soldiers of Perón: Argentina's Montoneros*, Oxford: Clarendon Press, 1982.

2   The Military Junta was made by the Commanders-In-Chief of the Argentinean Armed Forces: Lt. General Jorge R. Videla, Brigadier Orlando E. Agosti and Admiral Emilio E. Massera. Following a previous agreement Videla took over as president.

3   Jo Fisher, *Mothers of the Disappeared*, London: Zed and Boston: South End, 1989.

4   Ariel C. Armony, *Argentina, the United States, and the Anti-Communist Crusade in Central America 1977-1984*, Athens, Ohio: Ohio University Center for International Studies, 1997.

5   The Peronist Party got only 40.16% of the total vote.

The 'Dirty War'

The political persecution by the right-wing paramilitaries and the military of intellectuals and those involved in trying to create a more just Argentinean society in the years 1970-1983 might be exemplified by the case of Argentinean theologian Enrique Dussel, one of most prominent theologians of liberation. Dussel did not work as a parish priest, but as an academic dealing with historical and economic issues: his contribution to Argentinean models of politics and economics was considerable.[1] He influenced others through reconceiving an ethical and political project for Latin America at a time when the military regimes aligned themselves with capitalist policies, challenging those policies with Christian ideas of economic justice and equality.[2] The military regimes endorsed a common concept of 'the national security state', which would prevent the spread of communism and legitimise their policies by violating human rights on a massive scale. The first official reports by the Comisión Nacional sobre la Desaparición de Personas (National Commission of Disappeared Persons, CONADEP), established by President Raúl Alfonsín in 1983 to investigate forced disappearance in Argentina, suggested that there were 9,000 documented cases, while human rights organisations over the years have asserted that there were in fact 30,000 cases.[3]

Dussel recognised that his intellectual project about the sufferings of Latin America started years before after a conversation he had with the philosopher Emmanuel Levinas. Dussel asked Levinas why he thought only about the Jews, and did not think about the suffering of the indigenous peoples and black populations of Latin America. Levinas looked at him and said: 'That is for you to think about'.[4] However, the right-wing paramilitary groups in Argentina

---

1 Married to Joanna Dussel, they had two children, Enrique and Susanne.
2 A special issue of the journal *Anthropos* used that classificatory systematisation for Dussel's wide range of writings that comprises more than 50 books; see *Anthropos*, 180 (September-October 1998).
3 Jo Fisher, *Mothers of the Disappeared*, London: Zed and Boston: South End Press, 1989, Daniel Poneman, *Argentina: Democracy on Trial*, New York: Paragon, 1987, Luis Alberto Romero, *A History of Argentina in the Twentieth Century*, Pennsylvania: Pennsylvania State University Press, 2002 and Laura Tedesco, *Democracy in Argentina: Hope and Disillusion*, London and Portland, OR: Frank Cass, 1999, pp. 23-61.
4 Enrique Dussel and E.D. Guillot, *Liberación Latinoamericana y Emmanuel Levitas*, Buenos Aires: Bonum, 1975.

were suspicious of his intellectual project, and on 2 October 1973 a bomb destroyed part of his home.[1] Given the political situation it is likely that Dussel would have been killed if he hadn't sought refuge in Mexico. Mexico offered shelter to highly qualified professionals and intellectuals escaping the military regimes of the Southern Cone, as well as to the leaders of the ERP who left Argentina after the death of their leader Roberto Santucho in July 1976.

This could not have been a more difficult time to be provincial of the Jesuits; and Bergoglio's young age made it even more so. The role of the Jesuits within this particular period of Argentinean political and ecclesiastical history needs to be assessed in the context of the large and diverse Argentinean Catholic Church, which had more than eighty bishops and sixty dioceses. For the most part, there was an ecclesiastical acceptance of the military in all areas of Argentinean society – even within a national context of political repression. Individual responses, however, were more diverse. One bishop, Angelelli, and several priests, nuns and Catholic pastoral agents were assassinated by the regime because they lived in poor areas, and as a result of this they were labelled subversives by the regime.[2] The Jesuits did not have the power to confront the authorities within a nation whose security plan deemed all those involved in *any* opposition to the military government 'subversives'. The Argentinean security forces were aided by other Latin American security forces, commonly co-operating with the Chilean security forces in the transportation and elimination of political prisoners. My general assessment of Bergoglio's conduct during this period is that, just like anybody else, he might have done more to protect political prisoners. However, given the circumstances of a military dictatorship (and I experienced the dictatorship of Augusto Pinochet in Chile) it was impossible for him to show much opposition in the public sphere as it was completely controlled by the military. Such control included censorship of the press and educational organisations. The general blame, if any, should be placed upon the Argentinean bishops: they should have spoken openly and with a

1   Enrique Dussel, 'Preface to the Third Spanish Edition', in *A History of the Church in Latin America: Colonialism to Liberation*, Grand Rapids, Michigan: William B. Eerdmans, 1981, p. xx.

2   I commend the critical synthesis of the Argentinean Catholic Church provided by Jeffrey Klaiber SJ, 'Argentina (1976-1983): The "Dirty War"' in his work *The Church, Dictatorships, and Democracy in Latin America*, Maryknoll, NY: Orbis, 1998, pp. 66-91.

common voice about the political situation. It was difficult for the provincial of the Jesuits to do so with the same authority. Bergoglio protected his own Jesuits after indirectly exposing those who decided not to live in the Jesuit community under his leadership by suspending them (this withdrawal of protection caused their arrest by the regime). He undoubtedly tried to help them after their arrest, and when they were released helped them flee the country.

The Jesuits and the 'Dirty War'

During the years of the 'Dirty War', the Jesuits were confronted with the same dilemmas as any other religious order. They operated within a church that was mostly conservative, and within a socio-political situation where large numbers of men, women and children were being systematically arrested at their homes, their places of work, or even on the street, and accused of being subversives. They were taken to government-controlled buildings where they were tortured, killed and their bodies secretly disposed of.

During the 'dirty war', Jesuit priests continued to work in elite universities and schools, yet also within the shanty towns and poorer areas of Buenos Aires. As provincial, Bergoglio had to deal with Jesuits who were traditional and conservative, as well as with others who were more radical in their lifestyle and who had been strongly influenced by the General Meeting of Latin American Bishops in Medellin (1968) that had set the guidelines for the implementation of the changes of the Second Vatican Council in Latin America. For the Jesuits, such implementation had begun with the meeting of Jesuit provincials from all of the Latin American provinces that took place in Rio de Janeiro (6-14 May 1968), and which preceded the bishops' meeting at Medellin.[1] From this meeting, two areas of reflection emerged, along with guidelines and future aims, that became important for the role of the Jesuits within Latin America in the 1970s: the provision of education for those without access to it and a Jesuit option for a life of poverty. Thus, the Jesuit provincials asserted 'we must offer marginal groups the chance for an education, so

---

1 The conclusions of that meeting are available as Provincials of the Society of Jesus, 'The Jesuits in Latin America (May 1968) in Alfred T. Hennelly, ed. *Liberation Theology: A Documentary History*, Maryknoll, NY: Orbis, 1990, pp. 77-83.

that they may be able to contribute their talents to the life of the nation . . . providing a solid education to all'. Further, in relation to a life of poverty, the Jesuit provincials suggested that 'in addition to these activities, the Society finds another thrust to be fully in accord with its underlying spirit. It is the vocation to an apostolate of being present to the people and bearing witness among them, sharing their life of poverty'.[1]

The military takeover in Argentina brought with it a totalitarian political order, and priests, nuns and pastoral agents who were working with the poor and marginalised, following the guidelines of Medellin, were confronted with persecution, torture and death. First and foremost among those persecuted were the priests who, in December 1967, published a document supporting the declaration known as the 'Manifest of Eighteen Bishops of the Third World', which gave birth to the organisation known as Priests for the Third World. The organisation grew to almost 500 members, 9% of the Argentinean clergy in the early 1970s.[2] They worked in the *villas miseria* (Argentinean shanty towns), and became closely connected with the movement of political socialism known as *peronismo*. Consequently, they became the enemies of those who opposed Perón and his political movement. Carlos Mujica, the founder of the group, was shot dead outside his parish in May 1974, presumably by the right-wing paramilitary AAA. Mujica had presided over funerals for members of the Montoneros movement, a guerrilla-style, left-wing organisation that had attracted hundreds of Catholic youth and maintained a close association with priests who worked with the poor in Argentina.

Three other priests were killed: the popular Alfredo Kelly and two seminarians of the Pallotine congregation on 4 July 1976 at the parish of St Patrick's in the neighbourhood of Belgrano in Buenos Aires. The killers painted the walls with left-wing paramilitary slogans, but it was clear that the priests had in fact been killed by right-wing paramilitary fighters. Both the nuncio and Cardinal Aramburu visited the military to express their concerns, but, after a memorial Mass was celebrated in the parish, the incident was forgotten until the legal investigations undertaken after the collapse of the military government in 1983.

---

1 'The Jesuits in Latin America' § 6.
2 José Pablo Martín, 'El Movimiento de Sacerdotes para el Tercer Mundo', *Nuevo Mundo: Revista de Teología Latinoamericana*, Buenos Aires: Ediciones Castañeda San Antonio de Padua and Ediciones Guadalupe, 1991.

Further assassinations followed: on 18 July 1976, two priests who belonged to the Priests for the Third World movement were kidnapped and killed in Chamical, near Rioja.[1] On 4 August 1976, Bishop Enrique Angelleli, bishop of Rioja, died in a car accident, later disclosed as an assassination after a car ambush, because he had publicly condemned the Argentinean government for human rights violations. When he died he was carrying documents that implicated the military in the killing of the earlier two priests, documents that were stolen from the site of the accident and never found. A year later, Bishop Carlos Ponce de León of the diocese of San Nicolás and a friend of Angelleli, died in a suspicious car accident. In December 1977 two French nuns of the French Institute of Foreign Missions, who worked with the mothers of the Plaza de Mayo, were kidnapped, killed and their bodies 'disappeared'. The French President, Valéry Giscard d'Estaing, sent a personal envoy to the Argentinean government to ask for an explanation, but he was told in no uncertain terms that the military junta did not know anything about the killing of the French nuns or about the whereabouts of the group kidnapped at the same time.

Thousands of people were kidnapped and tortured in order to extract information about the Church's activities and aid to subversives. One of the well-known Church activists kidnapped, and disappeared was Mónica Mignone, daughter of Emilio Mignone, author of the classic analysis of the Church and military in Argentina *Iglesia y dictadura*.[2]

Bergoglio and the 'Dirty War'

On 23 May 1976, while Bergoglio was Jesuit provincial, Francisco Jalics and Orlando Yorio, both Jesuits, were kidnapped and held until October 1976 at the infamous Mechanical School of the Navy (Escuela de Mecánica de la Armada - ESMA). The ESMA is located in Buenos Aires, with Libertador Avenue to the west, Comodoro Rivadavia and Leopoldo Lugones streets to the east and Santiago Calzadilla street to the south. The army personnel assigned to interrogate and torture prisoners were known internally as Task Force 3.3. 2. They were stationed, together with the prisoners, in

---

1 'Bergoglio declara como testigo en la causa ESMA', *El Clarín*, 8 November 2010.
2 English edition: Emilio Mignone, *Witness to the Truth: The Complicity of Church and Dictatorship in Argentina 1976-1983*, Maryknoll, NY: Orbis, 1988.

the officers' mess, a three-storey-high building with a cellar and a huge attic.[1] Jalics and Yorio were initially held here, but later kept in a house in Don Torcuato, and released on 23 October 1976.[2] Yorio testified that they had been together at the ESMA and that they realised it was the ESMA because on 25 May 1976 a military parade took place nearby. Those broadcasting the parade said it was from the ESMA. When the priests were released, Yorio was taken blindfolded by helicopter to a field where he courageously removed the cloth from his eyes to discover that Jalics was in the same field.[3] Yorio testified that he had been without water, food, or toilet facilities for several days, and that he was verbally abused by his captors, who repeatedly told him that he was not a priest.[4] On the day of his release, Yorio had been injected with a drug and put in a truck. Whenever he awoke he was injected again. When he finally recovered consciousness in the field, he and Jalics walked to a house over one kilometre away and knocked on the door, where a surprised farmer told them that they were in a place called Cañuelas.[5] They realised that they had been transported in a truck to an airfield and loaded onto a helicopter; however, unlike the many thousands who were the thrown into the sea they were left unconscious on the field at Cañuelas.

The Jesuits were already widely regarded as 'subversives' by many in the military; partly because of their education and intellect, which meant that were always considered intellectual outsiders 'to the educational nationalistic ideas fostered by the regime.[6] As part of the legal investigations into human rights abuses perpetrated at

1   *Nunca Más: The Report of the Argentine National Commission on the Disappeared*, New York: Farrar, Straus and Giroux and London: Index on Censorship, 1986, a translation of the original document published in Argentina in 1984, pp. 79-84, with graphic diagrams of the rooms used for torture at pp. 80-81, 83.
2   Their case is mentioned in the 'List of victims' who were members of the clergy and of religious orders in the Report of the Argentinean National Commission on the Disappeared, see *Nunca Más*, pp. 337-354, Francisco Jalics § 14, pp. 344-345.
3   Testimony by Fr Orlando Virgilio Yorio, file number 6328, *Nunca Más*, pp. 344-345.
4   Orlando Virgilio Yorio § 23, 'List of victims' who were members of the clergy and of religious orders in the Report of the Argentinean National Commission on the Disappeared, see *Nunca Más*, pp. 347-348.
5   Testimony of Fr Orlando Virgilio Yorio, file No. 6328.
6   This is an interesting point well-argued by Mick Anderson in Martin Edwin Anderson to Mario I. Aguilar, 1 May 2013.

the ESMA, María Luisa Funes, a former catechist and prisoner at the detention and torture centre, declared on 23 September 2010 that the arrested Jesuits had lost their protection from the security forces once Bergoglio withdrew 'their religious license' to preach in the Villa del Bajo Flores, a week before their arrest. According to the witness, Bergoglio had asked them to leave Bajo Flores, to which they complained that he was trying to impede their service to the poor. It may be that Bergoglio, as provincial of the Jesuits, had received instructions from Pedro Arrupe SJ, the Jesuit Superior General, to ask them to leave their life in the shanty towns outside the immediate protection of the Jesuit community, or to leave the Jesuits all together if they could not comply. This idea would be consistent with the importance given to obedience within the Jesuits and Arrupe's concern for the fate of Jesuits working in poor areas of Latin America within the period of the military regime, expressed during his visit to Chile and Argentina in 1973.[1]

After the arrest of the two priests, Bergoglio wrote to the family of Francisco Jalics, intimating that he would do whatever he could to secure his release.[2] Jalics' brother showed two letters to Marie Kathatrina Wagner, a German reporter. In one of them, dated 15 September 1976, Bergoglio wrote:

> I have sought in many ways to bring about your brother's freedom, but thus far we have been unsuccessful. . . . But I have not lost hope that your brother will be released soon. I have decided that the matter is my ongoing task. . . . The differences that your brother and I have had between us concerning the religious life have nothing to do with the current situation. [Then, in German] Ferenke is a brother to me. . . . [later]' I'm sorry if I started writing in German, but this the way I think about it. . . . I have Christian love for your brother, and I will do all in my power to see him freed.[3]

A day after Jalics' release from prison, Bergoglio wrote to the priest's brother once again, stating that 'We also heard the false reports that Francisco had been assassinated, but I never believed it because I heard news about both priests. Usually people talk too much rather

1 Conversation with Fr Fernando Montes SJ at the Universidad Alberto Hurtado, Santiago, 23 May 2013.
2 The letters were published in the *Frankfurter Allgemeine Zeitung*, 17 March 2013 and reported in *La República*, 18 March 2013.
3 *Frankfurter Allgemeine Zeitung*, 17 March 2013.

than finding solutions'.[1] In November 2010, Bergoglio gave his version of events, his legal right, at the offices of the diocesan *curia* in Buenos Aires. Bergoglio's legal testimony, offered to the Oral Tribunal 5 of Buenos Aires (an ordinary criminal court) stated that he met twice with Jorge Rafael Videla, a member of the military junta that ruled Argentina in 1976, and he also met twice with Emilio Eduardo Massera, head of the Argentinean Navy, in order to request the liberation of the two priests.[2] The prosecution in the case, including Luis Zamora and Myriam Bregman, investigating accusations of crimes against humanity at the ESMA, suggested that Bergoglio hesitated during his testimony. According to them he was concealing information and possibly even lying to the courts.[3] The legal investigation of the case of the two Jesuits at the ESMA was carried out within the broader investigation into the disappearance of the French nuns Alice Domon and Leonie Duquet. Further, the prosecution argued that Bergoglio's passivity reflected the sinister attitude of the Catholic Church during the 'dirty war', and that Bergoglio, who heard the testimony of the Jesuits after their imprisonment, should have gone to the Argentinean courts to denounce these crimes, and later, when democracy was reimplemented, should have come forward to give testimony to the courts as well.[4]

Apart from his actions on the behalf of the two priests, Bergoglio had been involved with the others who were persecuted during the period of the 'dirty war'. In his long meetings with Sergio Rubin and Francesca Ambrogetti, he was asked about the imprisonment of the two Jesuits and his own role as their Jesuit provincial.[5] Bergoglio

1   *Frankfurter Allgemeine Zeitung,* 17 March 2013.
2   'Causa ESMA: Bergoglio declaró que pidió a Massera y Videla por la liberación de los sacerdotes', *Diario Ámbito Financiero,* 8 November 2010.
3   'ESMA: La querella acusa a Bergoglio de mentir en su declaración' M24 Digital 8 November 2010 at http://m24digital.com/2010/11/08/esma-la-querella-acusa-a-bergoglio-de-mentir-en-su-declaracion/
4   'El cardenal Bergoglio que tanto sabe, ahora casi no sabe hablar. . . . , Causa ESMA, 8 November 2010 at http://juicioesma.blogspot.co.uk/2010/11/el-cardenal-bergoglio-que-tanto-sabe.html
5   Sergio Rubin, an Argentinean journalist, responsible for religious affairs in the Argentinean newspaper *El Clarín* and Francesca Ambrogetti, Italian journalist and social psychologist, interviewed Bergoglio over a period of two years of meetings at Archbishop's House in Buenos Aires, and the original text was published in 2010 with a revised cover and title, being launched immediately after Bergoglio's election as Pope in March 2013, see Sergio Rubin and Francesca Ambrogetti, *El Jesuita: La historia de Francisco, el Papa argentino,* Buenos Aires: Ediciones B Argentina and Javier Vergara Editor, 2010.

clarified that, while he was resident at the Jesuit Colegio Máximo in San Miguel, Buenos Aires, he had sheltered some of the persecuted.[1] Also, after the assassination of Bishop Angelleli of La Rioja (4 August 1976), Bergoglio sheltered three seminarians from La Rioja who were studying theology[2] Those he helped were not hidden, but protected by the fact that the Jesuits often gave long retreats at the Colegio Máximo; therefore those in need of protection could remain at the retreat centre for a full month if necessary, without it being seen as suspicious.[3] Bergoglio also mentioned a young person who was being persecuted, and who happened to look very much like him. Bergoglio helped him leave Argentina through Foz de Iguazú on the border with Brazil, dressed as a priest and using Bergoglio's Argentinean identity card.[4]

During these conversations with Rubin and Ambrogetti, Bergoglio disclosed that he had met twice with General Jorge Videla and twice with Admiral Emilio Massera in order to enquire about the two Jesuits arrested in May 1976. On one of these occasions, Bergoglio had asked the name of the military chaplain who was going to celebrate a Saturday family Mass at Videla's residence, in order to request that the chaplain allow him to celebrate the Mass instead. Thus, Bergoglio managed to replace him and snatch a few minutes with Videla, to request information about the two Jesuits being held captive by the Argentinean Navy.[5] Bergoglio admitted that he had only visited one of the military detention centres, an air force base, close to San Miguel, in the locality of José C. Paz, in order to request information about a young person who was being held prisoner there.[6] Also, Bergoglio remembered receiving the sad visit of Esther Ballestrino de Careaga, the lady who had been his boss at the chemistry lab, who was a widow by the time of the 'dirty war' and who had two sons who were trade unionists and members of the Argentinean Communist Party. Both sons had been kidnapped, and she wanted help. Bergoglio made some

---

1   *El Jesuita*, p. 146.
2   *El Jesuita*, p. 147.
3   On the 30th anniversary of Angelleli's assassination, the bishop of Bariloche, Fernando Maletti, met one of the seminarians who had been ordained as a priest and lived in Villa Eloisa, in the province of Santa Fe, who told him his story. Maletti mentioned to Bergoglio that such story should be publicly heard, *El Jesuita*, 146-147.
4   *El Jesuita*, p. 147.
5   *El Jesuita*, p. 147.
6   *El Jesuita*, p. 147.

enquiries but didn't get any information to help Esther Ballestrino, who was eventually also kidnapped and killed.[1] There were also happy endings: he was asked to intervene on behalf of a young catechist, who was eventually freed by the military.

Bergoglio clarified that Frs Jalics and Yorio had been trying to establish a new religious community when they were taken. They had already written a possible common rule for such new institute, and had given a draft to Mgrs Pironio, Zazpe and Serra. When the Superior General of the Jesuits in 1976, Pedro Arrupe SJ, heard about this, he asked them to choose between the Society of Jesus and their new institute. These events, involving over a year of discussion among the Jesuits themselves had nothing to do with Bergoglio; but, as with any canonical change, they involved the Superior General of the Jesuits and the Argentinean bishops under whom the two Jesuits were serving. The transfer of the men out of the Jesuit order was accepted in the cases of Fr Yorio, and of Fr Louis Dourrón, who was working with Yorio and Jalics; however, the situation of Fr Jalics was more complex, since he had already taken solemn Jesuit vows and only the pope could declare them null. These decisions were made on 19 March 1976, just five days before the military took over of the government from President Isabel Perón. As a military coup was expected, Bergoglio was aware of the complexity of the situation, and gave the Jesuits in question the opportunity to reside at the Jesuit Provincial House, an offer that they rejected. Bergoglio thought they were in danger not because they were 'subversives' – he never accused them of collusion with the Montoneros – but because they lived in the exposed barrio of Rivadavia del Bajo Flores, a place where many left-wing militants resided. They and other priests were vulnerable to military raids. Yario and Jalics were arrested during one of these raids, known as 'operaciones rastrillo'. During military raids all houses were searched, all males interrogated and all documents checked. Dourrón managed to escape the military's search because he was riding through the streets on a bicycle, and when he saw the first signs of their arrival he took a short cut and quickly left the area.[2]

Other testimonies about Bergoglio during this period suggest that certain well-to-do families of 'the disappeared' who had been close to the Jesuits, and who had given them financial support, were directed to contact Bergoglio by Arrupe, the Superior General. Bergoglio did not grant audiences to these relatives of the disappeared, and therefore

---

1   *El Jesuita*, pp. 147-148.
2   *El Jesuita*, p. 149.

he became part of a passive ecclesiastical machinery. This passivity is exemplified by the case of María Isabel Chorobik de Mariani ('Chicha'), one of the founders of the association of grandmothers of the Plaza de Mayo (21 November 1977), who was told by the Church that her granddaughter, kidnapped at three months old, was probably well cared for by powerful people. Chorobik's granddaughter was never found, a fact that made Chorobik assert that 'it is very clear to me that the Church knew what was happening to the children who were being handed over and those who were born in prison. The Church aided the actions of the military'.[1]

There are those who have defended Bergoglio's actions at the time of the 'dirty war' have suggested that, without Bergoglio's warning, the Jesuits working in Bajo Flores would have been even more exposed to kidnapping; and that, without his conversations with members of the Argentinean military junta, they would have been killed. Bergoglio used the private forum in order to save the lives of the Jesuits who otherwise would have been thrown from the helicopter into the sea and today would be listed among the disappeared. However, he failed to support some of those who requested his help, who were women and lay people, at a time when he could have done so. It is clear that during the same period the Chilean Jesuits provided personnel who worked for human rights organizations. Several of them were arrested, including Fr Aldunate, who led a movement against the use of torture in Chile. Alicia Oliveira, a judge during the time of the military and a lawyer at the Centro de Estudios Sociales y Legales (CESL), argued that the two Jesuits did not take Bergoglio's warning seriously enough. She testified that Bergoglio had saved her life during the military crackdown against subversives.[2] Another of Bergoglio's defenders was Clelia Luro – the secretary and later wife of Mgr Jerónimo Podesta, former bishop of Avellaneda, who had resigned his office in order to marry her. She testified that Bergoglio had tried to protect the two Jesuits by warning them about the imminent danger to their lives.[3] It must be remembered

---

1 'Chicha Mariani: "No espero nada de Bergoglio porque jamás podré olvidar el rechazo de la Iglesia a nuestra causa"', Juicio a genocidas por robo de menores, 21 April 2013 at http://robomenores.blogspot.co.uk/2013/04/chicha-mariani-no-espero-nada-de.html

2 *La Nación*, 14 March 2013.

3 Luro recalls with affection that Bergoglio was the only Argentinean bishop who visited Podesta when he was dying in hospital in the year 2000, *Le Monde*, 26 October 2007.

that Bergoglio was the only bishop to attend the transfer of the human remains of the priest Carlos Mujica – spokesman of the Priests for the Third World and friend of the Montoneros – to his resting place at Villa 31 in Buenos Aires, where he worked until killed in 1974 by the AAA. Mujica's sister Marta suggested that, without Bergoglio's support, his brother could not have rested among those whom he loved.[1] This shows that Bergoglio was far from ignoring the plight of those who suffered under the junta, although he was unable to speak out against it as much as one with greater power would have been able to.

Some accusations that Bergoglio was complicit in the actions of the junta are founded on columns and documents provided by Horacio Verbitsky (born Buenos Aires 1942), an investigative journalist, who writes regularly for the Argentinean newspaper *Página 12* and heads the CESL.[2] A former *Montonero* (member of the Montoneros movement) intelligence chief, Verbitsky is linked to a book published by the Argentinean Air Force in 1979 entitled *El poder aéreo de los argentinos*. A special dedication is made to the military junta, and to Verbitsky as ghost writer.[3] Verbitsky published materials in 1999 suggesting that the Catholic Church had covered up cases of military violence against priests and others during the 'dirty war'.[4] In his work *El silencio* (2005), Verbistky accused the Church of ignoring the arrest of two Jesuits in May 1976.[5] A second book by Verbitsky, *Doble Juego* (2006), described the close alliance between the Catholic Church and the military, a feature of which was the Church's silence. It was published in the same year that Bergoglio published his *Iglesia y democracia en la Argentina*, in which the then-cardinal provided some key documents for enriching the understanding of relations between the Church and the military. Verbistky went on to claim that Bergoglio's book contained

1   *Le Monde*, 26 October 2007.
2   I am grateful to Barry Carr (La Trobe University) for his contribution to discussions on this period at H-NET Latin American History List, and I refer particularly to his communication to this scholarly list of which I am a member on 14 March 2013.
3   Martin Edwin Anderson to Mario I. Aguilar 1 May 2013; cf. Dossier Francisco I – Martin Edwin Anderson, 'Pope Francis and still some dirty secrets from Argentina's so-called dirty war' at http://www.offnews.info/verArticulo.php?contenidoID=44546
4   Horacio Verbistky in *Página 12*, 25 April and 9 May 1999.
5   Horacio Verbitsky, *El silencio: De Paulo VI a Bergoglio, Las relaciones secretas de la Iglesia con la ESMA*, Buenos Aires: Editorial Sudamericana, 2005.

serious omissions, and in April 2010 he published five further testimonies of victims of the military repression which, in his opinion, compromised Bergoglio's accounts.[1]

It must be clarified here that *Iglesia y democracia* is not Bergoglio's personal book, but a publication by the Argentinean Episcopal Conference, providing a continuity of the Church's thought twenty-five years after the publication of *Iglesia y comunidad nacional* (1981). Thus, the 2006 volume presented by Bergoglio provides key public documents written by the Argentinean bishops from 1981 to 2006. These books are a common product of Latin American episcopal conferences, and this particular volume was not a personal defence by Bergoglio. In this case, he was presenting the documents as president of the Argentinean Episcopal Conference.[2] In his verbal presentation at the press conference within Archbishop's House, Bergoglio alluded to the difficult times that Argentinean society and the Church had faced under the military government, and explained that, due to the complexity of issues related to human rights, '*Iglesia y democracia*' included documents dating from 1967 to 1982.[3] In Bergoglio's opinion, these documents expressed the thought of the Argentinean bishops, and, by providing information on the recent past, laid the foundations of the future.[4]

It is understandable that Bergoglio – as Jesuit provincial and not yet a bishop – would have had less influence than suggested by commentators and critics of the Church in 1976. However, as argued by Pablo Palomino: 'More important is Bergoglio's silence after the dictatorship – when unlike in 1976, there were no reasons to feel terrified'.[5] The Jesuit provincial could have been more outspoken against the former regime, and the bishop of Buenos Aires more open about those times and horrors.

After the two priests, Yario and Jalics were released, Jalics, born

1   Horacio Verbistky, in *Página 12*, 8 April 2010.
2   'Iglesia y democracia en la Argentina' – Palabras del cardenal Jorge Mario Bergoglio, arzobispo de Buenos Aires y presidente de la Conferencia Episcopal Argentina, en la presentación del libro Iglesia y democracia en la Argentina (6 marzo 2006).
3   'Iglesia y democracia en la Argentina' – Palabras del cardenal Jorge Mario Bergoglio § 4c.
4   'Iglesia y democracia en la Argentina' – Palabras del cardenal Jorge Mario Bergoglio § 5.
5   Pablo Palomino's comment on H-Net Latin American History List, 27 March 2013.

in Hungary but a naturalised Argentinean, left for Germany. He remained a Jesuit all his life. Three years after his release, Jalics wrote to Bergoglio from Germany, requesting help to renew his Argentinean passport. Jalics feared that if he returned to Argentina he would be re-arrested. Bergoglio received the letter and wrote to the Argentinean authorities supporting Jalics' request; he even went in person to deliver the letter alongside Jalics' application form, stating that a journey back to Argentina was going to be very costly, and requesting that the Argentinean consulate in Bonn be instructed to issue a new passport to Fr Jalics. The officer who received Bergoglio's application asked him why Jalics had to leave Argentina, a question that Bergoglio answered truthfully by stating that Jalics and a companion had been arrested, mistakenly accused of being subversives. The officer told Bergoglio to leave the letter and application form, and that an answer would be forthcoming. Jalics' application for a new passport was rejected, and the officer that spoke to Bergoglio wrote a note on the application suggesting that Bergoglio had said that Jalics had been arrested for being a subversive – without adding that ultimately Jalics had been declared innocent of any charges.[1]

Another accusation against Bergoglio is that he supported the appointment of Admiral Massera to the teaching staff of the Universidad del Salvador, a Jesuit foundation that, at the time of the incident, was not affiliated with the Jesuits in Argentina. However, Bergoglio did not attend Massera's inauguration ceremony, and in my opinion he was not involved in selecting Massera as an adjunct member of staff; he also challenged a group who, in one of their meetings, discussed public politics in relation to university matters.[2] Bergoglio's actions have been consistently questioned from all sides by groups from all parts of the political spectrum, one of the reasons he has given to explain his silence on the subject of the many of the incidents he faced as Jesuit provincial.

There are other witnesses who testify that he helped others during the dirty war. One of them, Alicia Oliveira, a judge at this time, met Bergoglio at her office in 1975 before the military takeover. He requested help for a person in legal difficulties.[3] Oliveira and Bergoglio enjoyed their conversation, and other meetings followed. In these, Bergoglio expressed his concern that there was going to be

1   *El Jesuita*, pp. 150-151.
2   *El Jesuita*, p. 151.
3   *El Jesuita*, pp. 152-157.

a military takeover, and Oliveira as a judge, with a certain risk to her life, committed herself to uphold the law and to become close to human rights organisations. Bergoglio offered her residence at the Colegio Máximo for a short period of time, an offer that Oliveira declined, suggesting foolishly that she would rather be taken care of by the military than by the clergy. Oliveira did, however, suggest to her secretary, Dr Carmen Argibay – later minister of the Supreme Court of Argentina – that maybe she should leave her two children in Argibay's care for a while and go into hiding. In the end, Oliveira did not do so. Argibay was taken prisoner by the military on the same day of the military takeover, and Oliveira managed to find out days later that Argibay was being held in the jail of Devoto where she spent a few months of prison. It is clear from these testimonies that Bergoglio also aided individuals who were not connected directly to the Jesuits or to the Catholic Church.

Oliveira was subsequently sacked by the military, but she continued working as a human rights lawyer, requesting hundreds of *habeas corpus* writs for illegal detentions and forced disappearances. She also became one of the first members of the executive commission of the NGO, CESL. She recalled the early opinion she shared with Bergoglio, that the military perceived the nation as composed of friends and enemies: thus anybody connected to the poor and to places where the poor lived, and who had not been born there, was perceived as a terrorist and an enemy of the state. During their meetings, Bergoglio always showed concern about the risks that the Jesuits who worked in the poorer areas of Buenos Aires were taking, because they were already known and suspected by the military. Oliveira mentioned that Bergoglio did whatever he could to find out where the two kidnapped Jesuits were being held, and made representations for their release on their behalf. She also witnessed many farewell meals at the Jesuit retreat house, wishing good luck to people who had been able to secure safe passage out of Argentina as a result of Bergoglio's help. Bergoglio was the custodian of the library of Mrs Ballestrino de Careaga's daughter (Mrs Ballestrino was his former boss at the laboratory where he worked in his youth) – a library with many Marxist authors – because the military were watching her. Later, the military arrested Mrs Ballestrino's daughter but released her, while Bergoglio's former boss was arrested and killed.

Oliveira lectured at the Universidad del Salvador at the School of Law, alongside Eugenio Zaffaroni, who was also appointed to the Argentinean Supreme Court. She described to her students some of the forceful practices used by prosecutors in the middle ages in order to extract a confession, and she linked those practices with facts about the military in Argentina. Bergoglio warned her that this put her at risk of abduction by the military. However, she and Zaffaroni continued to call for candidates for the presidency of Argentina who would affirm Argentina's support for human rights and democracy. An opportunity for fostering political change came when Charles Moyer, former Secretary of the Inter-American Court of Human Rights, expressed a wish to visit Argentina to talk with the presidential candidates. This was important because until then Argentina had not ratified the Inter-American Convention of Human Rights (Pacto de San José de Costa Rica). During the military regime, the Secretary General of the Organisation of American States was the Argentinean Alejandro Orfila, a man closely linked to the Argentinean military. All human rights agreements were ignored by Argentina at this time. Charles Moyer was even threatened with dismissal if he went to Argentina. However, Bergoglio made it possible for Moyer to deliver a public lecture on the proceedings of the Inter-American Court of Human Rights at the Universidad del Salvador. Those attending were for the most part mostly academic staff teaching international law; however, Moyer had the chance to meet with presidential candidates after the talk. He wrote to Bergoglio to thank him, and Raúl Alfonsín, who was elected president of Argentina, later ratified the Pacto de San José de Costa Rica.

These were times of obscurity for Bergoglio, but the day his selection as a bishop would soon arrive, when he would be able to lead Christian public reflections on the living, the dead, the Church and the nation.

3. From Auxiliary Bishop to Cardinal

After six years as Jesuit provincial, Bergoglio became rector of the Jesuit Colegio Máximo in Córdoba and director of the faculties of theology and philosophy at the same institution.[1] At the same time, he undertook the duties of a parish priest in the Parroquia San José, in the newly-founded diocese of San Miguel.[2] Bergoglio was the first parish priest to organise the parish catechesis within the diocese. He later founded four chapels and three soup kitchens for disadvantaged children in the parish. It was in this context that Bergoglio discovered his pastoral vocation, and the simplicity of life that would become a hallmark of his ministry as auxiliary bishop of Buenos Aires.

In March 1986 Bergoglio travelled to Germany to complete his doctorate on the theology of Romano Guardini (dealing with liturgy and spirituality), but ultimately never completed his studies.[3] He went to the Philosophisch-Theologische Hochschule Sankt Georgen, a theological school located in Frankfurt am Main that had been founded as a seminary for the diocese of Limburg by

---

1   The Colegio Máximo was founded in the early seventeenth century by the Jesuits. After their expulsion from Latin America, the Franciscans took over the learned institution, and in the late nineteenth century it became an integral part of the Universidad de Córdoba, today a state university.

2   The Catholic diocese of San Miguel was erected by John Paul II in 1978 and its first bishop was Monsignor Horacio Alberto Bózzoli (1978-1983).

3   Romano Guardini (1885-1968), an Italian priest who worked, studied and taught mainly in Germany, had a considerable influence in the renewal of liturgy in Germany with his seminal work *Vom Geist der Liturgie* (*The Spirit of the Liturgy*, Crossroads, 1998), a work that was to aid the renewal of the liturgy that took place after Vatican II. Guardini's *The Lord* (Regnery, 1996), published originally in the 1940s, remained in print in its English translation for decades and was one of the most read books on the subject by Catholics all over the world.

the Jesuits in 1926.[1] In 1951 it became a Jesuit faculty of philosophy and theology. Famous alumni include Cardinal Friedrich Wetter, the Salvadoran theologian Jon Sobrino SJ, and Muslim theologian Farid Esack. Bergoglio went there to find a director for his doctoral thesis on Guardini, but the idea never came to fruition. Bergoglio felt rather lonely during that year in Germany, wishing to return to close contact with parishioners in Argentina.[2] His wish was soon granted, and he returned to Argentina, where he became spiritual director and confessor at the Colegio de El Salvador, later holding a similar position the Parroquia de San Ignacio in Córdoba.

As Auxiliary Bishop

After years as a confessor and professor of theology, Bergoglio was ordained as titular bishop of Auca on 20 May 1992, becoming an auxiliary bishop of Buenos Aires who worked closely with Archbishop Antonio Quarracino (1923-1998), the cardinal primate of all Argentinean bishops, archbishop of Buenos Aires from 1990 to 1998.[3] Quarracino became well known for his ongoing dialogue with Jews, a dialogue Bergoglio was to continue during his time as archbishop. During his 1992 visit to Israel, Quarracino

1   Albert Schorsch to Mario I. Aguilar, 8 June 2013.
2   Some biographers and media have suggested that Bergoglio was forced to return to Argentina as a punishment, and that he was closely monitored by the Jesuit authorities, see for example Evangelina Himitian, *Francisco: El Papa de la gente*, Buenos Aires: Aguilar, 2013, p. 97. This judgement is completely inaccurate, and those Jesuits from Chile involved in his return to Argentina – the two countries were ecclesiastically united – denied that there was any coercion behind Bergoglio's return to Argentina. This point was made by Fr Fernando Montes SJ in a conversation we had at the Universidad Alberto Hurtado in Santiago on 23 May 2013.
3   Cardinal Antonio Quarracino was born in Italy on 8 August 1923 in Pollica, Salerno, Italy and emigrated to Argentina with his parents when he was four years old. He was ordained on 22 December 1945 and became a lecturer at the Diocesan Seminary of Mercedes and the Catholic University of Argentina. He was appointed bishop of Nueve de Julio in Buenos Aires on 3 February 1962, and took over the diocese on 8 April 1962. On 3 August 1968, he was moved by Paul VI to the diocese of Avellaneda and later by John Paul II to the archdiocese of La Plata on 18 December 1985. He was moved to the archdiocese of Buenos Aires on 10 July 1990 as primate of all Argentina. From 1990 to 1996 he served as president of the Argentinean Episcopal Conference and was named Cardinal of Santa Maria della Salute a Primavalle in the consistory of 28 June 1991.

was decorated by Jewish institutions for his work in promoting inter-faith dialogue. In 1997, Quarracino had a mural painted on the wall of the cathedral of Buenos Aires that commemorated the victims of the Holocaust, those who died in the bombing of the Israeli Embassy (17 March 1992) and those who died at the Argentine Israelite Mutual Association (AMIA, 18 July 1994).

Bergoglio's episcopal appointment by the Vatican was advocated by Quarracino after the pair met in Córdoba at a spiritual retreat. Bergoglio impressed Quarracino with his easy manners and his striking authority when he spoke. Quarracino mentioned this feeling to José Carlos Camaño, lecturer in Dogmatic Theology at the Catholic University of Argentina, telling him that he was quite sure that he had found a talent and that he would petition the Vatican to appoint Bergoglio as his auxiliary bishop.[1] Quarracino thought that Bergoglio was the right man to assume the leadership of the southern part of the city, where the less well-off suburbs of the archdiocese were located. However, every time Quarracino tried to get Bergoglio appointed he failed because of the well-placed objections of Esteban Caselli, President Menem's ambassador to the Vatican, who had powerful contacts with the Vatican's Secretariat of State and the Vatican Embassy in Buenos Aires.[2] Caselli distrusted Bergoglio because of his Jesuit education, and because he was an independent thinker who didn't foster contacts within the Argentinean political world. After several attempts to appoint Bergoglio from a distance, Quarracino got tired of outside interference and flew to Rome to meet John Paul II in person, requesting that Bergoglio be appointed as his auxiliary bishop, a wish that John Paul II granted immediately.

Following John Paul II's decision, Mgr Ubaldo Calabrese, the papal nuncio to Argentina, called Bergoglio as he customarily did to follow up on enquiries about possible candidates for episcopal appointments.[3] Calabrese asked Bergoglio to meet him in person,

1   Evangelina Himitian, *Francisco: El Papa de la gente*, Buenos Aires: Aguilar, 2013, pp. 111-112.

2   When Bergoglio became archbishop of Buenos Aires, Caselli sent him a first class ticket to travel to Rome for the ceremony. Bergoglio posted back to Caselli a letter with the ripped envelope he had received, containing the ripped ticket inside, with the clear message that he was not going to rely on Caselli's financial aid to the Catholic Church.

3   Monsignor Ubaldo Calabrese (1925-2004) was born in Sezze Romano and later studied civil and canon law at the Lateran University. He was ordained on 27 March 1948. On 3 July 1969 he was named titular bishop of Fundi and Apostolic Delegate to the Sudan and ordained as bishop on 28

and sooner rather than later. Bergoglio was living in Córdoba, and, as the nuncio was travelling by plane from Buenos Aires to Mendoza and changing planes in Córdoba, they agreed to meet at Córdoba Airport while the nuncio waited for his connection. They discussed various matters until the call came for passengers including Mendoza to board; then the nuncio told him that he had been appointed auxiliary bishop of Buenos Aires, and that the public announcement would take place a week later. It was 13 May 1992, and Bergoglio's life was about to change dramatically. Bergoglio's reaction was one of numbness, his typical reaction to any kind of unwanted news; he had certainly never wanted to become a bishop as he had known that this was very unlikely for any Jesuit. Later, on 27 May 1997, Calabrese called him mid-morning to invite him for lunch. After coffee, when he was just starting to prepare for a return to the cathedral, he saw that a cake and a bottle of champagne had been placed on the table, and he assumed that it was Calabrese's birthday. A minute later, Calabrese told Bergoglio that he had been appointed to succeed Cardinal Quarracino as archbishop of Buenos Aires, with the title Coadjutor Bishop of Buenos Aires.

However, Bergoglio was a Jesuit, and since the time of St Ignatius, their founder, the Jesuits have understood their role as being to serve within the Church without occupying clerical roles of leadership. Thus, Bergoglio told the nuncio that he could not accept the appointment since he was a Jesuit. Calabrese communicated as much to the Vatican, and John Paul II reminded Bergoglio that the Jesuits take a special vow of obedience to the pope. Bergoglio finally consented to be appointed auxiliary bishop of Buenos Aires in 1992, at the age of fifty-five.

The Jesuits have been traditionally very reluctant to allow their members to become bishops; nevertheless, Bergoglio's appointment followed that of Cardinal Carlo Maria Martini (1927-2012) to the archdiocese of Milan in 1980, a Jesuit biblical scholar who was considered by many worthy of being elected pope by the conclave of 2005.[1] Martini's appointment as bishop followed a

September 1969. He was nuncio to Venezuela (1978-1981) and then nuncio to Argentina (1981-2000). Calabrese was one of the participants in the papal mediation between Argentina and Chile over the diplomatic problems surrounding the Beagle Channel. He retired from the diplomatic service on 4 March 2000, and died of Parkinson's disease in Rome on 14 June 2004.

1   See Obituary of Cardinal Carlo Maria Martini by Peter Stanford, *The Guardian*, 3 September 2012.

brilliant academic career as a biblical scholar and his appointment as rector of the Roman Pontifical Biblical Institute in 1969. This was an unusual appointment for the Jesuits, who, since their foundation, understood themselves as missionaries. They had deliberately avoided clashes with diocesan authorities and the papacy from the time of their period of suppression from Spain, Portugal and most of the European Catholic world (1750-1773).[1]

Despite being ordained auxiliary bishop of Buenos Aires, Bergoglio remained a Jesuit; however, he was relieved of his vow of poverty and his vow of obedience to the Superior General of the Jesuits, becoming accountable only to the Sacred Congregation for Bishops and to the pope himself.[2] Within the Society of Jesus, Bergoglio, like any other Jesuit appointed as bishop, ceased to have a 'voice'. This is an important point to grasp in order to understand Bergoglio's spiritual background: a diocesan bishop spiritually formed as a Jesuit, and grounded in the ecclesial developments of Latin America. It might be truly said of Bergoglio that, 'once a Jesuit always a Jesuit'.[3]

Identity within canon law was discussed again after Vatican II and incorporated into the text of the revised Code of Canon Law. A canonical question regarding members of religious orders who become diocesan bishops was posed: are they still members of their

---

1 I am grateful to Fr Fernando Montes SJ, rector of the Jesuit University Alberto Hurtado, Santiago, Chile, for expanding on the topic of the great difficulty felt by the Jesuits in allowing their members to become bishops during our meeting in Santiago on 23 May 2013. This difficulty is only mentioned in a small number of the works on Pope Francis, but see the discussion on Jesuits and bishops and their vow of obedience to the Pope in Saverio Gaeta, *Papa Francisco: su vida y sus desafíos*, Buenos Aires: San Pablo, 2013, pp. 39-40.

2 Fr Gero McLoughlin SJ to Mario I. Aguilar, 1 May 2013. I am extremely grateful to Fr McLoughlin for guiding me in the canonical understanding and interpretation of the 1983 Code of Canon Law, and the appointment and 'voices' of bishops who are members of religious congregations within the Catholic Church.

3 Four months after his election as Pope Francis, Jorge Bergoglio had a candid dialogue with journalists on the occasion of the Feast of St Ignatius of Loyola, founder of the Jesuits. Pope Francis stated that 'I feel like a Jesuit in my spirituality, it is the spirituality of the Exercises that I carry in my heart (. . .) I feel like a Jesuit and I think like a Jesuit', 'Misa del Papa Francisco en la fiesta de San Ignacio', Radio Vaticana 31 July 2013. On that morning Pope Francis celebrated the morning Mass at the Roman Chiesa del Gesú, a church very dear to St Ignatius, a private Mass shared with the Jesuits of Rome.

religious orders? Is Bergoglio the bishop still a Jesuit? It was clear that the 1983 Code of Canon Law (see canons 705, 706, 707) still applied. However, when doubts arose on this matter, the response and interpretation by the Vatican authorities was clear: all bishops were bound to the authority of the Holy See. On 29 April 1986 the Pontifical Commission for the Authentic Interpretation of the Code of Canon Law discussed and voted on the following question: do members of religious congregations who are bishops have an active voice within their institute? The answer that became binding in the interpretation of canon law was negative; bishops such as Bergoglio were members of their religious congregation no longer.

The text central to understanding the independence of Bergoglio's decisions from those taken by the Jesuits, reads as follows in the original:

Patres Pontificiae Commissionis Codici Iuris Canonici Authentice Interpretando propositis in plenario coetu diei 29 aprilis 1986 quae sequuntur dubiis, respondendum esse censuerunt ut infra:

I

D. Utrum Episcopus religiosus gaudeat in proprio instituto voce activa et passiva.

R. *Negative.*

Summus Pontifex Ioannes Paulus II in Audientia die 17 maii 1986 infrascripto concessa, de omnibus supradictis decisionibus certior factus, eas publicari iussit.

Rosalius Iosephus Card. Castillo Lara, *Praeses*
Iulianus Herranz, *a Secretis*[1]

The Development of a Bishop

Bergoglio, in the company of Fr Raúl Omar Rossi, was ordained bishop in the cathedral of Buenos Aires on Saturday 27 June 1992. The bishops who ordained Bergoglio were the Nuncio Ubaldo Calabrese, Archbishop Antonio Quarracino, and the Bishop of Mercedes-Luján, Emilio Ogñénovich. It was a warm afternoon, and

---

1   http://www.vatican.va/roman_curia/pontifical_councils/intrptxt/
    documents/rc_pc_intrptxt_doc_20020604_interpretationes-authenticae_
    lt.html *Cann. 705-707* (cf. *AAS*, LXXVIII, 1986, 1323-1324).

among the thousands who attended the ceremony were friends of Bergoglio who came from Córdoba, and who remembered him as having lived a legacy of simplicity, humility, real poverty, and intense prayer while among them. They also remembered his intuitive intelligence and well-prepared intellectuality.[1]

Bergoglio, like any auxiliary bishop, was given a diocese that does not exist today, but that was part of the ancient Roman Church. In this case, the diocese of Auca, in the territory of today's Villafranca Montes de Oca, Burgos, Spain. With his ordination, the archdiocese of Buenos Aires acquired a sixth auxiliary bishop, one more than expected within the diocesan structural plan of that time. This plan remained more or less intact under Archbishop Bergoglio, and later followed the lines of geography and pastoral diocesan care elaborated by Archbishop Quarracino and his *curia*. Thus, the archdiocese of Buenos Aires was administered by a vicar general in charge of the general vicariate, assisted by four other heads of vicariates related to the cardinal locational points of the Greater Buenos Aires area: the northern vicariate of Belgrano, the eastern vicariate of Centro, the western vicariate of Devoto, and the southern vicariate of Flores.

Bergoglio's first address to the faithful on the occasion of his ordination as auxiliary bishop signalled the start of an episcopacy dedicated to listening to those suffering within Buenos Aires and centering the Church on the margins: a missionary movement that did not give false importance to self-centered ecclesial reflection. He told them: 'The Lord is faithful to his words. He didn't forget his promise to be with us until the end of the world. There are brothers and sisters that today ask us to stop for a moment so that we could see in their wounds those of the Christ'.

Following the custom of giving cards with a holy image on them (*estampitas*) and a prayer to be said for those ordained or who have received the sacraments, Bergoglio gave to those present at his episcopal ordination prayer cards with the image of the Virgin Mary, with the title 'she who can undo knots' (the Virgin Desatanudos). This was quite an unusual choice, as the most fashionable image of Mary for Argentineans was the Virgin of Luján, patroness of Argentina and of the Argentinean Armed Forces. However, Bergoglio had become a devotee of the Virgin Desatanudos since his time in Germany. On returning from his studies in Germany in

---

1 P. Ángel Rossi, Jesuit superior in Córdoba 2013, interpretation by Savero Gaeta, *Papa Francisco*, p. 39.

1986, Bergoglio had brought with him a deep devotion to an image of the Virgin Mary that had moved him most, a painting of c. 1700 attributed to the Bavarian artist Johann Georg Melchior Schmidtner. The painting was placed within the Church of St Peter am Perlach in Augsburg, and while most people who visited this particular church did not give any special importance to this painting, Bergoglio became very attached to the image during his solitary time in Germany. The painting portrayed the Virgin Mary undoing a sash of knots presented to her by angels, giving an impression of patience and graciousness. The Lady dealt with big and small knots, some close to each other, others far apart. Bergoglio was amazed at the painting, knelt down in front of the Virgin Desatanudos, prayed, and felt that some of his own personal knots were being undone. Thus, when Bergoglio returned to Buenos Aires, he gave images of the Virgin to those who worked at the Universidad del Salvador. Ana María Betta de Berti, an administrator within the university, was one of those who received the image. She later painted a copy of the original over the weekends in September, October and November of 1996, and donated the painting to the Church of San José del Talar, in the neighborhood of Agronomía in Buenos Aires.

In September 1996, three devotees of the Virgin Desatanudos visited the Church of San José del Talar and spoke to the priest-in-charge, Fr Rodolfo Arroyo. They were looking for a parish where they might put a painting of the Virgin Desatanudos so that others could know her and receive her graces. Arroyo consulted with Archbishop Quarracino, who advised him to talk to Bergoglio, stating that he himself was a devotee of the Virgin of Luján. Arroyo remembered that he had sent Christmas greetings to Bergoglio, and had received from him an image of the Virgin Desatanudos, a card that carried the sentence: 'The knot that all carry through disobedience, the Virgin undoes with her obedience'. Arroyo called Bergoglio, who asked not to be involved; he had only been the person who brought the image to Argentina. However, if Quarracino gave his permission, Arroyo might see to the image of the Virgin Desatanudos was placed within the church. Thus, on 8 December 1996, Arroyo blessed the painting of the Virgin Desatanudos and placed it on one of the empty walls of his parish. On this occasion the parish church was full of devotees, and over the years thousands more went to see the painting and became her devotees. The characteristics of the Virgin Desatanudos image include being maternal, very human and very close to those who look at it, creating a closer connection between the devotees and the Virgin Destanudos than devotees and the Virgin de Luján. The arrival of the Virgin's image in Arroyo's church led to thousands of people visiting and requesting prayers to be said, Masses celebrated, and confessions heard. Later on, devotion to the Virgin Desatanudos expanded to Brazil, and of course with the election of Bergoglio as Pope Francis, more people than ever before arrived at the Church of San José del Talar to pray to the Virgin Desatanudos.

Bergoglio's Episcopal Coat of Arms

When a bishop is elected within the Catholic Church he chooses a motto, a phrase that marks his episcopal service to others. Following ancient customs associated with Christendom, he also articulates his life of ministry graphically in a coat of arms. Bergoglio's chosen motto was *Miserando atque eligendo* (by having mercy and by choosing him).[1] This motto is taken from the homilies of the Venerable Bede, a reading chosen for the Feast of Matthew the apostle, and read during the liturgy of the hours. The full text reads as follows: *Vidit ergo Jesus publicanum, et quia miserando atque eligendo vidit, ait illi, 'Sequere me'* (Jesus therefore sees the tax collector, and since he sees by having mercy and by choosing, he says to him, 'follow me').[2] On the feast of St Matthew in 1953, at the age of seventeen, Bergoglio listened to this reading and felt his call to a religious life. These words, treasured by the young Bergoglio, became his episcopal motto, and were later featured within his papal shield, which used the same symbols and words from his episcopal shield. This shield is light blue in colour, and contains the letters IHS, letters used as a seal by St Ignatius when he became superior of the Jesuits in 1541. The three letter symbol had been used by persecuted Christians in the third century, and was understood in Greek as shorthand for 'Jesus Christ the Son of God the Saviour'.[3] Within Bergoglio's shield, the letters are

1 Bergoglio spoke many times about the difficulties in translating the action of God towards Matthew, which is, translating the Latin word *miserando*. Bergoglio suggests the creation of a new Spanish word 'misericordiándolo', which finally he translates as 'envolviéndolo en la misericordia'; in English, 'covering him with mercy', see Cardenal Jorge Mario Bergoglio, *Coloquios*, con las Hermanas Cruzadas de Santa María, Residencia Rovacías, Madrid, 23 January 2006.
2 Venerable Bede Hom. 21, CCL 122, 149-151.
3 Wenceslao Soto Artuñedo SJ, 'IHS', *Revista Jesuitas* 120, Madrid, Autum 2009.

crowned with a cross, and have three nails underneath; the shield also bears the symbols of a five pointed star and a spikenard flower located on an image of a shield at the centre of the coat of arms. The star symbolises the Virgin Mary and the spikenard flower St Joseph, who, in the Spanish tradition, always appears with a vine in his hands.

Bishop Bergoglio's early days as auxiliary bishop in Buenos Aires were difficult. Bergoglio was entrusted with the southern vicariate of Flores – where his parents' home was – but the southern vicariate was extremely large in size and very complex when it came to diocesan pastoral care. It had well-to-do areas, blocks of flats for those with fewer financial resources, and even temporary urban dwellings known as shanty-towns (*villas miseria*). Bergoglio was an ecclesiastical outsider and an unknown priest in Buenos Aires; the central pastoral roles were held by parish priests who had come from the different areas of Buenos Aires and who had studied at the Buenos Aires Seminary.

It was here, at the start of his episcopal ministry, that Bergoglio began one of his preferred activities: walking. He walked everywhere, taking public transport, greeting people and talking to them, becoming familiar with streets and neighborhoods, which facilitated his pastoral ministry. Priests who worked with him at that time discovered that Bishop Bergoglio's pastoral organisation had not been developed by a diocesan office, and was not organised during private telephone calls to his priests. Bergoglio lived his ministry in his daily walks, his knowledge of people and their realities, and his unexpected visits to parishes, homes and schools. Bergoglio had time and an attentive ear for his priests, and he helped them whenever he was needed. Bergoglio visited them, rather than waiting for priests in need to visit him. Fr Fernando Gianetti, parish priest of Nuestra Señora de la Misericordia in the neighborhood of Mataderos – an area where Bergoglio had played as a child – remembers that, in one instance, the child of a family that was not very familiar with the Catholic liturgy was to be confirmed. Bishop Bergoglio, instead of dwelling on their lack of knowledge, guided them through the liturgy with love, explaining everything that was going to happen and its meaning so that they would feel at home in the church.[1] Bergoglio was adamant that his clergy should not stress people's mistakes, but instead foster their closeness to God. He visited the parishes bringing second-hand clothes and

1   Evangelina Himitian, *Francisco*, p. 123.

donations for the poor, and visited the poor in their own homes frequently. Fr Gianetti remembers one night when Bergoglio had been invited to celebrate their patron feast with them, and it was raining heavily. The doorbell rang, and there stood Bergoglio in rain boots, drenched, having taken the metro and the public bus number 103 to reach them. Gianetti testifies that the bishop was not willing to cancel his visit because of heavy rain.[1] Bergoglio did not have a car, and he did not call upon supporters or friends to transport him to different places. He simply took public transport, returning home very late from parish celebrations, despite offers, pleas and protests by parishioners and priests who would have gladly have taken him back to his residence by car. Residents in the dangerous area of Bajo Flores regularly saw him walking down their streets, dressed in clerical black, and completely unafraid of those around him; sometimes violent characters involved in criminal activities from petty theft to drug dealing. If the police could not enter those neighborhoods, Bergoglio did: he was known by people, and he knew them all by name.

Bergoglio was convinced that those who lived in the *villas miseria* had a strong piety and a deep faith, and he told them to be very proud of their faith. In 2007, Bergoglio would convey this belief to his fellow Latin American bishops at the meeting of Catholic bishops in Aparecida, Brazil. Bergoglio was absolutely convinced of this truth, and his life as a priest and as a bishop was enriched by his walks and conversations with the poor and the marginalised in southern Buenos Aires.

A year after his episcopal ordination, Bergoglio was named vicar general of the archdiocese of Buenos Aires because of his involvement with the faithful and the parish communities – once again to his surprise. Many had considered that the most likely candidate for vicar general was Mgr Héctor Aguer, the current archbishop of La Plata, who was also one of Quarracino's auxiliary bishops and who was connected to President Menem and his ambassador to the Vatican, Esteban Caselli.

As the new vicar general, Bergoglio did not get involved in diocesan politics; instead, he continued to work with the poor of Buenos Aires. In 1993 the Mayor of Buenos Aires, Jorge Domínguez, decided to demolish Villa 31, a *villa miseria*. This announcement triggered protests by those living there, who were supported by priests living and working in the villas (*curas*

1   Evangelina Himitian, *Francisco*, p. 124.

villeros). President Menem verbally attacked those priests, calling them 'tercermundistas', which referred metaphorically to the group of priests who had become close to the left-wing guerrillas and political activists in Argentina during the 1970s. Bergoglio was called in to mediate this difficult situation, and he acted promptly, convincing Quarracino to celebrate a Mass in support of the *curas villeros*.[1] It is possible to argue that, while Bergoglio seemed to be a conservative and traditional priest, his personal life and theological discourse embraced the habits of a *cura villero*. He lived close to shanty-towns and was immersed in the daily toils of those living in these poor neighborhoods, whose homes could be destroyed by the civil authorities' decrees at a moment's notice. The priests working in shanty-towns influenced Bergoglio greatly. Years later he wrote the prologue to a book containing some of their testimonies, asserting that 'the testimony of many men and women who follow Jesus Christ very closely edify the Church, makes her grow. Precisely because the Church grows by attraction rather than by proselitism'.[2]

His work as auxiliary bishop within the periphery of Buenos Aires laid the foundations for Bergoglio's thoughts about a poor Church for the poor, a reality already lived in the past by Saint Francis of Assisi. It is no mere coincidence that in 1993 Bergoglio attended the performance of a play about Saint Francis of Assisi, *El loco de Asís*, written and directed by Manuel González Gil with music by Martín Bianchedi. The play was performed at the Cervantes Theatre of Buenos Aires after having been played in many venues all over the world since 1984, and Bergoglio was one of the first to attend its performance in Buenos Aires. It was a polemic play criticising certain sectors of Argentinean society and some quarters of the Catholic Church in Argentina, but Bergoglio attended and wished those producing it every success in the future. As he had done in the case of Villa 31, he supported those who were challenging social injustice and inequality in Argentina.

As auxiliary bishop, Bergoglio undertook pastoral work that

---

1 Later, and as archbishop, Bergoglio created a new pastoral vicariate comprising all those priests working in the shanty towns in order to support their apostolate, and increased the number of parish priests involved with the *villa miseria* from ten to twenty.

2 Cardinal Jorge Mario Bergoglio SJ, 'Prólogo', in P. Fernando Lobo, *Tú eres mi prójimo: Testimonios de sacerdotes que acompañan al pueblo en el seguimiento de Jesús*, Buenos Aires: Editorial Claretiana, 2012, p. 7.

included office work, public appearances, the encouragement of others and many hours of prayer. Within such a multi-tasking priesthood, Bergoglio recognised that 'between the priest and the religious functionary there is an abyss, they are qualitatively different'. By just perfoming his duties a priest can become a functionary, a civil servant who performs but does not have a heart for the people.[1] Bergoglio believed that all people belonged to God, and demonstrated inclusivity in his weekend visits to all types of people. The following vignette provides an example of a cleric who, despite his busy schedule, was able to recognise the needs of an individual even as he departed for yet another engagement. As auxiliary bishop in Buenos Aires, Bergoglio remembers closing a folder on the desk in his office, looking at his watch, and realising that he had just enough time to visit the Blessed Sacrament at the cathedral before taking the train to preach at a retreat in a convent on the outskirts of Buenos Aires. It was summer, and Bergoglio enjoyed the silence and coolness inside the cathedral. While he was at prayer, he was asked by a young person to hear his confession. Bergoglio noticed that the young person did not seem to be mentally stable. Bergoglio felt annoyed because of the time pressure he was under, but managed to conceal his real feelings about missing the only train that would take him to his next appointment on time. Bergoglio thought that the man was about twenty-eight years old and he spoke as if he were drunk, or under the effects of some psychiatric medication. In a moment of confidence Bergoglio told him that he needed to be somewhere else, and that another priest would come – knowing that such priest would only arrive at 4 pm, two hours later. His thoughts were that the man, because of his state, would not realise that this would be a rather long wait. He started walking away, but in shame decided to hear the man's confession after all. After the confession, Bergoglio led the man to Our Lady's altar to ask for Our Lady's protection, and then left for the train station, knowing that the train he had been going to take had already left. However, on arrival at the station he learned that the train was late and he was able to take it to his destination and arrived on time – it was a sign from God for him!

Around the time of this incident, when Bergoglio was serving as vicar general of Buenos Aires, he experienced another revelation about humility. It was the summer month of January and it was

1 Jorge Bergoglio SJ, *Mente abierta, corazón creyente*, Buenos Aires: Editorial Claretiana, 2013, p. 15 § 1.

very hot. However, he remembered feeling confident that he could complete many pending matters despite the heat of the season. In the mornings he fulfilled his duties as vicar general, and every afternoon by 2 pm he took the train from Once Station to Castelar Station, the station close to the nuns' convent, where he was leading spiritual exercises. He later realised that he was committing the sin of pride because he felt that he could achieve many things on his own. In a 2010 interview with Rubin and Ambrogetti, he recognised that the virtue of patience was particularly important for him, mainly because he found it so difficult.[1] By reading the book *Teología del Fallimento* (a theology of failure), he started realising that Jesus had learned how to be patient with others. There are many occasions when our patience reaches its limit, according to Bergoglio, and it is at that limit that we learn patience; with the result that time is able to lead us and form us. He considered that there are roads to virtue and there are short-cuts: we are often tempted to take short-cuts that are ethical traps. Bergoglio recognised an enriched meaning of the parable of the prodigal son in his consideration of the virtue of patience. The story is of a son who asks for his inheritance and departs from the family home in order to see the world, and in doing so spends all of his father's inheritance. Upon his return, his father welcomes him back with open arms; the second son doesn't understand why a person who has misused material goods and has not looked after his father is so readily welcome. Bergoglio remarked that what impressed him about this story was the fact that the father saw his son approaching from far away, a clear signal that he was waiting for his son for years with enormous patience.

From Bishop to Archbishop and Cardinal

On 4 June 1997, the Argentinean newspapers reported that Pope John Paul II had chosen Bishop Bergoglio to succeed Archbishop Quarracino after his retirement at the expected canonical age of 75. John Paul II had made this decision in order to avoid any delay on the appointment of a new archbishop of Buenos Aires, as had happened in 1987; at that time, the appointment of Quarracino took longer than expected because of opposition by the then-Argentinean President Raúl Alfonsín. Thus, Bergoglio was appointed as bishop of Buenos Aires on 3 June 1997; and, after Quarracino's death, archbishop of Buenos Aires on 28 February

1   *El Jesuita*, pp. 68-71.

1998 and Primate of Argentina. On 6 November 1998, Bergoglio was also appointed ordinary bishop for the Eastern Catholics of Argentina. John Paul II made him cardinal at the consistory of 21 February 2001, with the title St Roberto Bellarmino. Over the years as a cardinal of the Catholic Church, he served as a member of the Pontifical Commissions for Latin America, the Congregation for the Clergy, the Pontifical Council for the Family, the Congregation for Divine Worship and the Discipline of the Sacraments, the Ordinary Council of the General Secretariat for the Synod of Bishops and the Congregation for Institutes of Consecrated Life and Societies of Apostolic Life. Within Argentina he was twice elected president of the Argentinean Episcopal Conference (2005-2011).

The news of Bergoglio's appointment as archbishop did not surprise those who knew him. After all, the press had consistently stressed that his pastoral approach had made the Catholic Church accessible to the people, and that it had changed relations between Church and State in Argentina. However, those following Church-State relations were surprised that other worthy candidates closer to the Argentinean government and less critical of Argentinean politics had not been chosen. Among the front-runners mentioned were Mgr Estanislao Karlic, archbishop of Paraná and President of the Argentinean Episcopal Conference, Mgr Domingo Castagna, bishop of Corrientes, and Mgr Eduardo Mirás, archbishop of Rosario. Bergoglio was seen as an unknown, a candidate who would continue the ecclesiastical criticisms of the presidency of Carlos Menem. These criticisms had started in 1997 with the release of an episcopal conference document that criticised the growing alliance between the executive power and the judiciary – a charge that President Menem quickly denied. The Argentinean bishops publicly stated that 'the administering of Justice requires today a clear independence from all other state powers, and from the professional associations, the trade unions, and the financial networks'.

With Bergoglio as leader of the Argentinean Church, criticisms of the government by the Church were frequent, often administered during the homilies delivered by the archbishop of Buenos Aires at the annual liturgical Te Deum (a hymn of thanksgiving to God), which was celebrated on national feast days associated with Argentinean independence and national identity. These were the 25 May and the 9 July, occasions attended by the Argentinean president and members of the government. In front of President Carlos Menem, Bergoglio spoke against 'those who serve a table for very few'; while in front of President Fernando de la Rúa, he spoke of those who follow a funeral cortège and worry about the living attendants rather than the dead body still to be buried. The late President Néstor Kirchner attended one of those occasions, and Bergoglio's words were so unpalatable to him that he and his wife Cristina subsequently celebrated national feasts elsewhere, rather than listen to Bergoglio's preaching on behalf of those facing injustice, those without work and those without bread for their families. Bergoglio spoke clearly and openly about national sicknesses such as corruption, exhibitionism and misleading policy announcements, and the Argentinean authorities didn't take these criticisms kindly.

Bergoglio started changing the profile of Argentinean Catholicism with his theological emphasis on the primacy of the poor within the Church. On 8 August 1997, two months after being appointed as the successor to Cardinal Quarracino, Bergoglio led a procession in honour of San Cayetano, the patron of bread and work, at the shrine of Liniers, where 600,000 people gathered to pray to the saint. The year was one of enormous financial hardship for Argentineans. The shrine of San Cayetano is in a small church in a neighbourhood with narrow streets, which must have been overflowing with such a crowd of pilgrims.[1] The pilgrims called loudly for roofs over their heads, bread, and work, in a massive public challenge to the Argentinean authorities. Two long queues spanned a couple of kilometres – a real shock to the Argentinean government – one line of the faithful wanting to kiss the saint's feet, the other waiting for their medals, printed images, statues and wheat palms to be blessed. Bergoglio addressed the crowds in a clear voice, saying, 'Work as well as bread is there to be shared. Everybody has to work a little bit. Work is sacred because it is through work that the human person is being formed. Work teaches and educates, it is culture. If God has given us the gift of bread and the gift of life, nobody can take away the right to work for that bread'.

When Cardinal Quarracino died in the Sanatorio Otamendi on 28 February 1998, Bergoglio became archbishop and Catholic primate of all Argentina. Bergoglio presided over the funeral Mass that was attended by President Menem and the Argentinean Ambassador

---

1 I visited the shrine of San Cayetano in August 2013 and it was clear to me that only a couple of hundred people would have filled the church and the shrine's compound to the full. The shrine is located at Cuzco Street 150, Liniers, Buenos Aires, see http://www.sancayetano.org.ar

to the Vatican, Esteban Caselli. John Paul II sent a telegram of condolence addressed to Bergoglio as archbishop of Buenos Aires, confirming his appointment. Ten years later, and within the context of an anniversary Mass for the repose of the soul of Quarracino, Bergoglio spoke kindly of the archbishop who had chosen him to be a bishop, saying, 'We remember him who announced and witnessed the Gospel and with the freshness and courage of his words was a true shepherd that courageously kept its values. He was a true shepherd'. On 1 March 1998, Bergoglio went on retreat, and upon his return his first engagement as archbishop of Buenos Aires was a celebration organised by President Menem to commemorate Nuncio Ubaldo Calabrese's fifty years of priesthood (on 18 March). Amidst these celebrations, in the White Room of the Pink House (the Argentinean presidential palace), and sitting at the left-hand side of President Menem, Bergoglio was asked questions about his identity by civil servants. Bergoglio was unknown to the Argentinean political world, because he had immersed himself in the world of those unknown by the Argentinean government.

Bergoglio realised that he didn't have the appropriate clothes for the many official and public engagements the archbishop of Buenos Aires must undertake. His assistants at Archbishop's House contacted a tailoring house to make an appointment for him, but requested an estimate for the new clothes. When Bergoglio examined the proposed budget he rejected it immediately, stating that it would be not be possible to spend all that money on him. He requested that his assistants retrieve the late Quarracino's suits, and, when he tried them on, realised that his predecessor had carried a few more kilos than he did. Bergoglio summoned the nuns who prepared his food, and asked them to alter the clothes, which the nuns succeeded in doing. Consistent with his practice of a simple lifestyle, Bergoglio rejected the idea of taking up residence at the archbishop's house in Olivos (Azcuénaga Street 1800), a few blocks away from the presidential palace. Instead, he chose to stay on the third level of the *curia* building, next to the Metropolitan Cathedral, where he had resided since being appointed auxiliary bishop, occupying a single room.

On the Solemnity of Saint Peter and Saint Paul of 1998 (29 June), Bergoglio received from the hands of John Paul II the *pallium* that all archbishops receive. The *pallium*, a circular band made of wool, symbolises the authority of an archbishop to serve his flock, as well as his communion with the pope, whom he represents within an archdiocese. The *pallium* is made from the wool of two lambs blessed each year on 21 January at the Basilica of St Ines in Rome. Thus, the connection is made with Christ's words spoken to Peter, the first pope, 'tender my sheep'. As a token of recognition, the Argentinean government paid for his air ticket to Rome, and a first class ticket was delivered to the archiepiscopal offices in Buenos Aires. Bergoglio visited the presidential offices in person to request that the ticket be exchanged for one in economy class, since he never travelled in business or first class.

The relations between the archbishop of Buenos Aires and the government of Carlos Menem were not too difficult, as Bergoglio had a direct style of communication. If there were any matters to be discussed with the government, Bergoglio picked up the phone himself. He was not afraid to speak out publicly to the Argentinean nation about matters of common concern that might be ameliorated by following the Gospel. Further, Bergoglio did not wait for the permission of the government to carry out his work in Buenos Aires – he just did it. In fact, Bergoglio's simple style of life and his preoccupation with the suffering and the dispossessed did not make him a rival to the state or a critic of the state – a more combative relationship was to come later when he was made cardinal, when he would not accept financial help from the government in return for ecclesiastical recognition of state policies. For Bergoglio, the Catholic Church did not need to be officially recognised, but she did need to serve others; and this ministry of service did not have the Church at its centre but Christ. At the time of Bergoglio's appointment as archbishop of Buenos Aires, President Menem was in his second term of office, and was searching for ways to press a constitutional change allowing him to be elected for a third term. The Argentinean Episcopal Conference, led by Mgr Estanislao Karlic, was very critical of the Argentinean president, and Menem hoped to find a benevolent interlocutor in the person of the new archbishop of Buenos Aires who, in most cases, did not say much, and might prove an excellent mediator between the president and the Argentinean bishops. Two presidential envoys approached Bergoglio but failed in their mission of enlisting his help to keep the survival of Menem's government.

Bergoglio saw his episcopal ministry as eminently pastoral, and had almost no interest in normative extra-pastoral pronouncements, a trait recognised by the Argentinean media.[1] If he spoke in the

---

1   *La Nación*, 13 October 1998.

public sphere, it was from the point of view of the poor and marginalised within Argentinean society, and on specially selected occasions – particularly if he felt that a large number of people were expecting his guidance in the name of the Church. However, at the Te Deum at the Metropolitan Cathedral on 25 May 1999, the first national occasion following political approaches by the Menem administration, Bergoglio spoke firmly in the presence of the Argentinean president about the difficulties ahead. These difficulties included the violence that awaited Argentina if basic privileges were not extended to all; the social fibre of the nation being destroyed if only a few enjoyed its benefits; and a national situation in which the gap between the rich and the poor grew ever larger. Bergoglio addressed the politicians who had failed to confront the national problems that had resulted in a society of disillusioned citizens, fatigued by official solutions that were out of touch with the real problems of Argentineans. In Bergoglio's view, political failure had created general apathy and a lack of interest in the common good, one consequence of which was the growth of individual consumerism. Bergoglio felt that the fragmentation of society was proceeding at a great rate, and those discussing solutions were unable to see this and aid society as a whole. The source of all hope within society and politics, for Bergoglio, was in the greatness of the Argentinean people, and politicians were failing to draw from this resource.[1] Bergoglio had changed the type of homily given at the Te Deum. Previously, the homily was intended for the Catholic Church in Argentina; Bergoglio, following a change already made by Cardinal Raúl Silva Henríquez in 1970s Chile, converted it into an address to the Argentinean nation on a national day celebrated by all Argentineans, Catholics and non-Catholics, and particularly the civil authorities elected by the people to serve the nation as a whole.[2]

During his time as archbishop, Bergoglio changed the pastoral understanding of what constitutes the centre and what the periphery. During his term in office, he always focussed his attention outwards. Thus, when the celebrations of Holy Week and Easter 1998 were being planned, Bergoglio delegated the washing of feet at the Metropolitan Cathedral to his auxiliary bishops – a ritual customarily carried out on Maundy Thursday

1 *La Nación*, 26 May 1999.
2 Ascanio Cavallo C., *Los Te Deum del Cardenal Silva Henríquez en el régimen militar*, Santiago: Ediciones Copygraph, 1988.

– and departed to the Francisco J. Muñiz Hospital for Infectious Diseases of Buenos Aires where he washed and kissed the feet of twelve patients with HIV/AIDS. All present were welcomed to the evening Mass: doctors, auxiliaries and the patients' relatives. People at the hospital were moved by the sight of the new archbishop visiting patients, sitting with them, listening to their life stories and blessing them, appearing as comfortable with them as if they were his own family. The photographs of Bergoglio kissing HIV/AIDS sufferers – at a time when the disease was not as fully understood as it is today – appeared time and again in the media and in publications about Bergoglio.[1] An archbishop with few words for politicians was nevertheless speaking loudly in the public sphere through his actions and the locations in which they took place.

A pattern began to emerge in Bergoglio's method of running of the archdiocese: a constant refocussing on the marginalised. During Holy Week in 1998, Bergoglio visited a hospital in order to share the Maundy Thursday Eucharist with the sick; in 1999 he visited a prison. Bergoglio took the bus to visit Villa Devoto Prison of Buenos Aires, where he washed the feet of twelve inmates, talking at length with many of them and giving them tips on how to better their situation. He even exchanged addresses with them, and kept in touch with those who wrote to him or visited him at the cathedral. On that Maundy Thursday, Bergoglio left the prison late at night and took bus number 109 back to the cathedral. In the following weeks he answered all letters he received from the prison inmates, using a typewriter that he had brought back from Germany in 1986. Over the following years the inmates continued corresponding with Bergoglio: unusually for an archbishop, who would customarily dictate letters to a secretary, Bergoglio wrote each letter himself, or picked up the phone to greet the caller and to exchange news. He stated that, 'I answer each one of them. It takes time but I would never like not to do it'. Further, he explained that, 'Jesus in the Gospels tells us that in the Day of Judgement we would have to account for our behaviour. I was hungry and you gave me food; I was thirsty and you gave me to drink; I was sick and you visited me; I was in prison and you visited me. The mandate of Jesus puts an obligation on all of us, but especially

1   The photograph of Bergoglio kissing feet on a Maundy Thursday appears, for example, on the front cover of his work, *El verdadero poder es el servicio*, Buenos Aires: Editorial Claretiana, 2007, 2013.

on the bishop who is the father of all'. Bergoglio referred to the text of Matthew 25:34-40, which has long been an inspiration for all kinds of works of Christian charity. It has also been the special motto of the priests working within the *villa miserias*.[1] For Bergoglio, the mandate of this text is summarised by the service of others. The fruit of such service is not seen until later, when 'face to face' charity requires a step further: love, a love in which we serve others without understanding most of the time what the results might be, a service based on love.[2]

Bergoglio's movement towards the marginalised continued. On his third Holy Week as archbishop of Buenos Aires, he visited the Hogar San José in the neighbourhood of Balvanera, a shelter and home for the homeless where about 80 homeless people slept daily, and where 250 or so destitute individuals were provided with lunch by the staff. Bergoglio washed the feet of 12 homeless people, and asked all of those in their condition 'to be slaves of one another, serving each other, as Christ had done washing the feet of his disciples'.

Over the following years, Bergoglio continued visiting the marginalised, including children at the paediatric hospital Juan P. Garrahan, and those who earned a living by collecting paper and empty boxes throughout the city of Buenos Aires, known as *cartoneros*. In 2008 Bergoglio celebrated Maundy Thursday at a shanty town, the Villa 21-24 of Barrancas. He visited Hogar Hurtado again, and washed and kissed the feet of twelve young people who were fighting to rehabilitate themselves from drug addiction, particularly to cocaine. Years later when Bergoglio was elected pope in 2013, these same youths gathered at the church of Nuestra Señora of Cacupé to pray for Bergoglio, knowing that they were still clean thanks to his ongoing support.

Bergoglio's years as archbishop were distinguished by his personal closeness to people, and by his special mission of bringing the Church to people rather than expecting people to come to the Church. On 12 October 1998, Bergoglio organised two large, public and open-air Masses in the neighbourhood of Palermo, opposite the Buenos Aires Zoo, which were attended by

---

1   The text from Matthew's Gospel appears in the first page of P. Fernando Lobo, *Tú eres mi prójimo*, before Bergoglio's prologue to the book.

2   Jorge Bergoglio SJ, 'Somos un pueblo con vocación de grandeza: Mensaje a las comunidades educativas', 2006, reproduced in *El verdadero poder es el servicio*, pp. 83-107; I refer in my commentary to pages 98-99.

95,000 people and in which 21,000 people received the sacrament of confirmation. The ideas behind this massive celebration of the sacrament were to improve the public Catholic understanding of this sacrament, and, at the same time, to bring together in the Eucharistic celebration Catholics from all localities, pastoral areas, and diverse social situations within the archdiocese of Buenos Aires. Thus, the faithful from shanty towns and from rich neighbourhoods in Buenos Aires all took part in a celebration together, where the archbishop stressed their unity in faith, witness, apostolate and life, regardless of their social or political differences. Bergoglio himself administered the sacrament of confirmation to fifty disabled people by making the sign of the cross on their foreheads with holy oil, while auxiliary bishops and senior clergy administered it to the thousands of others attending the liturgical celebration. During the Mass a woman with a poster painted with the colours of the Bolivian flag could be seen clearly. The words on the poster read: 'Mamita, may they return Edith!' It was a request to the Virgin Mary by a mother from the neighbourhood of Bajo Flores; her daughter had been kidnapped there. Bergoglio stopped the Mass and asked all present to say one Hail Mary for her daughter's return.

Following his own understanding that he was representing 'the people', Bergoglio spoke at the Te Deum in December 1999, celebrated at the Metropolitan Cathedral as part of the inaugural ceremonies for the new Argentinean President, Fernando de la Rúa. Bergoglio asked the new authorities, which included the vice-president Carlos 'Chaco' Alvarez, to look above to request wisdom and to look beside them to serve, because to govern is to serve each one of the brothers and sisters that make up the Argentinean people. On the one hand, Bergoglio continued, if authorities do not look for wisdom from above they become self-sufficient, with anti-values of pride and vanity. On the other hand, if they do not look beside themselves, they look only at themselves and their environment and forget to serve the people. Bergoglio was direct and paternal in his treatment of the two men. When the time came to ask for God's guidance for the new authorities, he asked using their first names, Fernando and Carlos.

The episcopal admonition continued on 25 May 2000, when the yearly Te Deum for Argentina took place at the Metropolitan Cathedral. Bergoglio revealed his developing political thought by telling those in attendance that the political system was surrounded by a shadow, the shadow of distrust. In this speech, Bergoglio used a sentence that was subsequently his signature with the people of Argentina: 'Arise Argentina!' He asserted that, until Argentineans recognised their double standards (they spoke of making Argentina a just society while taking bribes), there would be no trust or peace; and until Argentineans changed their attitudes there would be no joy or happiness. Thus, the archbishop's instructions resounded loud and clear within the Te Deum, insisting that, just as Christ did, the authorities should be ready to renounce the kind of power that is exclusive and makes people blind. They should exercise the kind of authority that accompanies and serves others. It is a fact, he continued, that only a few hold financial power and the power of technology, while a few others exercise state power; nevertheless, only an active community, based on common solidarity and support, could safely steer the common boat, the Argentinean nation.

Bergoglio's words were intended to challenge the government; President de la Rúa celebrated his political triumph by blaming all present-day problems on the past and on the market, while doing very little to improve social and family policies. During the following days, when the journalists asked President de la Rúa about the archbishop's comments, he avoided any clear answer, instead saying that the archbishop was a holy and wise man, and that de la Rúa was in total agreement with his assessment of the social crisis that was present in Argentina. A year later, on 25 May 2001 – and before the Argentinean financial crisis – Bergoglio returned to the same themes, President de la Rúa sitting in front of him. This time, the archbishop said that often politicians say they are listening, but in reality they are not. In the words of Bergoglio: 'they clap ritually without meaning to do so'; 'they believe that criticisms are aimed at others, never themselves'. In a further socio-political exegesis, the archbishop identified politicians as vultures who only want to stay in power, and lamented that any vocation of service in Argentina had become selfishness. This theme was fully expressed in his address on the Feast of San Cayetano on 7 August 2001, at the saint's sanctuary at Liniers, where Bergoglio spoke of his fear of a full social crisis in Argentina, the poor persecuted because they demand work, and the rich, while avoiding justice, praised by the powerful despite their avoidance of taxes and exploitation of the poor.

4. From Archbishop to Cardinal

On 21 January 2001 it was announced that John Paul II had asked Bergoglio to take part in the eighth papal consistory of his papacy, where Bergoglio would be made a cardinal of the Catholic Church. Messages of congratulation soon started to arrive, and the first was from Bergoglio's first-grade teacher. Others included a personal message from President de la Rúa. When Bergoglio was asked if he felt that he had ascended to the top he denied such feeling, and reiterated that any ascent must be preceded by a descent to the ongoing service of others. Bergoglio felt that he was being called to serve more than he ever thought he would by becoming a cardinal, and he certainly thought that any idea of his being chosen as the next pope was nonsense. Further, he spoke of the pope's honour to the archdiocese rather than to his own person; and said that, if being cardinal would entail no longer hearing confessions, he would miss those moments as he loved to be with other pilgrims and sinners. He told the press that he heard confessions not only at the Metropolitan Cathedral, but also at San Pantaleón, in the Buenos Aires neighbourhood of Mataderos, every twenty-seventh day of the month. Bergoglio also mentioned that, during the pilgrimage to the Virgin of Luján, he very much enjoyed listening to the confessions of the young: they allowed him to be in touch with them, to know what was happening to them and to understand their world.

After travelling to Rome in economy class and taking public transport to his accommodation at the International House for the Clergy, a house for priests in Rome, Bergoglio departed on foot for St Peter's Basilica. All the other cardinals-to-be took private cars, some provided by the country they represented. On the way to the basilica Bergoglio and an assistant, all dressed in red ready for the ceremony, stopped for a coffee. Once the ceremony and the celebrations at the Vatican were over, he proceeded to walk once again back to his accommodation. These simple habits would continue even after his election as Pope Francis, and his preoccupations would remain the same: poverty, education and inter-religious dialogue. These three theological themes have dominated Bergoglio's life and ministry.

In September 2001, bishops and cardinals from all over the world met for the Synod of the Third Millennium, called by John Paul II in order to discuss the role and life of bishops for the twenty-first century.[1] While Paul VI had created the occasion of the Synod of Bishops, John Paul II had given these meetings a theological foundation, stating that the Synod of Bishops was the 'expression and the very valuable instrument of episcopal collegiality'.[2] John Paul II asked bishops to live an effective poverty. The convenor of the Tenth Ordinary General Assembly of the synod was to be Cardinal Edward Egan, Archbishop of New York. However, a few days before the start of the synod, the terrorist attacks of 9/11 took place in the United States, and Cardinal Egan returned to New York as soon as he could to comfort his flock. After Egans' departure, John Paul II decided to appoint Bergoglio as convenor of the bishops' synod.[3] Before departing for Rome, Bergoglio spoke to

---

1 The Synod of Bishops was established by Paul VI by Apostolic Letter, Motu proprio *Apostolica Sollicitudo,* on 15 September 1965 (AAS 57, 1865, 775-780). Paul VI gave the definition of the Synod of Bishops at the Sunday Angelus of 22 September 1974 as follows: 'It is an ecclesiastic institution, which, on interrogating the signs of the times and as well as trying to provide a deeper interpretation of divine designs and the constitution of the Catholic Church, we set up after Vatican Council II in order to foster the unity of cooperation of bishops around the world with the Holy See. It does this by means of a common study concerning the conditions of the Church and a joint solution on matters concerning her mission. It is neither a Council nor a Parliament but a special type of Synod'. Vatican II had expressed the wish that bishops throughout the world would co-operate in a collegial manner with the Bishop of Rome in the Decrees *Christus Dominus* § 5 and *Ad Gentes* § 29.

2 John Paul II, 'Speech to the Council of the General Secretariat of the Synod of Bishops', 30 April 1983 and words during the 'agape' of the VII Ordinary General Assembly of the Synod of Bishops, 30 October 1987, held at the Domus Sanctae Marthae, Vatican City. Later, Benedict XVI confirmed the existence of the Synod of Bishops for discussing the Church's activity in the world and as a 'great act of true collegial affection', see Benedict XVI, *Meditatio horae tertiae ad ineundos labores XI Coetus Generalis Ordinarii Synodi Episcoporum* (AAS 97, 2005, 951).

3 The definition and functioning of the Synod of Bishops is outlined in the *Code of Canon Law* § 342-348 and the *Code of Canons of the Eastern Churches* § 46.

President de la Rúa about the terrorist attacks in the chapel of the
Pink House and they prayed together for peace. Bergoglio prayed
that peace would prevail and that there would not be reprisals
that would generate more violence. He also prayed that those
who were the leaders of world nations would finally discover the
grace of God that allows people to realise that human beings and
peoples of the world can live in peace. Later that day, Bergoglio
took part in a public ecumenical service of prayer at the Obelisk
in Central Buenos Aires, where he chose to pray the prayer of St
Francis: 'Lord, make me a channel of your peace'. At the end of
the service he walked back to the cathedral, meditating on those
words.

The Tenth Ordinary General Assembly lasted from 30 September
to 27 October 2001, with 247 bishops in attendance discussing the
topic 'The Bishop: Servant of the Gospel of Jesus Christ for the
Hope of the World'. As a result of the Synod, and with the help
of the X Ordinary Council of the General Secretariat, John Paul
II drafted the post-Synod Apostolic Exhortation *Pastores gregis*,
promulgated on 16 October 2003, which marked the twenty-fifth
anniversary of the election of John Paul II. Bergoglio did very well,
and other bishops were surprised by the ease with which he spoke
of bishops adhering to poverty, being credible witnesses, and
being close to the marginalised of society. Bergoglio became more
widely known because he had to face the press in the Vatican
press room, and he spoke of the strength of the Catholic Church in
its communion; for Bergoglio, the weakness of the Church lies in
division and antagonism. *Pastores gregis* reminded bishops all over
the world about issues of collegiality, something that strengthens
the ties between local bishops and the pope, but that also allows
for the possibility of rethinking the lifestyle of each successor of
the apostles. This is a very poignant reflection; John Paul II was
giving an example of suffering through his illness, and Bergoglio,
the convenor of the Tenth Ordinary General Assembly, lived the
call to poverty and simplicity in his own life. It is possible to argue
that, after the death of John Paul II in 2005, some of this work to
alleviate poverty was unappreciated. The theologian Benedict XVI
was elected, and he was uncomfortable appearing in the political
world and preferred to write philosophical encyclicals rather
than pastoral ones. However, Bergoglio's recognised authority as
convenor would extend further during the 2007 general meeting
of Latin American bishops in Aparecida, Brazil.

The year of the Synod and of 9/11 was also a year in which Argentina craved peace between diverse sectors of the populace. In August 2001 the Argentinean Episcopal Conference had warned the nation of an impending financial and social crisis, blaming crude liberalism (understood as the enrichment of the private sector at the expense of the poor) as one of the most serious social illnesses in the country. The document requested that a social network be built that would embrace the poor, and clearly condemned tax evasion and the waste of public money by the Argentinean government, money that came from the people. It raised questions about the foreign debt that prevented the country from growing, a topic that had never been discussed by any Argentinean government. Reports from parishes in Argentina were clear: more and more families were not able to cover the cost of their basic needs, debt was increasing and there was growing social tension and widespread financial uncertainty. Bergoglio could vouch that requests for aid by poor parishioners that had previously been sporadic had increased enormously, to the point that the archdiocese was becoming a separate welfare state. Bergoglio's priests were encouraged to draw closer to the people and to help in whatever manner they could, while Caritas Argentina put together a report that was devastatingly critical of the role of the government, and alerted people to the fact of a full social crisis unfolding within a country in possession of enormous financial and human resources. In October 2001, the government of President de la Rúa lost the parliamentary elections and proceeded to implement a financial plan in response to the ongoing crisis: in December 2001 bank accounts were frozen, and it became impossible for Argentineans to withdraw cash from financial institutions.

On 18 December 2001, a day before the banking measures were made public, Bergoglio invited different people involved in the crisis to a meeting at the headquarters of Caritas (Calle Defensa 200), where the Church, together with the United Nations, were set to launch a combined report on the issue of poverty in Argentina. Invitees included governors, civil servants, lawyers and judges, businessmen and businesswomen and trade unionists. Among those who had confirmed their attendance at the meeting were Carlos Menem (former Argentinean president, member of the Partido Justicialista, the political party concerned with social justice, previously the Partido Peronista, founded in 1947); Rodolfo

Daer, leader of the official trade unions (Confederación General del Trabajo); Raul Alfonsín (former president and senator); José Manuel de la Sota (Governor of Cordóba); the government envoys Ramón Mestre (Minister of the Interior) and Chrystian Colombo (head of the cabinet). The meeting never took place: the crisis forestalled it, erupting with chaos in the streets, violence at the banks and a sense of anarchy as Argentineans were not able to withdraw cash to cover their basic needs.

During the previous month, the Catholic Church had mediated an ongoing dialogue between the different social players in Argentina in a process known as *la concertación*. This had allowed Bergoglio to help, but in a way that did not compromise the critique by the Catholic Church of those who were in government and those who headed the financial institutions in Argentina. Bergoglio had been reminded by Nicolás Gallo, Secretary General of the Government, that not all politicians stole or received bribes, but Bergoglio was relentless in his critique of a system of selfishness and broken policies that was not aiding the poor, the marginalised and the Argentinean nation as a whole.

For two days chaos reigned in Buenos Aires and throughout Argentina. Protestors looted and marched in the streets, striking their cooking pots, and clashing violently with police. 39 died and 350 were injured. The media – national and international – focussed on Buenos Aires. Bergoglio witnessed the protests at the Plaza de Mayo from his window at the archdiocesan offices, seeing a policeman hit a middle-aged woman who was protesting about the fact that her savings had been stolen. Bergoglio picked up the phone and called the Minister of the Interior, firmly requesting that the government make a distinction between those who wanted to create chaos and ordinary protestors who had the right to demand answers about the state of their savings and bank accounts. On the following day, Bergoglio wrote a public note that was delivered to the press by the Media Office of the archdiocese of Buenos Aires, stating that a new form of protest had arisen in Argentina. This was undertaken by those who see injustice, who do not belong to any given political party, who no one had called to protest, but who publicly requested an end to corruption in Argentina. Once again, Bergoglio had quietly intervened in support of the suffering within society. On the evening of 20 December 2001, President de la Rúa resigned, after days of social discontent and chaos.

It is during this period in Argentinean history, and the time of his appointment as cardinal, that Bergoglio began to be revealed in a new pastoral and socio-political light. As an auxiliary bishop of Buenos Aires, Bergoglio had supported local protests by the poor and marginalised within Argentinean society. As archbishop, he had given pastoral support and had spoken from the pulpit to address socio-political issues before government functionaries and civil servants. As cardinal, Bergoglio acted as a socio-political mediator within the Argentinean crisis, offering the best of Christian understanding and dialogue to bring together groups with different interests, even irreconcilable aims. It was a difficult task because Argentina – as well as her neighbour Chile – had experienced a long period of authoritarian military rule, a situation that had not helped to foster dialogue among citizens but instead had promoted order and obedience. Dialogue, be it social or political, was not natural to Argentineans in the 1990s, and had been suppressed again in the early years of the new millennium, this time not by a political regime, but by a financial order that expected financial obedience and had no interest in dialogue for the common good.

As mediator, Bergoglio would not be a mere public consultant content to sit quietly through meetings and dinners. He would be behind the scenes encouraging very different parties to dialogue about difficult issues, to include all sectors of Argentinean society in such conversations, and to realise that this dialogue served the nation, not individual agendas. Before the days of crisis in December 2001, Carmelo Angulo, the Spanish Ambassador to Argentina, requested to meet Bergoglio with some of Angulo's aides in order to exchange views and discuss how Spain might help to solve the crisis. Bergoglio agreed that they should come to the cathedral offices, and told them to sound the horn when the cars were approaching the side gates of the archdiocese buildings. On a quiet Saturday afternoon, Angulo, himself driving the diplomatic pick-up, pulled up in front of the gates and hooted. He was very surprised when Bergoglio himself opened the gates. When asked, Bergoglio remarked that it was the archbishops' task to 'open gates'. Bergoglio kept a small black diary in his pocket in which he wrote his appointments. Its contents were kept fairly secret, and he sometimes took meetings in the morning and the evening without establishing a clear timetable; he was open to meet at a very short notice if he saw a need – and those privileged in his diary were society's suffering and destitute.

Immediately after the Argentinean financial crisis, Bergoglio met in private with trade unionists, businessmen and women, and opponents of President de la Rúa, to ask them to collaborate in a dialogue that would help Argentina emerge from the crisis. When the interim president Eduardo Duhalde was appointed, Bergoglio had already secured some support for the difficult decisions that awaited the nation. On 7 January 2002, Duhalde held a ninety-minute meeting with Bergoglio and Mgr Karlic, head of the Argentinean Episcopal Conference. Bergoglio told Duhalde that the Church was going to take a very proactive role in the political transition, offering spiritual space and encouraging dialogue between different sectors of Argentinean society – something they had already started by calling a general meeting of interested Argentineans at the headquarters of Caritas in December 2001. This was the start of the 'Mesa de Diálogo'. Improving the Argentinean situation was not easy because the needs of the poor and the marginalised in Argentina were so great, and the country was bankrupt. Bergoglio encouraged Argentineans from different political sectors to dialogue, not through public documents, but by picking up the phone and speaking to each other directly. At the same time, Bergoglio did not stop criticising the Argentinean state. A month after the start of the dialogue, the Argentinean bishops wrote to the president describing the issues that should not be forgotten by the new political rulers. The main critique of the bishops was the failure of co-operation between different sectors of society, and the neglect of public interest by banks, private enterprises, businesses and the judiciary. Bergoglio's words were quite clear: the Church was tired of cleaning up the mess produced by those who had control of the taxes of the nation, and he pointed to the fact that according to his calculations only 40% of the financial resources assigned to the poor were actually reaching them; the rest, he added, was lost to financial corruption.

The reaction by those in business and government was unprecedented. Due to popular unrest, they were grateful for Bergoglio's intervention. For the cardinal did not envision a solution to the crisis that excluded any of the parties involved, and, while pressurising them to dialogue, he did not ask them to surrender office. Some of them were in fact strengthened in their religious beliefs as a result of Bergoglio's sound guidance, while others were more pragmatic, and appreciated Bergoglio's connections to many groups in Argentinean society they would have been unable to reach without his help.

On 25 May 2002, the annual Te Deum took place. The new president and his government congregated at the cathedral, and Bergoglio took to the pulpit and addressed the nation in the name of the Church. He spoke of the task of reconstructing the nation by following established law, and he spoke out against those who, despite Argentina's near collapse, still believed it was possible to hold on to their privileges and illegal financial gains. Bergoglio spoke about their 'rapacidad', or rapacious predation: a word associated with vultures that wait to steal meat after other big carnivores have done the work of stalking and killing prey. Bergoglio told those present that vultures are passive recipients of the suffering of others within daily life. The expression 'rapacidad' was a very strong rebuke to sectors of the government and civil service. Further, Bergoglio spoke of a silent war between groups in Argentinean society blinded by their own interests and only able to operate because of the immunity they were given by those enforcing the laws that should apply equally to every person in society, regardless of their income. The values that needed to be rescued were, according to Bergoglio, work, generous solidarity, egalitarian efforts, social achievements and creativity.

At the end of the Te Deum, President Duhalde avoided interviews with the press, shrugging his shoulders and looking to the heavens as if to say, 'What can I do?' He was certainly annoyed, but he later expressed gratitude to Bergoglio for having challenged the Argentinean government to do better. When Bergoglio became pope, Duhalde said that Bergoglio had been a key actor among those attempting to solve the 2001 Argentinean crisis, and, through his quiet actions and manners, he had helped the Argentinean nation to arise out of the ashes. Bergoglio had introduced more and more participants into the national dialogue and supported governmental reforms of education, health and the functioning of the different state powers. At the same time, he was always reminding those he spoke to that social justice must be at the centre of a strong nation and a strong people.

The political transition of 2003 was successful and on 25 May Néstor Kirchner took over the presidency. Kirchner didn't invite the Argentinean bishops to a meeting for a few months, a surprising course of action given Bergoglio's important role during the financial crisis. It is difficult to know why, but one of the reasons suggested is that Kirchner was not spiritual, and therefore did not see why the Catholic Church should suggest policy to his government. These first few months were to signal the start of a very uneasy relationship between Cardinal Bergoglio and President Kirchner. A cordial diplomatic meeting between the president and the bishops took place, but no more. However, the new president was obliged to attend the Te Deum of 25 May 2004 in the Metropolitan Cathedral. This proved to be the only one Kirchner attended, and in the following years he made excuses to avoid it. For instance, on 25 May 2005 Kirchner went to Santiago del Estero to hear Mass, where the local bishop, Juan Carlos Maccarone, was more sympathetic to the president's view of the nation.

In his homily at the 2004 Te Deum, Bergoglio criticised governmental exhibitionism and enthusiastic announcements, and clearly indicated that Argentineans had hopes for the future, but were not seduced by promises of a magic formula for all their problems, or by empty promises. Bergoglio spoke of his concern that those in the public sphere could not recognise that the abolition of institutions to acquire individual power would never be approved of by Argentineans. He used the term 'weak thought', and pointed out that anybody with strong thoughts and opinions, experts such as scientists or people in the arts, were ignored because they did not follow the dominant discourse that seemed to be absolute: the discourse of consumerism and exhibitionism.

On 30 December 2004, a large fire broke out at the Buenos Aires discotheque República de Cromañón, located in the Once neighbourhood, while the band Callejeros was playing. 194 deaths and 1432 injuries resulted. The fire triggered all sorts of questions and investigations into the laws governing the safety of people in public places. They were not being adhered to: with the collusion of the police, the laws were not being implemented for the sake of profit. When the news of the fire hit the media, Bergoglio was seen comforting relatives, visiting hospitals and ministering to all involved. He administered the sacrament of the sick to the injured, heard many confessions and gave absolution to the dying and the dead, embracing their families without tiredness, with tenderness and with closeness. He described the event to the media as a mindless tragedy, and received a telegram from John Paul II who was saddened by the news of many deaths, particularly of the young people. Bergoglio naturally assumed the pastoral care and support of the victim's relatives, and a month later celebrated a Mass for those who had died along with their relatives and friends. His homily resembled that of a Te Deum: an angry and adamant Bergoglio spoke of the need for prayers to awaken the city, so that never again would people place their trust in the powerful, but instead put their trust in the Lord. He cried loudly that children and the young are not objects for political or financial gain. His personal pastoral approach was evident throughout his homily: he did not try to explain suffering and evil in a philosophical manner, but suggested that 'we tell the Lord what has happened. We tell him that we are neither powerful nor rich nor important but we suffer much. We ask him to comfort us and not to abandon us because we want to be a poor and humble people that seek refuge in the name of the Lord. The pain cannot be expressed with words, a pain that hit full households; we come to seek refuge in the name of the Lord. We ask him for justice, we ask him that this humble people would not be laughed at'. Over the years, Bergoglio celebrated a Mass for these victims every 30 December, expressing each time that their lives must not be forgotten. Bells were rung 194 times, reminding all citizens to be active against a culture of death that allowed personal profit to be more important than human beings. Over the years Bergoglio telephoned the relatives of those who died on dates important to them, such as birthdays or wedding anniversaries, or just to ask them their news.

The 2005 Conclave

There is no doubt that Bergoglio was changed by his election as cardinal. Bergoglio not only appreciated the 'Polish Pope's' example of contact with all the different peoples of the world, but also appreciated his writings on philosophy and his focus on establishing the truth about the relation between God and human beings through the Church. In 2003 Bergoglio, who was Grand Chancellor of the Pontifical Catholic University of Buenos Aires at the time, created the Cátedra Juan Pablo II, coinciding with the twenty-fifth anniversary of the beginning of John Paul II's pontificate as well as the tenth anniversary of the encyclical *Veritatis Splendor*. The *cátedra*, in the Latin American tradition, consists of a lecture or a series of lectures given by a specially appointed lecturer who follows the theme already picked out for the *cátedra*. The John Paul II *cátedra* emphasised the prophetic charism of John Paul II, and his stress on acquiring the necessary tools for understanding the contemporary world as diversified, fragmentised, and situated within a contemporary secularised culture. John Paul II's response to the challenges of the contemporary world had begun in the universities, particularly in Catholic universities, with the philosophical development of a Christian humanism. For Bergoglio, it was clear that universities are places where human beings use their intellect to search for and convey the truth, under the related forms of wisdom and knowledge.[1]

In his 2003 *cátedra,* Bergoglio developed an introduction to the systematic and wide-ranging thought of John Paul II, touching the irreducible elements of society, the working world and the solidarity between human beings. Bergoglio suggested that 'from the start of his pontificate, the worker pope (John Paul II) invites us to enter into where the social life of a human being is disclosed: in the world of work and of solidarity'.[2] Bergoglio remarked that John Paul II had rejected a private and individualistic spirituality in favour of a spirituality of communion, meaning a spirituality that took into account the social dimensions of a human being. For John Paul II, neither the sacredness of the individual nor the eschatological promises of a world to come justifies spirituality without charity. There is no place for spirituality without engagement with social reality. Bergoglio connected John Paul II's thought with the wisdom of Vatican II, specifically how the Christian message does not separate human beings from the active construction of the world, but on the contrary makes humans more conscious of their obligation to engage in its construction.[3]

In his 2004 *cátedra* Bergoglio explored 'the clear analysis of reality', one of the major themes of John Paul II, who had experienced life under a totalitarian regime in Poland. As Bergoglio outlined, analyses of reality were necessary to combat the totalitarian ideologies of the twentieth century.[4] Among the

1   Cardenal Jorge Mario Bergoglio, Ponencia en la presentación de 'Consenso para el desarrollo', Universidad del Salvador, 17 June 2010.
2   'Desde el comienzo de su pontificado, el papa obrero nos invita a entrar allí donde la vida social del hombre se juega a fuerza de remos, a fuerza de echar las redes una vez más: en el mundo del trabajo y la solidaridad', Cardenal Jorge Mario Bergoglio, *Disertaciones,* Cátedra de Juan Pablo II, Pontificia Universidad Católica Argentina, 7 June 2003.
3   Bergoglio was referring here to the general tenets of *Gaudium et Spes,* and particularly to chapter III, § 33-39.
4   The term used by John Paul II as translated in Spanish and used by

risks to nations outlined by John Paul II, elaborated upon within the context of Argentina by Bergoglio, were ethically relativistic governments. Ethical relativism strips contemporary society of any moral reference point, badly affecting civil relations and hindering society's recognition of the truth. Bergoglio was clearly convinced that, if there is no ultimate truth, political activity is reduced to mere struggles to acquire power. As a result, a democracy without values can be easily converted into a visible or covert totalitarianism.[1] Bergoglio sees *Veritatis Splendor* as a kind of Magna Carta that protects the freedom of people, families, and humanity because it lays the foundation for an integrated humanism that is called to be the soul of a new universal civilisation of love and life.

John Paul II died on 2 April 2005, aged eight-four, having served as pope for almost twenty-seven years (one of the longest pontificates in history). Cardinal Josef Ratzinger, his right-hand man and head of the Sacred Congregation for Doctrine, was elected as pope and took the name of Benedict XVI. The details of the conclave that elected him remain secret and confidential, as the cardinals had promised, but some details have emerged; Bergoglio had been a strong contender for the position, and he had received the second most votes – ultimately, he had not been elected only because he asked others to support the election of Cardinal Ratzinger. The 117 cardinals participating in the conclave posed the same questions to one another that Cardinal Bergoglio had considered as the convenor of the 2001 Synod of Bishops: what characteristics should a pope for the twenty-first century have to lead the Catholic Church in a globalised era? Bergoglio had joked that true shepherds ought to smell a bit like sheep, rather than command like shepherds; but others didn't share his vision. The cardinals were certainly divided in their opinions regarding the role of the Church in a globalised world. Two main groups emerged: those who perceived the Church as a fortress of immanent truth against a diverse and secularised world, and those who perceived the Church as building bridges, the servant of all. The latter understanding of the Church's role, already present at

---

Bergoglio is 'lúcido diagnóstico de la realidad', Cardenal Jorge Mario Bergoglio, *Disertaciones*, Cátedra de Juan Pablo II, Pontificia Universidad Católica Argentina, 25 September 2004.

1   Bergoglio is paraphrasing the text from *Veritatis Splendor* § 101, text that in turn cites *Centesimus Annus* § 46.

Vatican II, had been accused by traditionalists as contributing to a world without a centre of reference. This group of traditionalists firmly believed in a strong and centralising Vatican, and rejected calls for renewal and streamlining; their candidate was Cardinal Josef Ratzinger, the enforcer of doctrine in the Church, who didn't avoid confronting and correcting those theologians who were leading the Church into orthopraxy rather than orthodoxy, such as Gustavo Gutiérrez.

Bergoglio was celebrating the Eucharist in the Villa 21 neighbourhood of Buenos Aires when the Argentinean media released the news of John Paul II's death. The Argentinean cardinal appeared shocked and uneasy on receipt of the news. As a cardinal of the Catholic Church, he had to prepare for a journey to Rome to take part in the conclave. Cardinals have assumed the role of electing the pope since 1059, and the practical details of the election and arrangements for the cardinals to stay and gather in Rome have evolved over the centuries. In 1996, John Paul II led a review of the conclave's procedures and decided that the cardinals' vote would be given by secret ballot, and the new pope would be elected by a two-thirds majority: that is, an absolute majority. The number of cardinals who could elect the pope was restricted to 120, and the historical practice of gathering within the Sistine Chapel was maintained, along with strict rules of residence. There must be no contact between the cardinals and the outside world until a new pope was elected. John Paul II arranged for the construction of a residence within the Vatican, with 120 individual rooms and another twenty large rooms for communal meals and meetings. The residence was named Domus Sanctae Marthae, and was used for the first time during the 2005 conclave.

Once Bergoglio heard the news of John Paul II's death, he arranged for a Mass to be celebrated on 4 April 2005 at the Metropolitan Cathedral in Buenos Aires, an occasion to which he invited members of the government as well as the leaders and members of other Christian churches and other faiths such as Judaism and Islam. In his homily, Bergoglio spoke of John Paul II as a consistent man who communicated with his people daily after spending hours in prayer every morning.[1] Consistency, for Bergoglio, was the fruit of this kind of daily adoration of God, the service of others and habits of spiritual search. These three

1   Cardenal Jorge Mario Bergoglio, *Homilías*, Misa en memoria de Su Santidad Juan Pablo II, Catedral Primada de Buenos Aires, 4 April 2005.

activities, in turn, harmonise human beings and give them God's strength. In his opinion, John Paul II was consistent because he sought the will of God – and in doing so suffered hardships – but nevertheless allowed God to grow in him. Bergoglio also remembered that John Paul II had taken a hands-on approach to serving God: he blessed children, visited the man who tried to assassinate him, welcomed the homeless and workers, and made possible, using public diplomacy, the avoidance of armed conflict between 'brothers and sisters'. He was referring to John Paul's mediation between the governments of Argentina and Chile in the early 1980s, years in which a war between the two countries seemed imminent. Thanks to the intervention of the pope, the conflict was averted.[1] In his homily Bergoglio also highlighted John Paul II's words: 'What this century needs are not teachers but witnesses'.

Bergoglio arrived in Rome already a well-known cardinal because of his work during the 2001 Synod of Bishops, and he was already perceived as a possible successor to John Paul II. Among those cardinals who wanted change within the Church, and proposed a consensus for a reformist candidate, was the Italian cardinal Achille Silvestrini. Those who wanted to maintain the continuity of a 'fortress' Church were the Colombian cardinal Alfonso López Trujillo, the Spanish cardinal Julián Herranz (member of the traditional Prelature Opus Dei) and Cardinal Angelo Sodano, the Vatican Secretary of State and previously nuncio to Chile in the time of General Pinochet. They quickly moved to muster support for continuity with John Paul II's papacy. The cardinals started receiving anonymous documents with accusations against Silvestrini (progressive in religion and politically a close friend of Communists), against the traditionalists (whom John Paul II had challenged for denying any openness to the world) and against Bergoglio, accusing him of having not defended the two Jesuit priests arrested by the Argentinean military in 1976. Bergoglio commented upon this among those his close circle, and decided that he would not respond to anonymous accusations, especially as he was not interested in being elected as the successor of John Paul II. There were also attacks against Cardinal Ratzinger. The progressive wing of cardinals decided to support the Jesuit

1   John Paul II's visit to Chile and Argentina in April 1987 was a celebration of life because the Polish Pope had managed to aid the two neighbouring countries to avoid a war.

Cardinal Carlo Maria Martini, formerly archbishop of Milan, as their papal candidate. Martini was a biblical scholar, and was ill in Jerusalem at the time of the conclave, where he had retired to continue his scholarship. By supporting Martini, the progressives sought to send a clear message of reform to the conclave. They then intended to change their allegiance to an outsider, somebody who was not an obvious candidate to the papacy.[1] This tactic of sheltering an outsider to the Vatican for papal election had also been used in the conclave that elected John Paul II.

During the meetings that precede the papal election, cardinals gather to pray, and to be briefed on procedural and historical matters. They try to collectively discern what qualities might be required in the new pope, and try to get to know one another over meals and during communal discussions. The Franciscan priest Fr Raniero Cantalamessa, the official preacher to the papal household, spoke at one of these meetings. He called for more participation from all the bishops in the governance of the Catholic Church.[2] The issue of collegiality, founded on agreed principles at Vatican II, had slowly been eroding in practice due to the centralising of the Vatican and the distrustful doctrinal guardianship of Cardinal Ratzinger. Cardinal Martini advocated elegantly for a full restoration of collegiality, and a real engagement with the contemporary problems in the *Curia* and the Catholic Church.

When the Conclave started on 18 April 2005, Josef Ratzinger presided at the opening Eucharist. This Mass, dedicated to devotional prayer on the occasion of the election of the Roman Pontiff, was marked by Ratzinger's homily on the dictatorship of ethical relativism in contemporary society, and the dangers of a range of philosophies, including Marxism and Liberalism, posed to morality. Ratzinger remarked that in the contemporary world having a clear faith was seen as fundamentalist. He made a clear defence of the 'traditionalist' ecclesial position, a defence that was not applauded by all. At the start of the first voting session of the conclave, an occasion cameras were allowed to record, Bergoglio was shown positioned between the Indian Cardinal Varkey Vithayathil and the Portuguese Cardinal José da Cruz Policarpo, and he appeared to be concentrated in reflection and prayer.

---

1   Evangelina Himitian, *Francisco: El Papa de la gente*, Buenos Aires: Aguilar, 2013, pp. 253-254.
2   Fr Cantalamessa visited Argentina in October 2012 and was warmly welcomed by Cardinal Bergoglio.

Bergoglio had been singled out as a frontrunner by the Italian weekly *L'Espresso*; however, on the second day and in the fourth ballot, Cardinal Ratzinger was chosen as the new pope, taking the name of Benedict XVI. Bergoglio had been the only other candidate with sufficient support to be elected following the first ballot, when Cardinal Martini, who had been given a significant number of votes, had addressed the cardinals explaining that because of ill-health, if he were elected he would not be able to serve. In the next ballot Martini's votes were transferred to Bergoglio, who, although conservative in doctrine, was perceived as progressive because he envisioned the Catholic Church as servant of others. After the third ballot, during lunch time, Bergoglio asked some of his supporters to transfer their votes to Cardinal Ratzinger. Bergoglio has never spoken of the conclave: therefore any explanations of the fact he decided to request support for Ratzinger are only speculative.

Bergoglio's lifestyle and pastoral approach might suggest that he would never put himself at the centre of things, and that he felt that reaching a consensus was more important for the well-being of the Church than opposing Ratzinger. It was this altruistic attitude that meant Bergoglio was elected in 2013. Presumably the cardinals who were present in 2005 remembered his concern for the unity of the Church above any concern for his own interests. Quite apart from his focus on episcopal collegiality, Bergoglio admired Cardinal Ratzinger's tenacity, and described his main virtues as being humour, goodness, intelligence and courage – his courageousness exemplified not least by his acceptance of the position of pope at the age of seventy-eight, when he was not in the best of health.[1]

Bergoglio and the Kirchners

Bergoglio had become more recognisable in Rome after his work at the 2001 Synod of Bishops. He was already well known in Argentina, where he had pushed for the clergy and lay people to bring the Gospel to the margins of society and the message of Christ to the city streets. Thus, despite the distrust of President Kirchner,

---

1 See transcription of part of the talk given by Bergoglio to the religious community of the Hermanas Cruzadas de Santa María, Residencia Rovacías, Madrid on 23 January 2006, after the retreat he had given to some of the Spanish bishops provided by Fr José Antonio Medina in José Medina, *Francisco: El Papa de todos*, Buenos Aires: Bonum, 2013, pp. 93-94.

Bergoglio returned to Argentina in 2001 an internationally respected man, who was playing a central role in Argentinean socio-political affairs. On 25 May 2005 the Argentinean president did not attend the Te Deum at the Metropolitan Cathedral. Later that year, however, he had to witness the elevation of Bergoglio to the position of President of the Argentinean Episcopal Conference. On 8 December 2005, during the ninetieth meeting of the Argentinean bishops at the retreat house La Montonera in the city of Pilar, Buenos Aires, Bergoglio was chosen as the leader of all Argentinean bishops with an absolute majority. Bergoglio obtained the two-thirds majority required at the first round of voting, and became the successor of Mgr Eduardo Mirás, Archbishop of Rosario, who had just completed his three-year term of office. For the day of the selection, Bergoglio had prepared a reflection on the themes of sin and corruption, defining corruption 'not as an act, but a condition, a personal and social condition that one gets used to living in'.[1] This reflection, primarily considering politicians and businessmen, argued that 'the values (or anti-values) of corruption are integrated into a full culture, with doctrinal capabilities, its own language, its own peculiar way of doing things'.[2]

President Kirchner commented to his aides that Bergoglio's election was an open provocation from the bishops, a view that seemed confirmed for him when the Argentinean Episcopal Conference published the letter 'Una luz para reconstruir la nación', a document defined by the bishops, in the language of the Second Vatican Council, as 'una Carta al Pueblo de Dios' (a letter to the People of God). Once again the bishops' analysis spoke of the scandalous and growing divide between the rich and powerful and the poor and powerless in Argentinean society, and warned that this divide might again lead to social violence and unrest. The marginalisation of whole sectors of the population and the lack of work were identified by the bishops as among some of the worst tragedies experienced by the Argentinean nation. The bishops requested firm and lasting policies from the government

---

1   'La corrupción no es un acto, sino un estado, estado personal y social, en el que uno se acostumbra a vivir', Cardenal Jorge M. Bergoglio SJ, *Corrupción y pecado: Algunas reflexiones en torno al tema de la corrupción*, Buenos Aires: Editorial Claretiana, 2013 (8 December 2005), p. 36.

2   'Los valores (o desvalores) de la corrupción son integrados en una *verdadera cultura*, con capacidad doctrinal, lenguaje propio, modo de proceder peculiar', Cardenal Jorge M. Bergoglio SJ, *Corrupción y pecado*, p. 36.

to improve these issues, and offered severe criticism of problems in the areas of education and health. When he received the news about the pastoral letter, President Kirchner was at the ranch of El Calafate in the Santa Cruz Province working on ministerial changes. He was not pleased by its contents; especially as the Argentinean press interpreted the letter as a new attack on the president led by Bergoglio. Five days later, President Kirchner spoke from the Casa Rosada (the presidential palace), defending the government's policies and asserting that the bishops were not sufficiently aware of the social realities in Argentina, and suggesting that the bishops were behaving as if they were a political party. This reaction was the end of any hopes of close Church-State relations under Bergoglio and Kirchner. Kirchner perceived Bergoglio's actions as fostering opposition to his government, and consequently reminded the bishops that God was the God of everyone, but the devil also reaches everyone – those who wear trousers and those who wear cassocks. President Kirchner and his wife Cristina began advocating for the service of the poor within a wider united Latin American movement for the defence of human rights. Since the Kirchners could not accuse Bergoglio of ignoring the poor or the broader concerns of Latin America, they started accusing him of not having defended human rights during the period of the military junta. Such accusations against Bergoglio did not take into account the difficult circumstances he faced in 1976 when he was head of the Jesuits: a role significantly different to that of Archbishop of Buenos Aires or a cardinal of the Catholic Church.[1]

There were no meetings between Cardinal Bergoglio and President Kirchner for two years until the death of Néstor Kirchner and the election of his wife, Cristina Fernandez, as President of Argentina on 10 December 2007. The Kirchners had wanted to meet at the presidential palace, but Bergoglio was always adamant that if they asked for a meeting they should come to the offices of the archbishop of Buenos Aires – as was the practice when any citizen requested a meeting. By refusing to meet them at the presidential palace, Bergoglio refused to allow himself to be exploited by the Kirchners to foster their political power. He would not walk through the Plaza de Mayo to knock on the door of the powerful, whom Bergoglio had publicly challenged for many years.

1 In the correct words of Evangelina Himitian 'cargaron las tintas en su contra sin saber cuál había sido la verdadera participación de Bergoglio y cayeron en un reduccionismo tramposo de la historia', *Francisco*, p. 164.

There were tensions between President Fernández's government and the Vatican from the start of her first presidential term in office. In January 2008, the Vatican informed President Fernández, through informal channels, that the nominated Argentinean ambassador to the Vatican, Alberto Iribarne, was not acceptable because he was divorced. Further, the Vatican was not happy about the vacant see of the Bishop of the Armed Forces in Argentina, vacant since the retirement of Bishop Antonio Baseotto. They also objected to the position of the Argentinean government on abortion; the government had fostered health protocols from 2007 addressing legal issues around abortion and recognising that rape justifies an abortion request. The tensions dragged on until 22 October 2008 when President Fernández appointed Juan Pablo Cafiero as Argentinean Ambassador to the Vatican, an appointment approved by the Holy See.

Bringing the nation together was a major goal of the Argentinean bishops as they provided ongoing advice to the Argentinean nation. In Bergoglio's case, his advice always included some criticism of the Presidents Kirchner and Fernández. Bergoglio criticised their ongoing accumulation of wealth, as well as their accusations that the Argentinean bishops were politically rather than pastorally motivated. Once again the document released by the Argentinean bishops after the April 2008 Episcopal Conference was critical of inequality, and requested that all Catholics pray daily for the nation, asking Jesus Christ, as Lord of history, to guide Argentina.[1]

In May 2008 Cristina Fernández avoided Bergoglio's Te Deum homily by travelling to the cathedral in Salta for a thanksgiving liturgy, presided over by the local archbishop, Mgr Mario Cargnello.[2] During the crisis generated by Kirchner's death in October 2010, Bergoglio offered words of comfort and hope to Cristina Fernández, and, years later, made her the first head of state to be received at the Vatican when he was elected pope. This probably shows that relations between Bergoglio and Kirchner were more strained than between Bergoglio and Fernández.

---

1 'Concédenos la sabiduría del diálogo y la alegría de la esperanza que no defrauda. Tú nos convocas. Aquí estamos, Señor, cercanos a María, que, desde Luján, nos dice: ¡Argentina! ¡Canta y camina!', Conferencia Episcopal Argentina, Mensaje al Pueblo de Dios, 95ª Asamblea Plenaria de la Conferencia Episcopal Argentina, Pilar, 8 April 2008.

2 'Cristina Kirchner también esquiva homilía de Bergoglio por Te Deum del 25 de mayo', Radio Cristiandad, 13 May 2008.

On 27 November 2008, during President Fernández's first period in office, representatives of the Argentinean Episcopal Conference visited her, and cordial photographs were taken of the occasion. However, the strike and public protests by Argentinean farmers, particularly producers of soya, in March 2008 brought the Church and State head-to-head once again. When the government announced that the national retention rate of agricultural products would increase from 34% to 44% (by law a certain percentage of agricultural products must be sold within Argentina), the agricultural producers of Argentina held a 21-day strike, which involved protestors blocking public roads: an action that left Argentina with shortages of food and agricultural products. As a result of the strike, the law on agricultural products was not passed by Argentinean Congress. Fernández's vice-president, Julio Cobos, voted against it, inspiring others to object. Bergoglio met with the leaders of the agricultural sector and also requested that Fernández extend a grand gesture of public political confidence in Cobos even when he had voted against his own government. At the end of 2008, Bergoglio invited President Fernández to a Mass in Luján, which she attended. However, Bergoglio's words suggesting that poverty was as much a human rights violation as terrorism, repression, and murder were countered by Fernández's assertion that, while some are content to speak about poverty, others like her actively try to fight poverty every day. Although relations between the cardinal and the president could lead to constructive dialogue, for the most part this didn't happen once Fernández was settled in her presidential office.

There is no doubt that a major crisis between the Catholic Church and the Argentinean State occurred during the public debates over Argentinean marriage laws, particularly the proposed reform of the law to allow same-sex marriages in Argentina from 2010. Some, who thought of Bergoglio as a liberal archbishop because he was close to the poor and the marginalised, were surprised when he objected to the proposal. They should not have been: Bergoglio had always been a conservative in the matter of Catholic doctrine; otherwise he would not have supported Cardinal Ratzinger for pope.

Bergoglio's opposition to the possibility of a law approving same-sex marriage in Argentina started in 2008, when he publicly requested four religious orders to pray particularly hard for Argentina. In a letter to the orders, Bergoglio spoke of the 'unchangeable gift' of marriage and the family. His public words were forceful: he warned his addressees that the law represented the sabotage of the plan of God: 'a move by the Prince of Lies to confuse and lie to the children of God'. Some spoke quietly inside Catholic circles, saying that the issuing of the letter had been a mistake because it allowed President Fernández to catalogue Bergoglio as an ultra-conservative bishop. In her opinion, Bergoglio had not only failed to defend human rights at the time of military rule, but in the twenty-first century was failing to defend the rights of all Argentineans, including those who were gay. Fernández subtly expressed her reservations about Bergoglio's words, stressing the fact that, while his letter labelled gay marriage as a subversion of the natural and moral order, she and the government were simply pressing for the legalisation of human relations already present within Argentinean society.

If one good outcome came from Bergoglio's lack of co-operation with government policies, it was that he had more time to focus on the pastoral problems affecting Buenos Aires because he didn't attend official banquets or presidential receptions. He took a particular interest in the fight against drugs, and he denounced human slavery, and became close to mothers who had lost sons or daughters to violent crime. Two pastoral incidents that *porteños* (Argentineans from Buenos Aires) remember particularly occurred before his departure for Rome.

The first was the urban crisis faced by Mauricio Macri, mayor of Buenos Aires, when, on 7 December 2010, 200 families renting in Villa 31 of the southern area of Buenos Aires occupied the Parque Indoamericano.[1] Those without homes wanted to make the park their home; they occupied land near the bus station in Retiro and divided it into 200 plots with plastic strips, in the hope that it would be given to them. There were ugly scenes of violence. Tires were burnt and foreign immigrants attacked by angry neighbours who opposed the occupation of the Parque. Bergoglio was scheduled to celebrate Mass at the chapel of San Juan Diego within the Parque on the day of the liturgical calendar marked as the feast of one of the indigenous Latin American saints. Bergoglio's custom was to try to be present in a parish or chapel on the day of the liturgical feast of the Virgin Mary or one of the saints. Despite the fact that the chapel was located beside the Parque, Bergoglio decided to go in. When

---

1   Another 1000 homeless families took over land in the area of Bernal Oeste, Buenos Aires, while a few additional people tried to take over land in Florencio Varela, Berazategui, Villa Lugano and other locations of Greater Buenos Aires.

he arrived he found it surrounded by burned tyres, fifty policemen ready to charge against the occupants of the Parque, and around two hundred protestors shouting at the police. Bergoglio celebrated the Mass and proclaimed the unity of all Latin Americans, including the Bolivian woman who had been beaten up trying to get to the Mass. Afterward he greeted people outside, and, in the midst of the smoke and shouting, he walked down to the nearest bus stop in order to return to his room at the cathedral offices. The park was finally cleared of its occupants on 15 December 2010, when the national and federal government announced that homes would be given to the 5,688 protestors.[1] However, a year later, the promises by the national and federal governments had still not been fulfilled: President Fernández had promised to match any money given by the federal government of Buenos Aires, and Mauricio Macri, Head of the Autonomous Government of the Buenos Aires Province, did not give it.[2]

The second pastoral incident remembered by *porteños* took place only a few days before Bergoglio's journey to Rome to take part in the conclave that was to elect him as the new pope. The archbishop celebrated Mass at the Metropolitan Cathedral for the victims of a train crash that had taken place in Buenos Aires a year before on 22 February 2012, in which 51 people died and 701 were injured. The accident occurred because there were no technical checks on the train involved, and the company in charge of maintenance had not provided enough resources to make the train safe for carrying passengers. The clear cause of the accident was neglect due to corruption, whereby the train company had been permitted to operate without observing the legal requirements for doing so. Bergoglio had corresponded via e-mail with some of the relatives, and had encouraged them to seek justice and compensation by all available means; however, what surprised them was that the cardinal's communication came before any of them had approached him with their sorrow and suffering. On the day of the Mass he was waiting for them outside the cathedral; he embraced each one of them, kissed them, listened to their stories and sat with them even before they entered. During the Eucharist the relatives of the victims who carried large posters

1 'Liberaron el parque Indoamericano en Soldati', *La Nación*, 16 December 2010.

2 'A un año de la ocupación del Parque Indoamericano', *Alternativa Socialista*, 15 December 2011.

that formed the word 'justice' were given Bergoglio's permission to place photographs and posters on the altar. Bergoglio's words during the Mass were direct and strong, reminding those present that people were responsible for this tragedy: people who had not fulfilled their duties.[1] He recollected that those who died were people who had taken the train in order to earn a living with dignity, and who had to journey like cattle in order to earn money to feed their families. Bergoglio asked those present never to get used to this situation. When Bergoglio was elected pope, these relatives returned to the Metropolitan Cathedral to give thanks to God for his presence.[2]

Fifth General Meeting of Latin American Bishops, 2007

Bergoglio had risen from auxiliary bishop to cardinal against the backdrop of an ever-changing Latin American Church, which had lost some of its centrality since the end of the military regimes. Both the end of these regimes, and the 500 year anniversary of the arrival of the Gospel in Latin America, had been marked by the Fourth General Meeting of Latin American Bishops in Santo Domingo (1992). Fifteen years after that meeting, Pope Benedict XVI agreed to call a fifth general meeting, which took place in Aparecida (Brazil) in 2007. One of the reasons such a long period had elapsed was because the Vatican was concerned about the spreading of liberation theology within the Latin American clergy and the influence that the Latin American bishops could have in the Catholic Church. However, anticipation for the Aparecida conference had grown enormously among those who were still active in theological reflection. The number of Catholics in Latin America had fallen dramatically, particularly in Brazil, and a whole generation of progressive theologians from Latin America had already been ostracised in official Church circles, partly because their leaning towards liberal theology was seen as suspicious. They had continued meeting in globalised reflective

1   'Bergoglio sobre la tragedia de Once: "Hay responsables irresponsables que no cumplieron con su deber"', *La Nación*, 23 March 2012.
2   In June 2013 the relatives of the victims were still fighting to bring the issue to public trial, given that those responsible for negligence were supported by the Argentinean Congress, and the fact that the judge initially appointed to deal with the judicial demand was a relative of one of those accused of financial fraud and manslaughter, see 'Para los familiares es "un paso positivo"', *La Nación*, 7 June 2013.

congregations, such as the Social Global Forum, but their writings and experiences seemed largely ignored within Latin America. One reason for this was the appointment of very conservative bishops in Latin America by John Paul II.

In a 2009 address to members of Caritas Argentina, Bergoglio spoke of three pillars that had aided the pastoral success of the meeting at Aparecida. The first pillar was the deliberate absence of a pre-composed working document dictating the agenda of the bishops' meeting and their deliberations. Instead of a document, there was only a print-out of all opinions, and suggested themes had been collected and consolidated by the national Episcopal Conferences throughout Latin America. The second pillar was the location of the meetings. The Church of Aparecida is a Marian shrine with 25,000-person capacity, and the bishops celebrated the Eucharist daily at the church with the participation of lay people, mostly pilgrims to the shrine. The bishops met beneath the ground floor of the church, where rooms and facilities were adapted for the meetings; thus, in Bergoglio's words, the 'music' that accompanied the bishops' deliberations were the voices, prayers, chants, hymns and homilies taking place just over their heads in the main church. The third pillar was the document. Its main last section was based on a mission – a mission of the Church which was still unfinished, to put Latin American people, rather than the Church, at its centre.

On 15 May 2007, the bishops at Aparecida voted to elect a commission that would write the final document arising from the meeting, and Bergoglio was elected president of the commission. In the midst of a crisis in the Catholic Church created by the large numbers of Catholics who had turned to Pentecostal and Evangelical churches, and the fact that the Catholic Church did not have the same authority within the national debates and concerns that it had previously, expectations for the meeting were huge. If the first meeting of Latin American bishops in Brazil in 1955 had been the structural beginning of a Latin American voice within the Catholic Church, the subsequent meetings in Medellin (1968) and Puebla (1979) had emphasised the poor and the marginalised as the centre of the pastoral concerns of the Latin American Church. The fourth meeting in Santo Domingo had, for some, been overshadowed by the Roman *Curia*. The Latin American pastoral practice had indeed feared for its very existence after Cardinal Ratzinger directed a full-blown doctrinal enquiry into the centrality of liberation theology for Latin America and the theologians who espoused it.

A day after his appointment as president of the writing commission for Aparecida, Bergoglio presided at the Eucharist with all the bishops and spoke quietly about his own interpretation of the general theme of the meeting: a Church that would not focus on herself and her self-sufficiency, but a Church that would reach out to every periphery, accepting an invitation to mission. This theme became central in the final document, even after group deliberations that were completely free and to which everyone was able to contribute. The difficulty was, of course, that most participants wanted a short document, but the democratic level of participation yielded enormous amounts of material for discussion which might be included in the final document. After two weeks of deliberation, five experts (*periti*) helped the commission to organise the text. The text was finally delivered to the participants after a long night of work. The *periti* all agreed that Bergoglio, who customarily sleeps for only five hours a night, was in better shape than anybody else in the morning.

There are discernible traces of Bergoglio's life and spirituality in the final document from Aparecida, a document that reminds Christians in Latin America that the life of all Christians is a joyful one, and that their mission offers happiness, joy and a better life. Some themes were excluded from the document, many suggested by conservatives among the Latin American bishops who wanted to stress Christian apologetics and the idea of a Church that was under attack from civil powers and other Christian churches in Latin America. Bergoglio's promotion of dialogue and common participation with other churches prevailed, and the final document stressed the theme of life (mentioned more than 600 times). Life for a Christian, in Bergoglio's terms, must be connected with those who suffer – reiterating the 'preferential option for the poor' present in the Puebla document – and involve the active participation within the mission of the Church of those who suffer, the poor and the humble of society. Popular religiosity in all its aspects returned very strongly as a theme, solidarity with the poor and promotion of the active participation and dignity of the marginalised, both within society and within the Church. Bergoglio also stressed the importance of devotion through pilgrimage and prayer, a theme that had been downplayed by the socio-political emphasis of liberation theologies in the documents of Medellin and Puebla.

However, the final document from Aparecida also expressed concern for just economic and financial models, and challenged free-trade agreements, which are sometimes signed between totally unequal parties.[1] Such free-trade agreements do provide possibilities of wealth creation and increased wealth for the disadvantaged, but the Church stressed that considerations of wealth creation must be accompanied by attentiveness to the quality of human beings' lives within society. The document continued – and Bergoglio's experience of the Argentinean financial crises is clearly important here – to say that the magnitude of exclusion and the numbers of the excluded in society had risen, challenging the 'success' of Latin American financial models.[2]

It is through the reading of the documents of Aparecida, whose conclusions Bergoglio treasured enormously, that his Latin American identity is revealed. For instance, once elected as Pope Francis, his gift to visiting heads of state from Latin America, such as the Uruguayan President José Mujica, has been a copy of the documents of Aparecida. For Bergoglio, Aparecida represents an episcopal reflection from Latin America that should be taken very seriously indeed.[3] It can be argued that at Aparecida Bergoglio managed to overcome the revolutionary legacy of the 1970s and 1980s as well as the dissatisfaction created by the meeting of Latin American Bishops in Santo Domingo. The post-Vatican II golden period of action had been replaced – due in large part to the return of democracy to many Latin American nations – by a 'fortress Church' perceived as being solely concerned with ethical laws and the threat of Evangelicals and Pentecostals. Cardinal Bergoglio was to change this inward gaze by insisting that God was to be found at the margins of society. Consequently, the missionary mandate for the Catholic Church was toward solidarity and love for the marginalised and dispossessed of the continent without seeking temporal recompense.

---

1 Aparecida § 67.
2 Bergoglio has continued his theme through his papacy and addressed the concerns of the excluded when he wrote to David Cameron, Prime Minister of the United Kingdom, before the meeting of the G-8 leaders in Northern Ireland in June 2013. Pope Francis wrote in this letter that 'the aim of economics and politics is to serve humanity beginning with the most vulnerable', Pope Francis to David Cameron, 15 June 2013.
3 María Fernanda Bernasconi, 'El Papa Francisco recibe al Presidente de la República Oriental del Uruguay', Radio Vaticana, 1 June 2013.

5. The Nation, the Poor and Others

Bergoglio's thought, as expressed at the conference of Aparecida, challenged Catholics in Latin America to live the kind of Christian life that he did. Thus, if Aparecida represented continuity with the past, particularly with the conferences of Puebla, Medellin and Santo Domingo and the challenges established by Vatican II, it also represented a challenge for the future, a point of departure.[1] This challenge had been prepared by Bergoglio's pastoral ministry in Buenos Aires, and can be summarised under three headings: concern for the nation, the poor within the nation and the 'others' within the nation – including Christians of other denominations, Jews, Muslims, people of other faiths and those of no religion.

The Church as Servant

The connection between these three themes helps us understand Bergoglio's years as archbishop, cardinal and pope. They result in emphasis on the role the Catholic Church plays as servant of others, a return to the main themes of Vatican II, and the ubiquitous assumption in Bergoglio's reflections that the Church is not centred on itself but on God's love and Christ's presence among others,. He stated that, 'the Church is a companion en route to our poorer brothers, even unto martyrdom'.[2] Bergoglio's

---

1 This point is discussed at length and in depth by Cristián del Campo SJ, who, even when critical of the absence of a proper theological reflection from Aparecida, applauds the option of the poor as a point of convergence in the Latin American magisterium; however, he cries for this option as 'point of departure' as well, see 'Conclusión' by Cristián del Campo SJ in his work *Dios opta por los pobres: Reflexión teológica a partir de Aparecida*, Santiago: Ediciones Universidad Alberto Hurtado, 2010, pp. 121-124.

2 Cardenal Jorge M. Bergoglio SJ, 'Homilía con motivo del V Encuentro Nacional de Sacerdotes', Villa Cura Brochero, 11 September 2008.

understanding of the Church proposed – and implemented – radical change: a Church that goes where needy people are, whose raison d'être is based on evangelisation to awaken the Christian memory of Latin Americans.[1] In his own words: 'we cannot remain passively waiting in our churches'.[2] Bergoglio believes that there is a constant imperative for Church leaders to re-examine the internal life of the Church. It must not attempt to regulate the faith more than actively pass on and facilitate the faith.[3] A properly functioning Church, according to Bergoglio, will be misunderstood and persecuted – yesterday, today and perpetually – unless she stoops: 'to avoid the cross (cf. Matt. 16:22), to compromise the truth, to diminish the redemptive force of the cross of Christ in order to avoid persecution'.[4]

In Bergoglio's opinion, one of the ills afflicting the Church is a clericalism that is pushed by the clergy and welcomed by the laity because it is easier to obey blindly than to lead as an agent of evangelisation.[5] The 'new evangelisation' that John Paul II had proclaimed at the assembly of the Latin American Episcopal Conference in 1983 was taken very seriously by Bergoglio. He not only renewed ecclesial pastoral structures, but also challenged any inward-looking tendencies.[6] When Bergoglio was playing a central role in the 2012 Synod of Bishops, the three tiers of the 'new evangelisation' suggested by Benedict XVI – which emphasised the importance of the sacrament of initiation, the mission *ad gentes*, and the revival of the faith of the already baptised – had been advanced with a new vitality by Bergoglio in the Argentinean context.[7] Bergoglio constructed a communal perspective on spirituality. It was based upon John Paul II's reflections on the centrality of the social doctrine of the Church in *Tertio Millennio*

---

1 Cardenal Jorge M. Bergoglio SJ, 'Plenaria de la Comisión para América Latina', Rome, January 2005.

2 Cardenal Jorge M. Bergoglio SJ, 'Sobre la nueva evangelización y la pastoral misionera', Discurso en el Consejo Presbiteral, 15 April 2008.

3 Cf. Cardenal Jorge M. Bergoglio SJ, 'El llama a cada una por su nombre, y las hace salir . . . ', Carta a los Catequistas, August 2007.

4 Cardenal Jorge M. Bergoglio SJ, Asamblea del Episcopado, April 2007.

5 Cardenal Jorge M. Bergoglio SJ, 'Entrevista concedida a AICA (Agencia Informativa Católica Argentina), Pilar, Buenos Aires, 9 November 2011.

6 John Paul II, 'Discurso a la Asamblea del CELAM (Consejo Episcopal Latinoamericano), Puerto Príncipe, Haiti, 9 March 1983.

7 Benedict XVI, Misa para la Clausura del Sínodo de los Obispos, Basílica Vaticana, 28 October 2012.

Adveniente (TMA) – specifically the parts that consider just relation between personal rights and dignity, work and money, and the promotion of peace.[1]

There is no doubt in Cardinal Bergoglio's mind that service to others is the essence of the Church's life: 'in service there is greatness; where there is service, there is vocation'.[2] The main actors of such ecclesial service are priests. Bergoglio has said that: 'priests who go out and know how to become close to others, who welcome gently, who take time to make people feel that God has time for them, wish to help them, wish to bless them, to forgive them and to heal them' are true servants of the Church.[3] If in the past the Church had sought to accumulate power within Argentinean society, Bergoglio maintained that 'the true power is love . . . because on the cross or in the deathbed one can love'.[4]

A Theology of the Nation

In Argentina, after the era of military governments, the Catholic Church was widely considered to be secondary to democratic government. The Church had failed in various ways under the military regime, and the military, in their clinging attempt to remain in power, had pushed the nation into a war with Britain in 1982. It would seem that the Argentinean presidents that followed this era – particularly Alfonsín, Menem and Kirchner – wanted to create a sense of common national identity that was less influenced by the military and the Catholic Church.

Bergoglio offered sound reflections upon the issue of the Argentinean nationhood during his Te Deum homilies.[5] He used

1   *TMA* 22, analysed by Bergoglio in Jorge M. Bergoglio SJ, '*Duc in Altum*: El pensamiento social de Juan Pablo II', June 2003.
2   Cardenal Jorge M. Bergoglio SJ, 'Con motivo del lavatorio de los pies del Jueves Santo en el Hospital Garrahan', 9 April 2009.
3   Cardenal Jorge M. Bergoglio SJ, 'Homilía en la Misa Crismal', 9 April 2009.
4   Cardenal Jorge M. Bergoglio SJ, 'Homilía con motivo del Te Deum', 25 May 2012.
5   See the collections of Bergoglio's homilies on the theme of the nation, published by Editorial Claretiana of Buenos Aires: Cardenal Jorge M. Bergoglio SJ, *Ponerse la patria al hombre: Memoria y camino de esperanza*, Buenos Aires: Editorial Claretiana, 2004, *La nación por construir: Utopía, pensamiento y compromiso*, Buenos Aires: Editorial Claretiana, 2005, and *Nosotros como ciudadanos, nosotros como pueblo: Hacia un Bicentenario en justicia y solidaridad 2010-2016*, Buenos Aires: Editorial Claretiana,

the expression *patria* (nation) in his addresses to the governments of his time. Even more potently, when addressing pilgrims who represented different sectors of Argentinean society, he intentionally addressed them as one. For example, during the National Eucharistic Congress of 2004, he reminded pilgrims of the will of the Virgin of Itatí: 'She invites you, people of the nation (*pueblo de la Patria*) let yourself be reconciled with God!', and 'the Eucharist may fill the heart of the Argentinean people and may inspire its projects and hopes'.[1]

Every 25 May Bergoglio returned to reflecting on the nation from a Christian point of view. On this occasion, the so-called Argentinean 'national day', Argentineans commemorate the Friday 25 May in 1810 when a group of patriots established the first revolutionary junta that deposed the Spanish Viceroy Cisneros, and for the first time a group of civilians, the majority of them born in Argentina, were able to direct the future of the united provinces that would later become the Argentinean state. The immediate political cause of this development was the fall of Andalucía at the hands of the French Army and the capture of the Spanish King Ferdinand VII. On the yearly anniversary of this day, the Argentinean Independence Day, a Te Deum is sung at the Metropolitan Cathedral in Buenos Aires, a liturgical occasion attended by the Argentinean president and most of the government, senate and civil service. Prayers are led by the archbishop of Buenos Aires who also, after readings from the Bible have been read, delivers a homily marking the occasion.

One of the hallmarks of Cardinal Bergoglio's homilies at these occasions was a systematic consideration of some pastoral topic, which, over the years, he worked into a larger theological vision. For example, when addressing the eighth annual meeting of social pastoral agents (2005), he spoke on three main topics he had considered at length during the previous seven years: utopia,

---

2011. These publications were very deliberately edited and corrected by Bergoglio, then published, in order to show the systematic thought of the cardinal and to open a reflective space for those involved in the social pastoral work undertaken by pastoral agents of the archdiocese of Buenos Aires, recipients of many of Bergoglio's addresses, see P. Carlos Accaputo, 'Prólogo', in Cardenal Jorge Mario Bergoglio SJ, *La nación por construir: Utopía, pensamiento y compromiso*, Buenos Aires: Editorial Claretiana, 2005, pp. 7-11.

1 Cardenal Jorge M. Bergoglio, 'Homilía', Congreso Eucarístico Nacional, September 2004.

thought and witness.[1] Many of his primary topics of reflection – such as 'power is service', or the role of the Good Samaritan within the building up of a just nation – appear time and again as summaries of previous reflections, yet also as starting points for new reflections directed at different pastoral groups or socio-political sectors within Argentina.[2] Bergoglio's themes were therefore connected year by year, and, unlike other archbishops who addressed the nation on the theme of historical commemoration, Bergoglio used the yearly commemoration of 25 May to develop a set of Christian approaches about community for the Argentinean nation, through reflection on readings he chose: the disciples on the road to Emmaus for the 1999 Te Deum (Luke 24: 13-35), the raising of Nain's son for 2000 (Luke 7: 11-17), the request by the mother of Zebedee's sons for 2001 (Matthew 20: 20-28), the meeting with Zacheus for 2002 (Luke 19: 1-10), the parable of the prodigal son for 2003 (Luke 10: 25-37), and Jesus in the synagogue at Nazareth for 2004 (Luke 4: 16-32). Thus, the set of yearly reflections forms a composite body of theology upon which Bergoglio built each year.[3] In the Te Deum, Bergoglio repeatedly returns to the concept of the people who constitute the nation, people as 'a mystical category' rather than a logical one, a group of active neighbours.[4]

On this topic, during the liturgy of 25 May 1999 Bergoglio made reference to Pope John Paul II's forceful address on his second visit to Argentina in 1987, when he coined the phrase: 'Arise Argentina!'[5] In Bergoglio's view, John Paul II was calling

1 'Presentación' in Cardenal Jorge Mario Bergoglio SJ, *La nación por construir: Utopía, pensamiento y compromiso*, Buenos Aires: Editorial Claretiana, 2005, pp. 13-14.

2 Arzobispo Jorge Mario Bergoglio SJ, 'La nación por construir: utopía, pensamiento, compromiso', Documento de trabajo, VIII Jornada de Pastoral Social, Departamento de Pastoral Social, Arquidiócesis de Buenos Aires, 2005.

3 For example in May 2000 he made clear mention of the concept of the 're-founding of a social link among Argentineans, a hopeful link that could diminish the gap between the rich and the poor' – 'Para esta misma fecha, hace un año, destaqué la necesidad de *refundar el vínculo social entre los argentinos, un vínculo esperanzador*: un vínculo que acerque la dolorosa brecha entre los que tienen más y los que tienen menos', Arzobispo Jorge M. Bergoglio SJ, 'Comenzar la aventura de una nueva nación', Homilía en la catedral de Buenos Aires, 25 May 2000.

4 Cardenal Jorge M. Bergoglio SJ, 'Somos un pueblo con vocación de grandeza', Mensaje a las Comunidades Educativas, 2006.

5 Juan Pablo II, 'Levántate y resplandece', Homilía en la Misa para los consagrados y agentes de pastoral, Estadio Vélez Sarsfield, Buenos Aires,

all Argentineans, regardless of their place in society, to seek goodness for all. To arise is a sign of resurrection: it is a call to revitalise the fibre of Argentinean society.[1] Commenting on the text of the disciples on the road to Emmaus, who recognised the Risen Lord in the breaking of bread (Luke 24: 13-35), Bergoglio suggested that the call to arise is made to the Church but extends to every member of Argentinean society. The call to the disciples at Emmaus – who were fleeing from the disastrous end of Jesus of Nazareth at the hands of the Romans – was to arise, to see with new eyes the life that they had missed by having missed witnessing the Resurrection of the Lord. Thus, for Bergoglio, the call to the Argentinean people is to see the many gifts that people receive as a result of belonging to the Argentinean nation. In the words of Bergoglio: 'Because we are a people able to feel our identity beyond circumstances and adversities, we are a people able to recognise ourselves in a diversity of faces'.[2] However, Bergoglio recognises that the nation is tired and fatigued due to socio-political projects that do not take them into account as a collective group. Among the worst of these problems is the blindness of most Argentineans to a major danger within this process: a process of globalisation that, while advancing economic power alongside a rhetoric that legitimises such power, presents a danger for men and women feeling undermined by low self-esteem, without a sense of purpose, without something essential to humanity and the possibilities of access to a more dignified life. Bergoglio reminded his listeners on that 25 May 1999 that John Paul II had warned of the dangers of globalisation, chiefly the danger that the laws of the market would benefit only the powerful, make the divide between the rich and poor even greater and create a culture of unjust competition that would discriminate against the

---

10 April 1987. John Paul II visited Argentina twice. The first time after the Malvinas/Falkland War of 1982 he visited Britain and Argentina to intercede for peace between the two nations arriving in Buenos Aires on 11 June 1982. In his second visit he arrived in Argentina from Chile on a pastoral visit that lasted from the 6th to the 12th April 1987 visiting both countries after having aided the solution of a conflict between the two countries over sovereignty that avoided an armed conflict between Chile and Argentina, see 'Las visitas de Juan Pablo II a la Argentina', *La Nación*, 1 April 2005.

1   Arzobispo Jorge M. Bergoglio SJ, 'Dejar la nostagia y el pesimismo y dar lugar a nuestra sed de encuentro', Homilía en la Catedral de Buenos Aires, 25 May 1999.

2   Arzobispo Jorge M. Bergoglio SJ, 'Dejar la nostagia'.

poor nations of the world.[1] This fatigue, and the political failure to respond to real problems, increases the wish to live only for the moment and to abandon oneself in consumerism. Social fragmentation looms as a cloud on the horizon, while those with financial interests are absorbed by an acquisitive game that does not help anyone else in society. Bergoglio appealed to a shared Argentinean memory, wherein it is remembered that people are united by the many historical moments in which obstacles and difficulties have been solved through hard work and a common effort. However, there also needs to be a renewed understanding at the centre of society: all citizens should be called to a common project for the good of all, all citizens should answer this call and all citizens should benefit from the ensuing effort.

On 25 May 2000, Bergoglio developed the theme of 'rising from the dead' as a metaphor for the Argentinean nation, reflecting on the raising of Nain's son (Luke 7: 11-17).[2] The homily was delivered in the context of hope for the new millennium, which had just begun, and the call by John Paul II to remember the prior twenty centuries of Christ's presence among humanity. Bergoglio reminded his listeners of the two facts that filled the new millennium with both hope and repentance: the first, God's transforming grace for humanity: the second, a resistance by human nature to such grace. The first memory inspires thanksgiving, the second a request for pardon. Bergoglio spoke of the hope of the founding fathers of Argentina that made them ignore the obstacles to their project; similarly, the Argentineans of the new millennium can trust with hope and happiness that greater equality between the rich and the poor can be restored, that young people can find a social role, and that forgotten and impoverished children will no longer be excluded. Social links will awaken concern for job losses, and prompt citizens to show solidarity towards immigrants. Further, Bergoglio proposed that a new social link could restore pensioners to a place of social importance in the role of wise teachers, teaching us that hope exists. 'To find again our social links with hope' was Bergoglio's cry to those present at the Buenos Aires Metropolitan Cathedral in 2000, a cry that followed a speech on the imperative to work for the common good and to form a community that shares its possessions justly, by leaving behind individual interests in

---

1   John Paul II, Apostolic Exhortation *Ecclesia in America*, § 20.
2   Arzobispo Jorge M. Bergoglio SJ, 'Comenzar la aventura de una nueva nación', Homilía en la catedral de Buenos Aires, 25 May 2000.

order to live in peace. Bergoglio invited all present to cease using privilege in order to exert power, exploit and abuse, but instead to seek encounters with others within a culture of hope.[1]

Bergoglio continued, saying that the call of the Gospel is for the dead to rise, and the call within contemporary history is for the Argentinean nation to rise. This process requires a personal conversion towards the values of the Gospel, the only process that leads to happiness and joy. Greed for power, money, and popularity only signifies a large emptiness inside.[2] In sum, those who do not transmit happiness or joy transmit suspicion, and do not create social links with others. Bergoglio's cry at the 2000 Te Deum was powerful: 'Touch Lord our Argentina still young, making her less self-centred but open to our neighbours! Show us your sign of love that make us lose fear! And let's try particularly to touch those marginalised by the system, seeing in them men and women who are more than potential voters'.[3] Bergoglio called Argentineans to give priority within national institutions to community organisations that foster participation such as the clubs for retired people and the soup kitchens. They give hope to those who are suffering. There will always be diverse kinds of speciality and expertise in society: it is only a community active in solidarity and common work that can steer the boat of the common good and guard the law and common life. This would also constitute a common initiative allowing a young Argentina to

1 I copy the original text here as these words have been cited as Bergoglio's trademark time and again by his commentators: 'Debemos reconocer, con humildad, que el sistema ha caído en un amplio cono de sombra: la sombra de la desconfianza, y que algunas promesas y enunciados suenan a cortejo fúnebre: todos consuelan a los deudos pero nadie levanta al muerto', Arzobispo Jorge M. Bergoglio SJ, 'Comenzar la aventura de una nueva nación', Homilía en la catedral de Buenos Aires, 25 May 2000.

2 This theme of the emptiness and confusion of accumulating riches is a *leitmotif* for Bergoglio that he continued using after being elected as Pope Francis. Thus, during the morning Mass at the Casa Santa Maria on 22 June 2013, he gave the following reflection during his homily: 'For one who is attached to riches, neither the past nor the future is important, he has everything here. Wealth is an idol. I don't need a past, a promise, an election: nothing', see Pope Francis, 'Serve the Word of God, not the idolatry of riches and worldly cares', Homily Casa Santa Marta, 22 June 2013, Mass concelebrated with Bishop Arturo González of Santa Clara Cuba with employees of the Vatican Museum in attendance.

3 Arzobispo Jorge M. Bergoglio SJ, 'Comenzar la aventura de una nueva nación', Homilía en la catedral de Buenos Aires, 25 May 2000.

give back the nation to those older people who feel that they were led stray into suspicion and scepticism. It will be at the moment when these priorities are realised that the young man who was dead will arise and will speak, as narrated in the Gospels.

During the Te Deum of 25 May 2001, Bergoglio spoke about the practice of service in the context of a Gospel passage. A mother asks Jesus for her sons to acquire power through him and to sit on his right and left sides in the forthcoming Kingdom (Matthew 20: 20-28).[1] Bergoglio began his reflection by suggesting that it was clear from the Gospel that this was not only a contemporary way for the powerful to obtain favours, but a common activity at the time of the Gospels. A mother requests power for her sons and the Lord's answer is unexpected: can they drink the chalice that their Lord will drink? It is clear that the disciples learned the hard way that *service* is power, and that love is the quality of service expected by God.[2]

On 25 May 2001, Bergoglio reflected mainly on the sentence 'the Son of Man did not come to be served but to serve' (Matthew 20: 26-28). For Bergoglio, service is attendance on others, which fosters brotherhood. It is the rejection of indifference and utilitarian selfishness. It is to do for others, and also to do *to* others.[3] Service is undertaken by all great people, and the great realisation for today, according to Bergoglio, is that gifts and opportunities have been given by God: to give ourselves and to give ourselves fully. To serve is to be faithful to who we are; to give who we are; to love to the extreme of our limits, or, in the words of Mother Theresa, to give until it hurts. In Bergoglio's opinion, the words of the Gospel apply to all believers, including ecclesiastical and political authorities, because they bring to light the true meaning of power. Power is service. Power only makes sense if it is put at the service

---

1 Cardenal Jorge M. Bergoglio, 'Beber el cáliz del servicio', Homilía en la catedral de Buenos Aires, 25 May 2001.

2 Service is an important theological theme within Bergoglio's ministry and public Christian reflection, see for example Cardenal Jorge M. Bergoglio SJ, 'Enviados para llevar esa unción con fervor apostólico a todas las periferias', Homilía, Misa Crismal, 2007.

3 The Spanish original in this text conveys two different meanings; the English language uses the same verb and conveys one meaning. Thus, the Spanish text reads: 'Es hacer por los otros y para los otros', Cardenal Jorge M. Bergoglio, 'Beber el cáliz del servicio', Homilía en la catedral de Buenos Aires, 25 May 2001.

of the common good.[1] Society will not be authentically human if it is based merely on a shared struggle to survive or a compromise of scattered interests. It will be authentic when it flows from the best of itself, from unselfish gifts from one person to another, and from the power on high. It is through service that thousands construct a communal sense of solidarity and avoid the xenophobia of a small group of people in Argentina. Citizens have gathered together in the solidarity of community organisations and spontaneous creative cultural groups, such as those that welcome immigrants or look after the poor in a neighbourhood. These organisations have rejected consumerism, considering it a nonsensical sign of mediocrity and lack of hope. Bergoglio asserted that Argentineans will discover a way out of the misery caused by lack of security, violence and drugs. Those who have listened to the Word are those who, without much 'ritual clapping', have exhibited the great cultural and moral reserves of the people. For example, Bergoglio praised the efforts of networks of Argentinean social organisations, researchers and academics who search for the truth (even when others relativise the truth or keep silent), teachers and lecturers who survive times of adversity, producers who chose to work, young people who study, work and start new families, the poor and those who look for work, those who fight destructive marginalisation and organised violence, and who, with faith, silently serve and love their country.

'Can we drink from this chalice of the silent Christs present among our people? Can we drink of the chalice of the pains of our nation's limits and miseries, while at the same time recognising the festive wine of assimilation with the people to whom we belong?', asked Bergoglio of those present at the 2001 Te Deum. This invitation to drink from the chalice of hard work and solidarity was familiar to indigenous Argentineans. For Bergoglio, the answer to the uncertainty in Argentina is drink from this chalice of work in solidarity and service. This is the best response to the uncertainty riddling a country that is damaged by those who use power to their advantage, by those who ask for sacrifices from others but avoid their own social responsibility by wasting resources, by those who say they listen but do not, by those who 'clap ritually'

---

1   Bergoglio had, in his writings of the 1980s, suggested that 'power is ambiguous and can operate as good or bad', Jorge M. Bergoglio SJ, 'Necesidad de una antropología política: Un problema pastoral', Lección inaugural del curso académico 1989 en las Facultades de Filosofía y Teología de la Universidad del Salvador, área San Miguel, § 18.

without making sound, by those who do not take responsibility for the nation's problems. Leaders must be self-giving and ethical because 'he who wants to be powerful must become servant of all' – to serve somebody rather than to use somebody.[1]

To move forward must be a sense of hopeful serenity (*serenidad esperanzada*) in a nation that seeks the common good in solidarity. It must bring together all its resources of art, history and religiosity to create this national frame of mind.[2] Serenity will allow Argentineans to avoid violence and claim their rights, especially those that are most urgent: the right to life, to an education, to health services. The responsibilities of supporting the old, promoting the family and the rights of children, often left aside and unappreciated, could also be considered. Without service there is no nation, only a land devastated by self-interested fights. The chalice of service draws us closer to one another and gives us dignity. Service allows us to come together, to mature, to establish a communion of differences whose fruit is the serenity of justice and peace: a plural communion made up of the talents and efforts of all, without focusing on origins, a communion of everyone who recognises human dignity. This is the gospel proposition for today, Bergoglio asserted at the end of his Te Deum, the best possible homage to the Argentinean founding fathers and contemporary Argentineans.

Bergoglio's words irritated 'those who ritually clapped without noise'; and those who were annoyed by Bergoglio's portrayal of a divided nation whose leaders were enriching themselves at the expense of Argentineans in the midst of a deep financial crisis,

1   In Spanish these words use the same verb and Bergoglio points to the clear distinction between the action of serving somebody and using somebody: '*Servir a* imponiéndose al *Servirse de*', see Cardenal Jorge M. Bergoglio, 'Beber el cáliz del servicio', Homilía en la catedral de Buenos Aires, 25 May 2001.

2   The theme of the 'common good' appears once and again in Bergoglio's thought, which is heavily influenced by the corpus of teachings known as the social doctrine of the Church. Bergoglio defined the citizen's association with the common good as the one who is called to the common good – citizen comes from *citatorium* – the one called to the common good, see Cardenal Jorge M. Bergoglio SJ, 'Citados al bien común' in 'Nosotros como ciudadanos, nosotros como pueblo: Hacia un bicentenario en justicia y solidaridad 2010-2016', XIII Jornada de Pastoral Social, Hacia un Bicentenario en Justicia y Solidaridad 2010-2016, *Nosotros como ciudadanos, nosotros como pueblo*, Comisión de Pastoral Social de la Arquidiócesis de Buenos Aires, Santuario San Cayetano de Liniers, 16 October 2010.

without homes, work or food. The 2001 Te Deum homily on service is a direct and beautiful reflection on the gospel's demands for a nation that, for the most part, recognises itself as guided by the Roman Catholic Church.

At the subsequent Te Deum on 25 May 2002, Bergoglio continued his train of thought on service, exploring some the implications of the dialogue between Zacheus and Jesus. Zacheus, a chief of tax collectors, encountered Jesus and, touched by the experience, proclaimed that he would help the poor and those he had treated wrongly (Luke 19: 1-10).[1] Bergoglio began his homily by claiming that Argentina had never had a greater need for the salvific presence of the Lord in its history. However, he remarked, living in certain conditions can prevent us from seeing the salvific presence of the Lord. According to Bergoglio, those who are supposed to serve too often retreat into the accumulation of power that prevents them from seeing painful realities. The suffering of others, to those with such near-sighted vision, takes on the significance of pawns on a board, numbers, statistics and variables. Once disaster strikes, the only solution for those in power is to demand more sacrifice. These are manifestations of spiritual illness – the impossibility of feeling guilt – that too often afflicts ambitious climbers who, despite their international qualifications and technical language, betray their lack of human knowledge and lack of humanity.

Afflicted by this lack of knowledge, their common response to crisis is to leave any response to others. It is as if the common good were some kind of foreign science, or as if politics were not a high and delicate form of exercising justice and charity. Myopia regarding these realities prevents us from seeing the presence of God among us, said Bergoglio. It prevents us from feeling grateful and preparing to receive many gifts unhesitatingly, while being dedicated to an unobtrusive openness towards our brothers and sisters. How much blood and suffering will be needed for Argentineans to recognise that they must work together? Zacheus climbed a tree and let himself be seen by the Lord; this is what we need to do. We must allow ourselves to feel the impact of pain, ours own and others', and allow failure and poverty to take away our prejudices, our ideologies and the fashions that desensitise, so that ultimately we can hear the call to climb down and to talk to the Lord.

---

1   Cardenal Jorge M. Bergoglio SJ, 'La grandeza de dar y darnos', Homilía en la Catedral de Buenos Aires, 25 May 2002.

Bergoglio's call for Argentineans on 25 May 2001 was to reject passivity, to position themselves in the best possible position to see God face to face, to look upon their brothers and sisters with kindness while recognising their own limits and potentialities. Bergoglio said: let us not return to last century's division between the urban centre, with its finances and investments, and the countryside, with its natural resources that can expand the tourist industry (*soberbia de la división centenaria*). Let us not return to a customary yet cruel national sport: the destruction of the good ideas and suggestions of our opponents (*internismo faccioso*). Such destruction is counter-productive, and persistent lying, with the aim of keeping one's privileges intact, is a sad act that shuts down possibilities and imprisons us. Like Zachaeus, we must come down to patient and constant work, without possessive pretensions but with solidarity. Bergoglio analogised the social fallacies of Argentina in terms of the biblical story of the 'golden calf', in which the Israelites strayed from their faith in the Lord and adored foreign gods, imagining them to be more powerful. In so doing they broke the covenant, and suffered exile and national disaster. In Bergoglio's opinion, the Argentinean adoration of the 'golden calf' is the fallacy of considering Argentina a first world country. Indulging in dreams of consumerist stability and lavish journeys abroad leaves the nation in financial ruins – the result is the impoverishment of millions of citizens who had never enjoyed the periodic consumerist stability that some Argentineans could.

According to Bergoglio, this illusion grips the leaders of society. Like Zacheus, they must look at the Lord, and climb down from the tree to join the real world of the multitude, the Argentinean nation. Bergoglio reminded his listeners that the only way forward is to obey a law that establishes the necessary conditions for uniting all in a common banquet of the same nation, rather than following, in Bergoglio's own words, a 'swallow's café' – 'birds that arrive only to extract and leave'. The law, Bergoglio continues, is the unchangeable power of justice, solidarity and politics. The law protects us when we climb down from the tree of temptation to confront chaos, violence and revenge. Bergoglio called those present at the 2002 Te Deum to witness the blood running in the streets, unnoticed by opposing factions, because they are too involved in crime networks that fester in the absence of sociability, decay of authority, legal vacuum and unjust immunity from the law.

Amidst these harsh words Bergoglio reminded his listeners that this reality does not call for shame, because we are all a bit like Zacheus – we all have value and talents as well as faults. The solution lies in the reconditioning of social links and a revived appreciation of the greatness of giving and of giving ourselves to others. The great challenge, following Zacheus' example, is renouncing the illusion of having all the truth, and clinging to privileges and an easy life. There is a third step in the process of meeting the Lord, shown in the story of Zacheus, which is to give back whatever is not ours and to share what is ours with others. Bergoglio suggested that what the Argentinean nation needed was to rescue from its soul the work of generous solidarity, justice and a spirit of creativity and celebration. Like Zacheus, nations can leave behind their brokenness and arise. There is also a need to put aside empty complaints, illusions and promises, and to take a course of solid actions. If this is done, hope will flourish: a hope that is a gift from God to the heart of Argentineans. For Bergoglio sees the hope of service and of giving ourselves to others as our gift.

During the Te Deum of 2003, Bergoglio expanded upon the theme of service, and explored the implications of the parable of the Good Samaritan (Luke 10: 25-37).[1] Bergoglio started his homily by summarising some of the points he had already made in previous commemorations of the independence of Argentina: the vocation of citizens to build new social links, and renew a sense of common purpose and structure the social and political towards the common good. The parable of the Good Samaritan, for Bergoglio, shows how a community can be reconstructed by men and women who feel and act like true partners (*conciudadanos*, or *socios*). They recognise the fragility of others and lift and rehabilitate the fallen; they come close to others, in order that the social good might be shared in common. Bergoglio reminded his listeners that from the days of the early Church, the Good Samaritan was identified with Christ, and that this parable does not offer a mere metaphor but a clear path of Christian action. We cannot be indifferent to pain of others, nor allow them to be left on the margins of life, on the margins of their dignity. Such injustice should trigger

---

1   Cardenal Jorge M. Bergoglio SJ, 'Ponerse la patria al hombro, los tiempos se acortan . . . ', Homilía en la Catedral de Buenos Aires, 25 May 2003.

sentiments of indignation in us.[1] The pain and marginalisation of others should disturb our serenity. Through self-giving we will find our own existential vocation, and become worthy of ownership of Argentina.[2]

Every day, according to Bergoglio, we have the possibility of being Good Samaritans or of ignoring the injured on the side of the road. We each exhibit some characteristics of each character in the parable; however, at the end the parable divides human beings in two types: those who stop to aid the suffering and those who do not. It is the difference of either including or excluding the wounded person on the side of the road, according to Bergoglio, that defines all economic, political, social and religious projects. He argues that the story of the Good Samaritan is visible every day: social and political fraud makes Argentina an arid road, by the side of which marginalised people are thrown. What would have happened to the wounded man if hate and anger had prevailed? Jesus Christ trusts, according to Bergoglio, that the best of the human spirit can manifest, even in the most unpromising of circumstances; and he is asking all Argentineans to love of God, integrate the wounded and build up a society worthy of the name.

Bergoglio pointed out that this parable contains thieves: those who abandon people, who use violence to facilitate their selfish accumulation of power, to entrench division and to seek positions of authority for their own glorification. He asked, 'Shall we ignore the injured again in order to focus on our divisions or to persecute

---

1   This theme of personal and communal indignation over pain and death returned time and again in Bergoglio's homilies and messages after his election as Pope Francis; see for example the homily in his first journey outside Rome when he visited Lampedusa, the island where most African and Asian illegal immigrants request asylum on arriving in precarious boats and being trafficked into Italy and the European Union. Pope Francis reminded those present that we have lost the capacity ourselves to cry, and to cry out to others responsible for unjust deaths 'Cain, where is your brother?', instead embracing a globalization of indifference, see Pope Francis, Homily in Lampedusa, 8 July 2013.

2   Bergoglio's local predication of the parable of the Good Samaritan for Argentina was extended to incorporate the universal Church and the world's nations when he became Pope; as he explained that the Good Samaritan was a Samaritan, somebody who was not expected to be good to the man on the road, but *he* was named the Good Samaritan rather than the priest or the Levite. Thus, Pope Francis asked all those listening to his words: 'Be the Good Samaritan!' Pope Francis, Homilía during the Angelus, Castel Gandolfo, 14 July 2013.

the thieves?' The lessons given by Martín Fierro, an Argentinean cowboy and hero of a literary classic with the same name, need to be remembered: because of our divisions, those from the outside devour us.[1] Bergoglio recognised that the people of Argentina had opted to be good Samaritans, and, in spite of the weaknesses of the system, return to the democratic method of deciding their future. Within the parable are those who will not stop for the wounded man: some are too focussed on themselves, some are indifferent, and some are too busy looking elsewhere. Bergoglio placed particular stress on those who look elsewhere: who consider other societies ideal, and fail to engage with the social realities of Argentina. At the intellectual level, this often involves blindness to significant local characteristics and processes and a disdain for what constitutes the Argentinean identity.

Furthermore, too often violent attitudes towards different opinions prevail. These attitudes amount to a bull-headed obsession with one's own opinions. Indirectly, in Bergoglio's analysis, the thieves have allied themselves with those who avoid helping the wounded, those who cheat people, with those who do not see national realities but prefer to remain out of touch with the realities of the nation. Some who profit personally from communal institutions ally themselves with others who do not hold any hope for the majority of people, and also live out of touch with national realities. They create an atmosphere of hopelessness, closing a perfect and perverse circle, an invisible dictatorship of interested parties who selfishly corner resources and even take away our capacity to express opinions and to think. In response to these injustices, Bergoglio cries: 'All of us, within our responsibilities in society, must carry the nation on our shoulders because the time left is short'.[2] Bergoglio reminded listeners during a previous Te Deum in 2000 that he had warned of the threat of the dissolution of the nation, a threat that some refused to accept by ignoring those who had fallen beside the road.[3]

1   During Easter 2002 Cardinal Bergoglio distributed a reflection on *Martín Fierro*, an Argentinean literary classic, to all educational communities in Buenos Aires, a meditation entitled 'Una reflexión a partir del Martín Fierro'.

2   This sentence in the Spanish original has become another well-known saying by Bergoglio: 'Todos, desde nuestras responsabilidades, debemos *ponernos la patria al hombro,* porque los tiempos se acortan'.

3   'Can we drink from this chalice of the silent Christs present in our people? Can we drink from the chalice of the pains of our nation's limits and miseries while at the same time recognizing the festive wine of assimilation

Examining the parable's wounded man, Bergoglio suggested that many citizens feel like the wounded, abandoned by the side of the road. They feel left out of national institutions, and estranged from the love of the nation. However, according to Bergoglio, we shouldn't expect those in government to do everything; we must each play an active part in the rehabilitation of a wounded nation. Let us courageously confront the circumstances that face us, Bergoglio enjoins, without fear of pain or impotence, because the Risen Lord is present. Where there was a tomb, life awaited. Where there had been a desolate land, our aboriginal fathers – and later others that dwelt in the land – prepared the way for a flourishing nation.

Difficulties that appear enormous ought to be engaged with as they provide opportunities to grow, and are not excuses for inert sadness that results in passivity. The Samaritan acted without expecting recognition or gratitude; his reason for serving was satisfaction from following God's laws. Bergoglio insists we do not have a right to be indifferent, to lack interest, or to look the other way. We have a responsibility towards the wounded in the nation as a whole. Bergoglio concluded in 2003: let us 'take care of our wounded people, each one of us with his own wine, oil and horse. Let's take care of our nation, each one paying from his own pocket whatever is needed so that our land becomes a true inn for all, without exclusion of anybody. Let us take care of each man, woman, child and old person with that attentive attitude of solidarity, an attitude of closeness to the Samaritan'.

During the Te Deum of 2004, Bergoglio again expanded upon his thoughts from the previous Te Deum, exploring the implications of Jesus' appearance in his own local synagogue at Nazareth (Luke 4: 16-32).[1] Bergoglio began his homily by suggesting that, during the liturgy, his listeners should return to the original and historical May of 1810 to find new hope. For the Christian faith teaches that from within the plenitude of memory we can discover new roads of possibility.[2] Those in the

---

with the people to whom we belong?', asked Bergoglio to all those present at the 2001 Te Deum, see Cardenal Jorge M. Bergoglio, 'Beber el cáliz del servicio', Homilía en la catedral de Buenos Aires, 25 May 2001.

1   Cardenal Jorge M. Bergoglio SJ, 'Nuestro pueblo sabe y quiere', Homilía en la Catedral de Buenos Aires, 25 May 2004.

2   Cardenal Jorge M. Bergoglio SJ, *Ponerse la patria al hombre: Memoria y camino de esperanza*, Buenos Aires: Editorial Claretiana, 2013, p. 79.

synagogue at Nazareth who listened to Jesus were also waiting for hope, and they found it in Jesus' 'Good News to the poor' – a new way of looking at life. Jesus' Good News is expansively inclusive: he asks those whom he liberates and heals to liberate and heal others. Jesus speaks with the absolute conviction that his prophetic words find immediate fulfilment as he says them, moved by the Spirit. His words were met with immediate claps and signs of admiration, but at the end of the story we are perplexed to hear that, when they found out that Jesus was Joseph's son, they tried to throw him over a cliff (Luke 4: 28-20). However, Jesus didn't confront them, but simply walked through the midst of his attackers, and departed for Capernaum, where he continued his preaching.

For Bergoglio, Jesus' teachings are clear: he challenged the privileged who exclude others. Jesus' way is the way of the poor, of any kind of poverty that requires an emptying of the soul, a trust and a self-giving to others and to God. The human being who has his possessions or health taken away, who suffers irreparable losses, should allow himself to be caught up in the experience of the wise, of the bright, of those freed in love, who work in solidarity and without self-gain, knowing some or much of the Good News. Bergoglio asserts that many Argentineans have experienced an array of these poverties, and that Christ walks alongside these poor today.

Those who attacked the Lord, Bergoglio suggests, were the learned, who had closed their hearts to the people; in today's Argentina, there are many left-wing atheists, as well as right-wing unbelievers, who, ensconced in their marginal securities, remain distanced from the people. They are blind and see neither the causes of injustice nor solutions for the future. We need the Lord's help, because so many times we too are blind. We entertain false illusions with which we cover our eyes. We quickly revert to intolerance. We do not recognise the greatness and virtues of others. We attack anybody who thinks outside the bounds of the dominant discourse. Self-giving, heroism and holiness are treated with contempt. When we are finally able to see the truth, like the disciples on the road to Emmaus, we see God walking amongst his people. We see Jesus preparing true food for the spirit that creates a communion between every citizen in the nation, a food of wisdom that unites all.

The blindness of the soul impedes our freedom. We want

liberation from captivity and oppression; but what kinds of captivity and oppression? First from ourselves, our disorientation and immaturity; secondly from external oppression. Internal oppression comes out of our own bleeding wounds and internal divisions; from our compulsive ambition; it comes from the power plays within our institutions. Our captivity is expressed in indifference, intolerance, excessive individualism and sectarianism.

Our challenge, according to Bergoglio, is to come out of our enslaving mediocrity. We are easily distracted by a sensational piece of news, yet cannot react emotionally to our daily lives. We have more information than ever, but we do not know what is really happening around us. Despite these negative trends in Argentinean society, however, citizens do have a strong sense of their dignity. It is a dignity shaped by a long history, and comes with the knowledge that the only escape from social discrimination is a road of constancy and determination.

The Theology of Martín Fierro

During Easter 2002, Bergoglio distributed a printed reflection on *Martín Fierro* (a classic of Argentinean literature), to all educational communities in Buenos Aires. The meditation was entitled 'Una reflexión a partir del Martín Fierro'.[1] Bergoglio had taught the classic when teaching literature at Jesuit schools, and would have also studied it as a child; it was a text that suggested a unified identity for immigrants to Argentina. The text idealised Argentina's open agrarian spaces (*pampas*) from the standpoint of city dwellers who longed to live the life of the *pampas*, with its freedom to roam, access to fresh agrarian products and to good fresh meat. Meat is the main food of Argentineans, who are known for their excellent beef, and preparation of it with sauces such as the *chimichurri*.

Because of its centrality in Argentinean national identity and

---

1   Later, Bergoglio made further reflections and commentaries on the original text on Martín Fierro in a volume aimed at Catholic teachers, see Cardenal Jorge M. Bergoglio SJ, *Educar: exigencia y passion: Desafío para educadores cristianos*. Buenos Aires: Editorial Claretiana, 2006, section 5 'Dar la educación TODO', pp. 152-178. For a thoughtful critical commentary of Bergoglio's reflection see José Medina, Un proyecto de Nación a la luz del Martín Fierro' in *Francisco: El Papa de todos*, Buenos Aires: Editorial Bonum, 2013, pp. 187-199.

historiography, and because it provides the ground for one of Bergoglio's most important meditations on encounter, Christian life and nationhood for the twenty-first century, it is worth exploring Bergoglio's reflection in detail. His text is a socio-hermeneutical analysis of the significance in the Argentinean nation of Christians and the Catholic Church. Some of the friction, and perhaps even animosity between the two Kirchners (the husband and wife who were successive presidents of Argentina) and Bergoglio arose out of Bergoglio's criticism of an affluent society where the hungry and the poor did not occupy a central place.[1]

Martín Fierro is an epic poem of 2,316 lines, originally published in two parts by author José Hernández: *El gaucho Martín Fierro* (1872) and *La vuelta de Martín Fierro* (1879). The poem provided a public and social recognition of the contribution by the *gaucho* (Argentinean cowboy) to the development of the Argentinean nation, as many *gauchos* fought for Argentina's independence from Spain. The text is seen by most Argentineans as an expression of Argentinean identity. The poem has been published in many editions and has been translated into seventy languages.[2] The work describes the independent character, heroism and personal sacrifice of Martín Fierro, as a symbolic representative of all *gauchos*. It was originally understood as a protest against European influences on Argentina, and as a critique of the Argentinean modern period under President Domingo Faustino Sarmiento.

The main character in the text, Martín Fierro, is a *gaucho* recruited to serve in a military post (*fortín*), one of the many built after Argentina's independence from Spain in order to keep the indigenous populations out of 'Argentinean' land, which was given to immigrants. Martín Fierro eventually challenges this

---

1   In August 2001 the Argentinean Episcopal Conference had responded to the increasing financial and socio-political crisis of Argentina with the document *Queremos ser Nación*, documento final de la 129 reunión de la Comisión Permanente de la Conferencia Episcopal Argentina, Pilar, Buenos Aires, 10 agosto 2001.

2   The whole text of Martín Fierro has been posted electronically with an introduction at www.martinfierro.org. A recommended edition that has been published in Spain and most Latin American nations is the one produced by Biblioteca Edaf with a prologue by José A. Oría, see José Hernández, *El gaucho Martín Fierro, La vuelta de Martín Fierro*, Madrid, Mexico, Buenos Aires, San Juan and Santiago: Biblioteca Edaf, 1983.

system and becomes a fugitive wanted by the police. He acquires a companion, Sargent Cruz, who helps him raises arms against the police, themselves symbols of the new Argentinean state. The first part of the epic ends with Martín Fierro and Cruz escaping from the police and settling among the indigenous population. Martín Fierro is a free soul and wants to remain that way, as he tells the reader: 'My glory is to live as free as the birds of the sky'.[1] However, in his present, the *gaucho* is no longer understood; he lives in a changing world dominated by the state. He reminisces of a past that is no more, saying 'I remember, how marvellous, how the gauchos moved around, always happy, on their horses and ready to work!'[2]

Bergoglio's meditation on *Martín Fierro* is similar to efforts by Latin American archbishops of the late twentieth century, such as Óscar Romero and Raúl Silva Henríquez, to reflect on the Christian sense of the nation, the state, and ultimately nationalism itself and the conflicts between the state and its citizens. The four homilies by Mgr Óscar Romero dismissed the possibility of an authoritarian state forming a social vision without integrating the values of the majority of its citizens, who instead become the subjects of violence, unlawful arrests, torture and ultimately death at the hands of the state. The reflections of the Chilean Cardinal Raúl Silva Henríquez challenged the obsessive and authoritarian nature of citizenship and nationalism formed by General Augusto Pinochet during the 1970s. Catholic reflections on the role of the state have therefore become a well-documented Latin American Catholic genre. Post-military reflections by democratic societies must now face the challenges of globalisation and secularism. These are themes addressed by Bergoglio in his pastoral reflections, and later incorporated by him and others into the conclusions and directives proceeding from the meeting of Latin American bishops at Aparecida (2007). Bergoglio brought to Aparecida some of his pastoral experiences with the poor, whose poverty was no longer due to underdevelopment as perceived by the theologian Gustavo Gutiérrez and the Latin American bishops at Medellin (1968), but the result of globalised financial growth and crises that impacted directly on the Latin American poor. Thus, the emphasis of Bergoglio's theological reflection shifted into a contemporary

---

1   *Martín Fierro* I § 16.
2   *Martín Fierro* II § 35.

context, but also presented a refreshed Latin American option for the poor. A new problematic has been outlined by Cristián del Campo in his analysis of the Aparecida conference: 'there is no doubt that the Latin American Church reaffirms the option for the poor; but, at the same time, it leaves a feeling that such "option" does not become a theology'.[1] Bergoglio managed to outline a pastoral option for the poor, but without affirming the centrality of one theology or another, as had been the case of liberation theology at the Puebla conference in 1979.

By Easter 2002, Argentina was emerging from the worst financial crisis of its history. In 2001, all Argentinean financial institutions collapsed, having been too closely allied with the US dollar, with the result that people were unable to withdraw their money from the banks. Protests were widespread. Bergoglio's Easter reflection considered the text of Martín Fierro. He expressed enormous hope for the formation of a great Argentinean nation. However, he reminded people that those dreams would be realised only if Argentineans exhibited solidarity with others. In the first part of his reflection, Bergoglio described *Martín Fierro* as a 'national' poem; in the second part as an inclusive poem; and in the third as a compendium of civic ethics.[2]

Bergoglio recognised that the historical context of *Martín Fierro* was almost completely removed from the experience of contemporary Argentineans, most of whom live in cities rather than in rural areas.[3] Bergoglio also recognised that, due to globalisation, Argentinean youth had become more familiar with Japanese comics than their own rural past. Within the globalised world, citizens of different countries across the globe buy and use the same products, and hear about each other's customs, religions and ways of doing things through the media and an increasingly available international tourism. Yet within this trend of globalisation there is a contradiction: on the one hand, people adopt the same ways of doing things, but on the other hand, they

---

1   My translation of 'De la lectura de Aparecida no queda duda de que la Iglesia latinoamericana reafirma la opción por los pobres; pero, al mismo tiempo, queda la sensación de que ese "optar" no se hace teología', in Cristián del Campo SJ, *Dios opta por los pobres: Reflexión teológica a partir de Aparecida*, Santiago: Ediciones Universidad Alberto Hurtado, 2010, p. 124.
2   I Martín Fierro, poema 'nacional'; II Martín Fierro, poema 'incluyente'; and III Martín Fierro, compendio de ética cívica.
3   This paragraph summarises Bergoglio's ideas in 'Una reflexión a partir del Martín Fierro' I.1 'La 'identidad nacional' en un mundo globalizado.

start realising the diversity of the world in terms of race, gender and culture. For Bergoglio, there have never before been such opportunities for building a world community with so much solidarity in diversity. However, despite this possibility, social inequality is increasing, there is increasing unilateral imposition of values and custom by some cultures onto others, a widespread ecological crisis, and the exclusion of billions of human beings from the benefits of development. Bergoglio concludes that the realisation of a fraternal human family living in solidarity with one another is still far off. However, he believes there are ways of educating consciences, and these ways are based on dialogue and love. Dialogue and love presuppose the acceptance of the other as they are: the acceptance of diversity. Thus, community is built by accepting human diversity. Any other attitude, according to Bergoglio, can only be associated with narcissism and imperialism. However, Bergoglio asks in the first section of his reflection, 'how can I dialogue, how can I love, how can I build something in common if I let my own contribution dilute itself, loosen itself or disappear?' He argues that globalisation at its worst is a unilateral imposition that provides a uniformity of values. These values create cultural imitation and subordination, both intellectual and spiritual. Thus, neither uniformity nor rejection of global processes can bring people into a global dialogue with their own cultural values intact, a dialogue in which they are equipped to receive from others, with respect and dignity, other cultures and other values.

In section one, part two of his reflections on *Martín Fierro*, Bergoglio developed some thoughts about the Argentinean nation and a common history.[1] The first premise, necessary for acquiring knowledge from *Martín Fierro* requires that Argentineans accept that the text has historical importance for the development of the nation, and that the text might speak to Argentineans, even if they do not live in the countryside. Thus, according to Bergoglio, *Martín Fierro* is a national poem. He suggests that Argentineans have a tendency to forget that they are connected to the past, and in so doing make mistakes that might be avoided. This assertion became a *leitmotif* in each one of his writings: 'We are a historical people. We live in time and space. Each generation

---

1   This paragraph summarises Bergoglio's ideas in 'Una reflexión a partir del Martín Fierro' I.2 'La Nación como continuidad de una historia común'.

needs the previous ones, and each generation has a responsibility towards the following generations'. For Bergoglio, these are the characteristics of being a nation: assuming that all citizens follow a generation that has already given their contribution: and understanding ourselves as builders of a common place, a home for all those who will come into society and the legacy of those who have contributed to society in the past. Bergoglio believed that Argentinean citizens can make a just society a reality, and can even change the global situation: learning from the difficulties of those who built the nation, and making the journey of a people of the present.

In section one, part three of his reflections on the text, Bergoglio outlined the importance of an ethical attitude towards life.[1] The financial crisis of 2002 had threatened the social link between people, and he asked questions about the nature of the link. What is it that actually unites one person with another? The union is a matter of ethics, a foundation that links the moral and the social. The ineradicable social nature of human beings provides the possibility of a contract between free individuals. Any talk of a worldwide crisis must include the examination of the human values recognised as universal that God has planted in human hearts. When the bishops speak of a moral crisis, they are not referring to an individual problem of conscience.[2] Rather, they are referring to collective values that are realised in attitudes, actions and processes. The free actions of human beings have long-term consequences: they generate structures that endure through time and foster a social climate in which some values occupy a central place in public life, or remain marginalised. We must reflect on our customs and strive to foster a community that lives in justice.

When Bergoglio resumes his reading of *Martín Fierro*, he suggests that it starts out describing an 'original paradise'. The gaucho lives in idyllic harmony with the calm rhythm of nature, working ably and happily, and having fun with his workmates. He leads a fully integrated, simple and humane life. Bergoglio

---

1   This paragraph summarises Bergoglio's ideas in 'Una reflexión a partir del Martín Fierro' I.3 'Ser un pueblo supone, ante todo, una actitud ética, que brota de la libertad'.

2   Bergoglio makes the distinction between a crisis that is 'moral' and 'moralina', an Argentinean slang word that does not easily translate into English.

sees this ideal as possible, given the dignity of the children of God and their vocation to live virtuous lives. Bergoglio recalls that God has established a natural law that provides for human endeavours, and also gives us the freedom to build our own societies.[1]

It is clear that Bergoglio considers *Martín Fierro* a text in which Argentineans can recognise themselves, through which they can retell their history and with which they can dream about the future. *Martín Fierro* is, for Bergoglio, an all-inclusive poem, and this fact is the subject of the second part of Bergoglio's reflection, in which an initial situation of order and justice is portrayed: an order that later becomes a disorderly Argentinean state. In the third part of Bergoglio's reflection on *Martín Fierro*, he points to the ethical lessons that come out of the text: operating from a framework of truth, working for one's keep, serving the weakest of society, remembering that being poor is not shameful but stealing from others is a personal shame, preserving unity and serving all who need it.[2] Bergoglio quotes from chapter XXXII of *La vuelta de Martín Fierro*, in which the author declares that unity between brothers is the most important law because, if brothers fight, others from outside the family will devour them.[3]

In a second reflection on *Martín Fierro*, which Bergoglio offered to Christian teachers in the context of a larger reflection on the nation and its condition, he suggests that after the public protests against Argentinean governments, a closer reading of the text could have the effect of uniting social and public

---

1 In a related homily Bergoglio argued that a good education consists in strengthening the youths' freedom and educating them in harmony, see Cardenal Jorge M. Bergoglio SJ, Homilía con motivo de la Misa por la educación, 18 April 2012 and Mensaje a las Comunidades Educativas, 23 April 2008.

2 The theme of truth, education into the truth and the search for truth in all realms of life – particularly in universities – appears in Bergoglio's writings time and again, see for example Cardenal Jorge M. Bergoglio SJ, Ponencia en la presentación de 'Consenso para el desarrollo', Universidad del Salvador, 17 June 2010.

3 *La vuelta de Martín Fierro* XXXII.17:
Los hermanos sean unidos,
Porque esa es la ley primera;
Tengan unión verdadera
En cualquier tiempo que sea,
Porque si entre ellos pelean
Los devoran los de ajuera.

purposes by stressing the importance of the common good. The purpose of the exercise was to find in the story of *Martín Fierro* some resonances that might be useful in education and for exploring national values, even though 86% of Argentineans of that time lived in urban centres.[1] *Martín Fierro* is an Argentinean national poem, and therefore a part of the 'real dynamic of history', whose developments have had a real influence on twentieth-century Argentineans; for Bergoglio one of the major faults of the Argentinean people is to think and act as if history had started that day, or at least very recently.[2] Cutting off the past can lead to cutting off the future, and it seemed that this had in fact happened in the early years of the twenty-first century in Argentina: past administrations and governments had not made provisions for the future, with disastrous consequences for the Argentinean nation.[3] Bergoglio's words were clear and prophetic: 'We are historical persons. We live in time and space. Each generation needs the previous ones and has a duty towards the following ones. That is what it means, for the most part, to be a Nation . . .'[4] In summary, Bergoglio believed that *Martín Fierro* showed the possibility of constructing a fraternal nation that loves justice and is indomitable.[5]

Ideas of inclusive social justice, and the prosperity of a nation belonging to all, are some of the ideas that Bergoglio's reflection on *Martín Fierro* presented to Catholic teachers, and indeed to all others who later read these reflections. Bergoglio felt that unity of purpose and inclusiveness should not permit an unfair distribution of resources and the existence of the poor in large numbers, and it shouldn't allow for sectarian attitudes towards other Argentineans, who are entitled to practice Christianity in different ways. Poverty, the nation and inter-faith dialogue were important markers of Bergoglio's episcopal ministry, and these themes would shape his vision for renewal for the Catholic Church as a whole – the subject of the following chapter.

---

1   Cardenal Jorge M. Bergoglio SJ, *Educar: exigencia y pasión*, pp. 154-155.
2   Ibid., p. 158.
3   Ibid., pp. 158-159.
4   Ibid., p. 159.
5   Ibid., p. 173.

6. Meditations on Poverty and Other Faiths

During his time as archbishop of Buenos Aires, Bergoglio paid close attention to the poor, as recommended by the Latin American bishops at the conferences of Medellin (1968) and Puebla (1979). The 'preferential option for the poor', proclaimed by the bishops at Puebla, was reaffirmed by Bergoglio at the conference of Aparecida (2007), and throughout his ministry in Buenos Aires. Bergoglio himself lead a life of poverty and simplicity, as did the priests who worked in shanty towns (*curas villeros*). These priests – supported and pastorally overseen by Bergoglio – attracted people to God by bearing living witness to the Gospel rather than by means of proselitism.[1] From the late 1990s, such priests realised the preferential option for the poor by using Church structures for the service of all, placing those at the periphery at the centre. According to Bergoglio, many experience a tension between a personal calling, which entails the ownership of a vocation, and service to the people, in which ownership disappears because personal goals and selfish interests start to disappear.[2]

Bergoglio believed that the challenge presented by the poor is to build a more just nation, a nation that can embrace each one of its citizens in a common project, and in which 'leadership is centred in service as an answer to a country damaged by privileges'.[3] In the 1960s, liberation theologians saw authoritarian regimes

1 Cardenal Jorge M. Bergoglio SJ, 'Prólogo' in P. Fernando Lobo, *Tú eres mi prójimo: Testimonios de sacerdotes que acompañan al pueblo en el seguimiento de Jesús*. Buenos Aires: Editorial Claretiana, 2012, p. 7.
2 Jorge M. Bergoglio SJ, 'Unidos para que el mundo crea', *Boletín de Espiritualidad* 122 May/April 1990 § 21.
3 Cardenal Jorge M. Bergoglio SJ, 'Conclusión' in Hacia un Bicentenario en justicia y solidaridad 2010-2016 Nosotros como ciudadanos, nosotros como pueblo: Documento de trabajo, XIII Jornada de Pastoral Social, Comisión de Pastoral Social de la Arquidiócesis de Buenos Aires, Santuario de San Cayetano de Liniers, 16 October 2010.

that needed to be destroyed in order to build up democracies. The challenges for Argentina in the early twenty-first century were slightly different. Democracy had already been realised, but powerful individualism and consumerism had obscured the dream of a just nation; many factions and divisions had arisen out of such dominant individualism.[1] Bergoglio was dismayed by these developments: by the Argentinean Catholic elites, the leftist atheists, and right-wingers disillusioned with the Church.[2] He urged the members of his archdiocese to go out and give witness, so that other people would convert to gospel values, reiterating that: '2000 years ago there was a man who wanted to re-enact an earthly paradise, and he came to do that'.[3] Bergoglio said: 'we don't have the right to stay put massaging our own souls'. There are thousands of people waiting for the Gospel message, which is a message of joy and should be conveyed with joy.[4] This message of joy and conversion was not aimed at individual human beings but also at institutions, peoples and the whole of humanity.[5]

Poverty and Nation

Over the years, Bergoglio developed a distinctively Latin American awareness of poverty. He believed that religious communities that did not embrace poverty contributed to division and inequality within society, and that they should make changes in order to

---

1 Bergoglio had already explored this phenomenon of a strong personal project that didn't allow others to exist as a Jesuit in the 1980s, and had concluded that it was necessary for every Jesuit to 'accuse himself' in order to keep solidarity with others. See his study of Doroteo de Gaza in Jorge M. Bergoglio SJ, 'La acusación de sí mismo', *Boletín de Espiritualidad de la Provincia Argentina de la Compañía de Jesús* 87, May/June 1984.

2 Jorge Mario Bergoglio SJ, 'La carne sacerdotal de Cristo', Retiro en La Plata, April 1990 § 12 in *Reflexiones en esperanza*, Buenos Aires: Ediciones Universidad del Salvador, 1992, p. 70.

3 Arzobispo Jorge Mario Bergoglio SJ, 'Homilía a los Catequistas, EAC, March 2000, in Jorge Bergoglio, *El verdadero poder es el servicio*, Buenos Aires: Editorial Claretiana, 2013 [2007], pp. 9-12 at p. 10.

4 Ibid.

5 Jorge Mario Bergoglio SJ, 'La manifestación del pecado' § 6 in Epifanía y Vida Retiro Espiritual 1989 in *Reflexiones en esperanza*, Buenos Aires: Ediciones Universidad del Salvador, 1992, p. 100 and Cardenal Jorge M. Bergoglio SJ, Homilía con motivo de la clausura del Encuentro de Pastoral Urbana Región Buenos Aires, 2 September 2012.

follow God more closely.[1] When interviewed in 2010, he drew a clear connection between his ministry, the Church and the poor, instead of assuming that Argentina was a prosperous country and trying to deny the existence of the poor. He reminded his audience that in the 1970s 4% of Argentina's population lived below the poverty line; but during the financial crisis of 2001 this figure rose to 50%. His words did not stress financial indexes or expert economic analyses, but his own deep feelings: 'Today there are so many people who are hungry'.[2] Their plight touched him deeply, and he stressed the human right to have bread on the table. He requested that people cry when confronted with poverty, because, in his assessment, there is a great a lack of sorrow when we are faced with the harsh financial realities of others.[3] He dwelt deeply on the social doctrine of the Church – and particularly the social thought of John Paul II – to challenge 'the temptation' of a 'private and individualistic spirituality'.[4]

As cardinal of Buenos Aires during the Feast of San Cayetano, the patron of bread and work, Bergoglio asked the congregation how it was possible that in Argentina, a land of plenty, people could go hungry and without work. He asserted that it was a great injustice and the clear result of an unequal distribution of resources. Throughout his time as archbishop of Buenos Aires, Bergoglio assumed that when the Church spoke out about poverty, inequality and hunger, the Argentinean government would accuse the Church of being involved in politics. However, his conclusion was clear and consistent: he argued that, as time went on, there was more and more poverty in Argentina. When asked if this increase in poverty in Argentina was a problem of economics or public policy, he stated that it was a problem of sin. Poverty is a sin because nobody feels responsible for those who are hungry or go without work, and these realities are the responsibility of all citizens, including the bishops and all Argentinean Christians.[5] Bergoglio gave clear examples of the

1 Jorge Mario Bergoglio SJ, *Reflexiones en esperanza*, Buenos Aires: Ediciones Universidad del Salvador, 1992, p. 150, personal notes of December 1990 § 9.
2 *El Jesuita*, p. 105.
3 Cardenal Jorge Mario Bergoglio SJ, Homilía con motivo del Aniversario de la Convención Internacional sobre la Protección de los Derechos de todos los Trabajadores Migrantes y sus familias, 1 July 2008.
4 John Paul II, *Novo Milenio Ineunte* (2001) in Cardenal Jorge M. Bergoglio SJ, 'Duc in Altum, El pensamiento social de Juan Pablo II', June 2003.
5 *El Jesuita*, p. 105.

topography of inequality in Buenos Aires – a city that he knows well – by reminding others that in the elegant area of Puerto Madero there are thirty-six restaurants where neither food nor drink are cheap. However, on one side of Puerto Madero there is a *villa miseria* called Rodrigo Bueno, and, on the other side of Puerto Madero, another *villa* known by the number 31 in the area of Retiro. In both *villas* there are people who are hungry, but nobody else seems to care, a fact suggesting a lack of social conscience.

As archbishop of Buenos Aires, Bergoglio reminded the Catholic faithful that some give alms to the poor but won't look them in the eye. Bergoglio told Catholics in his archdiocese that it was a Christian duty to share food, clothing, health and education with others, following the teaching of Jesus in Matthew 25 when he said that those who would enter the Kingdom would be those who clothed the naked, gave food to the hungry, visited prisoners and gave water to the thirsty. Bergoglio's aim was to highlight that people, as in the analysis by José Paradiso, must engage in 'the building up in common and the recognition of the other'.[1] Bergoglio advocated for the care for migrants, unknown brothers and sisters who should be approached with love, 'love, which is something concrete'.[2] He was very concerned with demonstrating care and love for those who were working as slaves in Buenos Aires, without freedom, rights or dignity Their presence was a sign of the moral degradation of those who elevated greed above human dignity.[3] Bergoglio demanded that people consider the biblical question 'Where is your brother?', a question addressed to us all.[4]

The formal homilies delivered by Bergoglio at the shrine of San Cayetano, the patron of work and bread, constituted a guiding influence for Argentineans. The workers and the poor gathering at the shrine were central to Bergoglio's agenda of pastoral care for

1 José Paradiso, 'Prólogo' in Cardenal Jorge M. Bergoglio SJ, *Nosotros como ciudadanos, nosotros como pueblo: Hacia un Bicentenario en justicia y solidaridad 2010-2016*. Buenos Aires: Editorial Claretiana, 2011, pp. 5-11 at p. 9.
2 Homilía con motivo del Día del Migrante, Santuario Nuestra Señora Emigrantes, 7 September 2008.
3 Cardenal Jorge M. Bergoglio SJ, Homilía con motivo de la Misa en memoria de las víctimas del trabajo esclavo a los 5 años del incendio del taller clandestino de Luis Viale 1269, 27 March 2011.
4 Cardenal Jorge M. Bergoglio SJ, Homilía con motivo de la 5ª Misa por las víctimas de trata y tráfico de personas, 25 September 2012.

those on the margins of society.[1] Through his homilies, Bergoglio challenged pilgrims to question injustice and corruption within Argentinean society, especially among politicians; in his view the power politicians exercised to govern and legislate was given by the voters, and 'power is ambiguous and can operate as good or bad'.[2] For Bergoglio, the roots of unemployment were to be found in corruption and the enrichment of the few who do not work, because they live on what they are given through bribes and false contracts. Sin and corruption are two different ways of being for Bergoglio. While repetitive sin can lead to corruption, corruption represents a qualitative phenomenon whereby corrupt habits deteriorate a person's capacity to love, and the soul sinks further and further into a selfish condition.[3] Prayer breaks such destructive individuality, because in prayer a human being is 'a person totally responsible for her acts, an "I" within a particular people'.[4] Each of Bergoglio's homilies address the readings assigned for the Eucharist celebrated for the thousands of pilgrims who journey to the saint's shrine in Buenos Aires. Each homily built upon the ideas of the previous year, giving cohesiveness and sense of consistency to the corpus of Bergoglio's public teachings.

San Cayetano, the Catholic saint celebrated particularly by those without work or food, was born Gaetano di Thiene in Vicenza, northern Italy, in October 1480 and died in Naples, southern Italy,

1   One of the seminal works for understanding the development of the notion of sainthood and the place of saints within the Catholic Church, is Robert Bartlett, *Why Can the Dead Do Such Great Things? Saints and Worshippers from the Martyrs to the Reformation*, Princeton, NJ: Princeton University Press, 2013.

2   Jorge M. Bergoglio SJ, 'Necesidad de una antropología política: Un problema pastoral' § 18 – Lección inaugural del curso académico 1989 en las Facultades de Filosofía y Teología de la Universidad del Salvador, área San Miguel.

3   Cardenal Jorge M. Bergoglio SJ, *Corrupción y pecado: Algunas reflexiones en torno al tema de la corrupción*, Buenos Aires: Editorial Claretiana, 2005, p. 17, see also 'Algunas reflexiones en torno al tema de la corrupción', Plática, Marzo 1991 in Jorge Mario Bergoglio SJ, *Reflexiones en esperanza*, Buenos Aires: Ediciones Universidad del Salvador, 1992, pp. 175-198.

4   Jorge Bergoglio, *Mente abierta, corazón creyente*, Buenos Aires: Editorial Claretiana, 2012, p. 201; this idea is taken from a retreat that Begoglio gave in La Plata in January 1990, see 'La carne en camino de regreso' § 5 in Jorge Mario Bergoglio SJ, *Reflexiones en esperanza*, Buenos Aires: Ediciones Universidad del Salvador, 1992, pp. 45-46.

on 7 August 1547. He studied law at the University of Padua and later became an apostolic notary at the court of Julius II in Rome, becoming well-known for his work advancing relations between the papacy and the Kingdom of Venice. After fostering the foundation of an association of priests, he was ordained in 1515 and founded a hospital for the terminally ill in Venice. In 1524 he founded the order of the Teatinos, in Spanish (known as 'regular clerics') to serve the poor, stipulating that they should not own anything and that they should not ask for anything to live on but the alms given to them by others. He also founded the charitable organisation, Monte di Pietà, later to become the Bank of Naples. His relics are located at the Church of St Paolo in Naples, and his annual liturgical feast takes place on 7 August. In Buenos Aires, his shrine is located at the church of Liniers, a neighbourhood in Greater Buenos Aires; other shrines are at Rosario (Decanato Centro, Santa Fe Province); and the San Cayetano Parish in La Plata. On the annual feast of San Cayetano, thousands of pilgrims gather at the shrine, singing hymns to San Cayetano and carrying the statue of the saint on their shoulders.[1]

As the patron of work in Argentina, the dedicatory prayer to San Cayetano requests his help with finding, keeping and improving work; the original reads as follows:

---

1   Hymn to San Cayetano – Himno a San Cayetano:
        Padre glorioso San Cayetano,
        Traigo en mis manos mi corazón,
        Con la esperanza y la confianza,
        Abro mi alma con mi oración.
        San Cayetano danos la paz,
        Danos trabajo, danos el pan.
        Siempre vivamos en alegría,
        En la justicia y en el amor.
        Cuando en mi alma sienta tristeza,
        Cuando en mi alma sienta dolor,
        Dame paciencia, dame tu fuerza,
        Ayúdame mi protector.
        Muestra siempre San Cayetano
        Al niño Dios, mi Salvador,
        Que en su mirada vea el amor
        Y en sus bracitos paz y unión.
        Siempre tú fuiste San Cayetano,
        Desde el cielo, mi protector,
        No me olvides en esta vida,
        Dame siempre tu bendición.

¡Oh, glorioso san Cayetano, Padre de la Providencia!
No permitas que en mi casa me falte la subsistencia
Y de tu liberal mano una limosna te pido en lo temporal y humano.
Oh, glorioso San Cayetano,
¡Providencia, providencia, providencia![1]

On 7 August 1999 Bergoglio delivered a homily in which he reminded pilgrims that San Cayetano's shrine is a place of hope and shelter, and that in the heart of God each individual, and the whole nation, has a place.[2] Bergoglio reminded pilgrims that too many people do not have a place in the city, feel excluded because they do not have a house or a stable job, or just feel generally disoriented. Often this disorientation is at least in part because they have abandoned their commitment to the common good, in order attain privileges that only give a temporary happiness. It is a fact that not infrequently one feels unwelcome, or deprived of a place in society, uninvited. Our place is the Father's house. With God we are always welcome, always accepted, always searching for friendly faces and helping hands.

To enter the shrine, one must wait; but there is hope in that wait. Those around us are not competitors, but brothers and sisters, and the person who is neediest and worst off is first in the eyes of God. We want to show God that we also care for our brother, following Jesus' example of caring for us. Thus, through the help we give others, we also experience God's care for us.

On 7 August 2000, Bergoglio visited the shrine of San Cayetano. The financial crisis was looming, and particularly threatened those who had money in the banks and couldn't withdraw it.[3] The reading of the day was Paul's exhortation to have the same sentiments as those of Christ, and Bergoglio stressed the common sentiment shared by all pilgrims to the shrine that day. This sentiment was hope, shared by those who had already queued

---

1 O glorious San Cayetano, Father of Providence!
   Do not let my home be without food
   And from your generous hand I ask for some human and temporal help
   Oh, glorious San Cayetano,
   Providence, Providence, Providence! [my translation]
2 Arzobispo Jorge M. Bergoglio SJ, 'Ponerle el hombro a la vida', Homilía en el Santuario de San Cayetano, 7 August 1999.
3 Arzobispo Jorge M. Bergoglio SJ, 'Con San Cayetano, por un milenio de justicia, solidaridad y esperanza', Homilía en el Santuario de San Cayetano, 7 August 2000.

for soup, and those who, in solidarity with those queuing brought packets of *mate* and sugar for those who needed them. Some came to the shrine to thank the saint for the jobs they already had, touching the saint's image with enormous devotion. The story of the Good Samaritan contains sentiments of justice, solidarity and hope, to which we should also aspire. These are Jesus' attitudes and pilgrims share them: they are wounded and in need of help, but at the same time, like the Good Samaritan, have good wishes to bring to the task of helping others. In their pilgrimage and prayers to San Cayetano pilgrims ask God for the grace to transform their hearts into hearts that share Jesus' sentiments more fully.

To be the Good Samaritan is to become ever closer to others, to provide others with wine and oil and to care for their wounds, to carry the wounded to the inn, to pay for their stay and to promise to return to visit them. In an age in which we can witness almost everything via technology, those who do not act upon what they see are those who do not draw close to others. For Bergoglio, the mediation of Our Lady can also help us gain the virtues that Jesus had that allow us to be more just, to live in solidarity and to be filled with hope.

On his visit to the shrine of San Cayetano on 7 August 2001, the newly-appointed Cardinal Bergoglio continued a reflection on the Good Samaritan that he had started the year before.[1] The readings of the day included the Sermon on the Mount, and Bergoglio remarked that pain and sorrow can be seen as marking human moments in which we need help from others, but also as blessings. Pain and sorrow can even bring a certain kind of happiness, a painful happiness, but true. In the Sermon on the Mount Jesus speaks of the poor, those who are hungry, those who cry, those who are unjustly persecuted, but with hope and consolation in his voice – 'Blessed are you who weep because you will be comforted'. His Word is already a consolation for all pilgrims at the shrine. Many weep in Argentina today; the poor and hungry who are ignored by the rich; the poor persecuted for demanding work while rich people evade the law and are applauded for their actions; those suffering from violence, while others enjoy themselves in safe areas; those going hungry while others throw food away. Jesus requests that our hearts remain open to those in difficult circumstances. Happiness is the reward of a heart that is open to receive God's gifts.

1 Cardenal Jorge M. Bergoglio SJ, 'El dolor reclama ayuda y exige soluciones', Homilía en el Santuario de San Cayetano, 7 August 2001.

During his homily at San Cayetano, Bergoglio choose to speak of the happiness that comes with tears. In it we taste the blessings of Jesus, and it opens our heart to God. The blessing of tears allows us cry for our nation. Tears are the ancient prayer of lamentation through which people repent from their sin and turning to God, leaving behind their empty illusions and false gods. Bergoglio paraphrased the Sermon on the Mount saying, 'Blessed are you who cry for your country with those tears that belong not to one but to many, with the tears of those who pray the Our Father; and when you say bread you say "our bread" and when you ask for forgiveness you say "and forgive us our financial debts"'. The best prayer of this world is in those tears of a mother or a father who cry for their children; they are comparable to the tears of Our Lady beside the Cross, praying for intercession.

Bergoglio exclaimed: blessed are you who cry, coming closer to San Cayetano, requesting bread and work; your tears petition God wordlessly, and you are sure that you have been heard and attended to. San Cayetano intercedes for his loyal people, for all the Argentinean people. And within these hard moments, we double our trust and confidence in Jesus Our Lord. He has promised us that He himself, in person, will wipe away our tears. Happy are we if we put all our hope in Him.

The blessing of those who mourn, Bergoglio said, reminds us of the tears of childhood. It is as if Jesus were telling us: 'Happy are you when you cried as you did when you were children and your mother consoled you'. It is true that we can only be consoled by our Lord and our Mother. We trust that Our Lady will console us, and we ask her to turn her merciful eyes on us and show us Jesus.

In 2002, after two years of extreme financial trouble in Argentina – Bergoglio escalated his message of solidarity with those without work, and also ventured to challenge the elites creating social problems. In his homily on the Feast of San Cayetano on 7 August 2002, he focussed on the words of St Paul. We must sacrifice ourselves for others as Christ did.[1] He encouraged pilgrims to request bread, to then share with others. Before giving up his life on the cross, Christ shared bread with his disciples, sharing himself and giving himself to others. Pilgrims should also request work that dignifies, because it is also through work that we give of ourselves to others.

1   Cardenal Jorge M. Bergoglio SJ, 'Reclamamos el pan que alimenta y el trabajo que dignifica', Homilía en el Santuario de San Cayetano, 7 August 2002.

Jesus takes upon himself the sins of all, including those who killed him, giving us an example of self-sacrifice. Nations determined to rise above their ruins and rebuild their societies in dignity give of themselves to others. Self-sacrifice is also displayed by people who live in solidarity with others and share whatever they have; and people who give themselves to prayer and put their trust in God. Bergoglio stated at San Cayetano that the act of pilgrimage is one of hope: hope manifested by the humble actions of queuing and walking, without stepping on anybody, without taking somebody else's place, without losing hope. The shrine includes everybody, as our offices and institutions should. The fortitude of the faithful people, who know how to offer their shoulders and carry the cross, must be recovered. We also want to recover the spirit of the Good Samaritan who does not pass by, ignoring pain and injustice – and nor does Jesus, who wishes to draw closer to those who suffer and to help them. We want to recover the grace given to those who hunger and thirst for justice – and receive from Jesus the consolation that we need. Bergoglio ended his homily in 2002 by requesting pilgrims to join him in the prayer composed for the novena (nine days of prayer) to San Cayetano, which ends with the characterisation of God as friend and a companion for the road.[1]

On 7 August 2003, at the shrine of San Cayetano once again, Bergoglio reflected on the Gospel passage in which a widow gives up two coins of small value and puts them in the collection box of the temple whose contents were used for the feeding of the poor.[2] It was clear that Jesus particularly noticed this action of love because it was remembered by those who composed the Gospels. She had little, but shared whatever little she had with others in

1   The text of the prayer is as follows:
     'Necesitamos ver tu rostro
     Guardar las palabras de tu boca
     Hablarte al oído
     Dejarnos mirar por tus ojos.
     Y al besarte, Cristo, encontrar en ti
     Los rasgos de tu madre,
     De tus santos, de tu pueblo sufrido.
     Queremos ver tu rostro
     Dios amigo
     Compañero de camino.'
2   Cardenal Jorge M. Bergoglio SJ, 'Encontraremos el camino para volver a empezar', Homilía en el Santuario de San Cayetano, 7 August 2003.

love. This kind of action is hardly noticed by those who select the daily news items. The pilgrims' motto that year was 'let us not lose hope, taking the hand of San Cayetano we will find the way to start again'. Bergoglio himself reflected upon the theme of hands.

The pilgrims to San Cayetano clutch the two coins for the alms to the poor in the one hand, and with the other touch the image of the saint, commending to the image the fragility of their families, their own failings, their petitions and their thanksgiving, their hopes wet with tears. Bergoglio said that hands break bread, absorb grace and give of what they have. These hands hold the promise of new beginnings, the possibility of setting out on a journey full of the hope that never deceives. Bergoglio asserted that we want to firmly clutch the hands of our families, particularly at times in which the family as a unit is under threat in society. The warm and firm hand of Jesus strengthens our fragility. Bergoglio believes that to clutch the hand of San Cayetano is to clutch the hand of all Argentineans – particularly of those who do not have hope – and this allows us to receive the gifts of bread and work. God wants to give to those who desire to include everyone in the good of society, and who claim justice for all. Bread and work are not alms, they are rights obtained because of justice. All gifts and all justice come from God, and then are channelled through governments or the invisible hand of economic system. When pilgrims give their two coins, they give them freely; even in their poverty and fragility they give first, and later ask for help.

Bergoglio prayed that he and his listeners might hold the hand of the child Jesus to enable the pilgrims to go forth once again into the world with courage, giving to the children who are the hope of the nation. He asked San Cayetano too to hold his hand, and the hands of the assembled pilgrims, so that their tired arms might be strengthened and they might work fairly for their bread. He asked God to lend His hand to the fragile people; and he asked the Virgin Mary to give her hand to families, so that their hands might be quickened at work and happy in charity. Finally, Bergoglio suggested that all the hands working and giving together will create a new beginning for pilgrims and citizens alike.

During his 7 August 2004 visit to the shrine of San Cayetano, Bergoglio spoke on the twin themes of the road to hope and the road to disillusionment.[1] The prophet Elijah and the disciples

---

1   Cardenal Jorge M. Bergoglio SJ, 'El camino de la desilusión y el camino de la esperanza', Homilía en el Santuario de San Cayetano, 7 August 2004.

at Emmaus found the strength for the journeys in bread broken by Christ.[1] This viaticum, this bread for the journey, renews the strength and hope of those walking the road. We have the Lord as food and therefore there is nothing that we should fear, there is neither obstacle nor challenge to hope that such food cannot transform into strength for fighting and ongoing travel. This divine bread is also represented by 'the small bread' that we share with co-workers halfway through the working day. It is this human bread that allows us to complete our working day. It is the bread that gives us our dignity. It is this bread, the Lord himself as Eucharist, that gives us the strength to push ahead, that makes us brothers and sisters, that makes us citizens of a nation, and that makes us the people of God (an expression that was central at Vatican II). In his prayer Bergoglio stressed the importance of bread, saying 'May the Virgin Mary who, like all mothers, puts a piece of bread for children and men in their bags for the journey, help us to search in our hearts with sure hope that we will find that bread which is Jesus. May San Cayetano give to all heads of families, male and female, the strength of that bread in order to search for that other bread that families need, the bread of energy and hope, and the inheritance we want to give to the next generations.'

During his 7 August 2005 address at San Cayetano's shrine, Bergoglio emphasised one of his favourite topics: service.[2] He took one of the Gospel passages that, in his words, 'one does not tire of reading and remembering': Jesus washing the feet of his disciples. In the Gospel of John, this was the last sign before Jesus' death: it was an extreme sign, similar to the sign of dying on the Cross; it was a beautiful sign that Jesus made by serving others in love. At that moment, the Gospel indicates that Jesus had all the power on earth, yet, as Bergoglio comments, Jesus choose to channel it into service, to reveal that the secret of happiness and true power is to practice service towards others. The washing of feet was also a sign of purification before the meal, teaching us that we should purify and clean ourselves by forgiving others.

---

1   The road to Emmaus was a favourite theme for Bergoglio; on Emmaus and 'closeness' to the Lord, see Cardenal Jorge M. Bergoglio SJ, Homilía con motivo de la clausura del Congreso Nacional de Doctrina Social de la Iglesia, Rosario, 8 May 2011.

2   Cardenal Jorge M. Bergoglio SJ, 'El verdadero poder es el servicio', Homilía en el Santuario de San Cayetano, 7 August 2005.

Jesus' powerful gesture makes obsolete all gestures made solely to accumulate power, to pretend to have power, to control others, or to become rich through power. When Pontius Pilate washed his hands in front of Jesus, he was following a logic that contradicts Jesus' values and example. Perhaps, and according to Bergoglio, one of the reasons Pilate decided not to intervene was because he couldn't understand the concept of service as power. For Bergoglio, power is service and service needs to be given up to the last detail in order to dignify the other person. Thus, the washing of feet proclaims a communion in which all are equal, the one who washes feet as much as the one whose feet are washed.

Bergoglio challenged pilgrims to emulate examples of self-sacrificing service from daily life: that of a person who invites guests to their house and prepares a barbeque for them; of the mother who, on her own birthday, cooks and serves a meal to others. People who hold the most power have the greatest responsibility to serve.

Because of the power of service, pilgrims who take part in religious rites remembering the saint are also taking part in a political act: they remind those in public office of the requirements of power, that is, service to others. The pilgrims' feet are tired and dirty, but are beautiful in the eyes of Jesus because they are the feet of people who are pilgrims of peace. They are the feet of people who allow their feet to be washed by the Lord in order to recover their dignity. They are feet that are cleansed and represent all human beings. Once a human heart is cleansed, they move to cleanse others and to integrate them into a community that treasures justice. All should work fairly for their bread and act to serve society, to unify, dignify and make human beings feel good about themselves. Bergoglio asserted that it was Jesus' mother who taught the Lord to wash feet, and Bergoglio requested pilgrims to pray to the Virgin of Luján so that she would teach all Christians how to wash feet and how to serve.[1]

1   Oración a Nuestra Señora de Luján:
      Virgen de Luján, Madre de nuestra patria;
      A vos recurrimos confiados
      Porque sabemos de tu inmenso amor
      Por nosotros.
      Al mirarte, contemplamos en tu imagen
      Al dolor y a la muerte ya vencidos.
      Pero, mientras andamos el camino
      de la vida,

What is clear from Bergoglio's engagement with pilgrims to San Cayetano is that he was deliberately connecting his yearly homilies and that they recognised that the dignity of a journey of pilgrimage does not only give hope to Argentineans of finding work and bread, but also teaches the Argentinean nation how to behave ethically. All must be included in the life of the nation. Bergoglio's sense of inclusion extended to other Christian churches and world religion, and a practical engagement with other faiths became central to his pastoral ministry after he became cardinal in 2001. If other archbishops stressed inter-faith committees and intellectual commonalities, Bergoglio followed a practical approach of holding prayer-meetings with other churches, meetings that grew into national conventions and occasions on which thousands of people met; not to talk about ecumenism, but to discover prayer and community life together.

Inter-Faith and Inter-Religious Dialogue

As archbishop of Buenos Aires, Bergoglio followed in the steps of his predecessor, and fostered encounters, dialogue and co-operation with Christians of other denominations as well as with leaders and members of other world religions present in Argentina. Bergoglio showed that he felt all religions offer something good and his co-operative gestures included the use of Pentecostal prayer when visiting a Catholic school, meeting with Jewish and Muslim leaders, visiting to the synagogue of Buenos Aires, weekly, hour-long prayer meetings with the gardener of the archdiocese gardens, a member of a Pentecostal church, and attendance at

---

necesitamos que hagas más fuerte
nuestra fe,
más grande nuestra esperanza,
más solidario nuestro amor.
Bajo tu manto se cobijan los más pobres,
Los enfermos y los que sufren
Soledad y tristeza en su corazón.
Que tu fuerza y tu cariño
Nos hagan más hermanos,
Para poder anunciar que tu hijo Jesús
Es el Salvador.
Madre buena de Luján,
Toda nuestra vida está en tus manos.
Cuídanos siempre con tu dulce bendición.

Muslim funerals when members of the Buenos Aires mosque whom he knew died. His first approach to inter-faith and inter-religious dialogue was through friendship, beginning with an invitation to meet over a cup of coffee, leading to further closeness with the other person; and then a prayer meeting at which all other faiths could be included. It was Bergoglio who pushed for the Te Deum of each 25 May at the Catholic Metropolitan Cathedral to be made ecumenical by inviting leaders and members of other Christian denominations and other faiths. For Bergoglio, in all religions there are common points where they encounter one another, and the beauty of every inter-faith moment is to try to find such points.

Bergoglio did not make grand public announcements about his meetings with religious leaders and communities of other Christian traditions and other faiths, but he worked consistently to open his diary to facilitate meeting them, getting to know them, and advancing a common agenda of unity and service of the people of Argentina. The most structured instance of inter-faith dialogue was the *Mesa de Diálogo Argentina*, a table to which he invited many leaders in order that they might get to know one another; it also fostered events during which religious leaders exchanged views about contemporary challenges within Argentinean society. Members of the *Diálogo Argentina* had a single united voice, for example, when it rejected the government proposal for a law legalising same-sex unions. It is not surprising that one of Bergoglio's last engagements before his election as pope was in December 2012, when he visited the synagogue at Arcos Street in the neighbourhood of Belgrano in order to light the candles of Hanukkah, coinciding with the Christian celebration of Christmas. Years before, Bergoglio had participated in a ceremony to mark Yom Kippur, the Jewish feast of repentance, in the synagogue of Libertad Street. On that occasion, a central day in the Jewish calendar, Bergoglio paid tribute to the Jewish leaders for inviting him to speak, an inter-faith gesture that was not welcomed by every Jew within the Jewish community of Buenos Aires. Another moment of encounter between Bergoglio and the rabbis was at the Mass celebrated after the death of John Paul II, a celebration attended by Rabbi Sergio Bergman and other members of the Jewish community; a third was the establishment of a dining-room for the needy, opened by Catholics and Jews at the synagogue of

Arcos Street and at the headquarters of Caritas; a third was the common work for the poor and the marginalised undertaken with leaders of the Jewish community in the 'emergency' neighbourhoods of the Great Buenos Aires.

Some of the conversations between Bergoglio and Rabbi Abraham Skorka, rector of the Rabbinic Seminary for Latin America – formal, explicit and public dialogues – have been made widely available in book form.[1] In 2012 Rabbi Skorka, as leader of the Jewish community Benei Tikva, received an honorary doctorate from the Catholic University of Argentina (UCA), in the presence of Bergoglio and the Apostolic Nuncio Paul Tscherrig. The rector of the UCA introduced the ceremony by stating that Christian institutions can welcome a rabbi's wisdom, regardless of the differences that exist between Christianity and Judaism.

In another important inter-faith development, Bergoglio, Rabbi Daniel Goldman (Bet-El Jewish community) and the Muslim leader Omar Abboud founded the Instituto de Diálogo Interreligioso, an institute for inter-faith dialogue supported by Christians, Jews and Muslims. This institute sponsored several conferences wherein, within the context of the sacred texts of the three world religions, other texts were studied (such as documents applying the sacred texts within society) and common social actions discussed. In 2001, during the Argentinean financial crisis, President Duhalde named the Catholic Church a custodian of social peace. Following the presidential call, Mgr Jorge Casaretto, bishop of the diocese of San Isidro, the northern part of Buenos Aires, called for a table of dialogue that included all social actors at the time of the crisis. It was Bergoglio who expanded the role given to the Church to include all other religions, because, as Bergoglio explained, the guarantor of peace was not only the Catholic Church, but all religions united in faith. Since his initiative, Jews, Muslims, Evangelicals and Orthodox Christians have come together, not only in sessions of inter-faith dialogue, but to collaborate in initiatives to aid the poor and the needy in Buenos Aires. They also keep watch over government policies regarding the poor and the marginalised.

The 2001 financial crisis in Argentina coincided with the terrorist attacks on the United States, and consequently

---

1   Jorge Bergoglio and Abraham Skorka, *Sobre el cielo y la tierra*, New York: Vintage Español, 2013 (original edition published by Random House Mondadori, Buenos Aires, 2010).

the media started demonising Muslims as followers of a religion of violence. Muslims in Argentina, who had always been marginalised anyway, suffered under increased public misunderstanding. Bergoglio and other religious leaders called publically for the study and true understanding of Islam. Thus, the Islamic Centre of Buenos Aires, through the initiative of its president, Adel Mohamed Made, fostered initiatives by which Argentineans' knowledge of Islam might be increased so they might see that Islam is a religion of peace. On behalf of the Catholic Church, Fr Guillermo Marcó took part in these initiatives, representing Bergoglio. Marcó introduced Bergoglio to the Muslim participants, and the Inter-Religious Dialogue Institute grew from these conversations in 2003 and 2004. Bergoglio was invited to visit the Islamic Centre, and there, in a public meeting, Catholics and Muslims agreed to work together for the defence of life and against terrorism and fundamentalism. Bergoglio wrote the following words in the guest book of the Islamic Centre: 'I thank God, the Merciful One, for the fraternal hospitality, for the spirit of Argentinean patriotism that I have experienced and for the witness of a commitment to the historical values of our nation'. In 2005 all those involved in the inter-faith initiative signed a manifesto against fundamentalism, a new and original venture that had not taken place in other countries. The document bore the signatures of Bergoglio, Helal Mahud (Islamic Centre), Jorge Kirszenbaum of the Delegación de Asociaciones Israelitas Argentinas (DAIA), Luis Grinwald (AMIA), Fr Guillermo Marcó, Rabbi Daniel Goldman and Omar Abboud. When Adel Mohamed Made died, Bergoglio took part in the funeral and gave the Muslim community his prayers and words of support.

At the time of the 2001 crisis Bergoglio also met weekly with leaders of Evangelical churches in Argentina to pray together for all its victims.[1] Formal meetings also took place between members of the Consejo Nacional Cristiano Evangélico and representatives of the bishops' conference, and even before the 2001 crisis they published a document together. On Saturday

---

1   Although there are no indications that Bergoglio organized meetings
    with members of the Anglican Communion or the Methodist churches in
    Argentina at a more public level, this surely does not reflect on the leaders
    of those communities but rather on the small numbers of Argentinean
    Anglicans in Argentina.

13 October 2012, 6, 000 people took part in the sixth fraternal meeting between Catholics and Evangelicals (Sexto Encuentro Fraterno de Comunión Renovada de Evangélicos y Católicos en el Espíritu Santo, or CRECES). Bergoglio was one of the prime movers behind the organisation of this public and open meeting that brought Catholics and Evangelicals together in prayer, united by the inspiring words of Fr Raniero Cantalamessa, preacher of the papal household, who was personally invited by Bergoglio to contribute to the ecumenical celebration. Bergoglio was among the crowds that day; he drank *mate*, ate *empanadas*, and gave a short message to all present, who responded with a loud ovation for the man who had brought the followers of Christ together. There were cheers and even songs before Bergoglio could utter a few words. Bergoglio's words were simple but direct: 'Jesus spent most of his time on the streets. He is still walking among us. During his time people didn't waste an opportunity to be with him, to touch him, to hug him, to receive from him. I do not have any fear towards those who fight Jesus, because they are already defeated. I have more fear towards Christians who seem distracted, sleepy, who do not see Christ when he passes. We have lost two things: the capacity to stand in awe in front of the Word of God, because we are consumed by news of those who are leaving aside the good news. Also, we have lost our tenderness. Jesus came close to the human wound and he healed it. Let us recover those two characteristics: let's not become accustomed to seeing the sick and the hungry without awe and without tenderness'.

Bergoglio took part in these meetings from 2004 onward and he always took part as one of the crowd, praying, singing and lifting his hands in prayer as is common among Evangelicals. At the 2006 meeting, in the Luna Park Stadium of Buenos Aires, Bergoglio appeared as a speaker. After climbing the stairs onto the main stage, he knelt down and asked pastors and priests to pray together for him in a humble gesture of unity that was not forgotten by those who were present that day. The priests prayed for him by laying-on hands, while the pastors prayed over him, lifting their hands to heaven. Among those praying for Bergoglio were Fr Cantalamessa, pastor Giovanni Traettino (bishop of the Evangelical Church of the Reconciliation of Italy), Mateo Calisi (president of the Fraternidad Católica de las Comunidades y Asociaciones Carismáticas de Alianza), Jorge Himitian (pastor of the Christian Community of Buenos Aires), Carlos Mraida (Centre Baptist Church) and Norberto Saracco (pastor of the Pentecostal Evangelical Church). Bergoglio finally spoke, stating that it was so nice that the participants were not trying to stone one another, and that nobody was making money out of a journey of faith. After speaking, Bergoglio disappeared among the crowds, talking to all and sharing part of his own journey with them. However, a group of Catholic protestors had come to the meeting to express their disapproval of Bergoglio's initiatives. One of them had a poster with the image of the Virgin Mary and tried to divide pastors and priests by requesting their response to the poster. Bergoglio gently requested to be given the poster, folded it, and put it inside his briefcase.

During this gathering, Fr Cantalamessa spoke of a new and unique Pentecost that was taking place in Buenos Aires. Christians had come from all over Argentina to pray together, and they celebrated the festival under the motto 'The Gospel, power of God'. The praises of God were led by Pastor Sebastián Golluscio and Pastor Jorge Himitian, who also read the 'Common Declaration of a Fraternal Encounter'. The Declaration included the following recognition of Christian unity: 'The Holy Spirit opened our spiritual eyes and we understood very simple but wonderful things. We understood that the Church is more than a physical building where God is worshipped. All of us who are children of God are brothers and sisters. Christ founded only one Church and he wants his Church to show the unity and holiness that characterises the gift of God to the world'.

Bergoglio was an unassuming archbishop who avoided being at the centre of attention; instead he preferred to bring people together to aid ecumenical and pastoral activities organised by the churches. Once, he agreed to appear in a series of television programs with Rabbi Skorka and the Evangelical Marcelo Figueroa, former director of the Bible Society of Argentina. At the invitation of channel 21, together with the television station of the archdiocese of Buenos Aires, they discussed themes of global interest. In the spring of 2010, Bergoglio invited Figueroa to take part in this public conversation; they had worked together in biblical initiatives over the past few years, and even outside ecclesiastical circles they were personal friends. The television program, with the title 'Bible, current dialogue' (*Biblia, diálogo vigente*), was organised by Figueroa, who thought that Bergoglio needed to participate. After several attempts, he managed to convince Bergoglio to appear on television. Together with Skorka, Figueroa and Bergoglio discussed contemporary topics of interest, providing three distinct contributions: Jewish, Evangelical and Catholic. Bergoglio surprised those who followed the program with his gift for listening, his acceptance that the truth is multi-faceted, and his diverse range of knowledge on many subjects from philosophical ideas to lyric verses appropriate to the tango.

Behind Bergoglio's openness was the surety of an educated man, a Jesuit who knew what he believed and who, during Lent in 2003, had asked educational communities to do only the one thing that would change nations and peoples: to speak the truth at all times.[1] It was clear to Bergoglio that 'education is one of the main pillars for the reconstruction of the sense of community'.[2] Personal maturity became for him a matter of central importance. It would allow the individual to acquire freedom within a society anchored in time and space; a freedom that would include the 'full affirmation of love as the link between human beings'.[3]

---

1   Cardenal Jorge M. Bergoglio SJ, Mensaje a las comunidades educativas, Buenos Aires, Cuaresma 2003.
2   Cardenal Jorge M. Bergoglio SJ, Mensaje a las comunidades educativas, Buenos Aires, Pascua 2004.
3   Ibid., 2005.

7. Conclusions

The life of the Argentinean Jorge Mario Bergoglio, the cardinal who would become Pope Francis in March 2013, has been shaped by his upbringing as the son of Italian immigrants, and his choice to follow the vocation of a Jesuit and a priest within the Catholic Church. A teacher, a spiritual director and later provincial of the Jesuits in Argentina, he was forced to face the political and religious challenges of the military junta in Argentina, a period from which he emerged for some as a hero, for others a passive servant of ecclesiastical policies of non-involvement.

Bergoglio's personal road to Damascus occurred when his superiors sent him to pursue a doctorate in theology in Germany. There he found himself lonely, wishing to return to Argentina. He did so without a doctorate, but with a clear sense of service to the people through parish ministry, spiritual direction and teaching. A man who had not endorsed the theologies of liberation, he nevertheless became a witness to the Gospel among the poor and the marginalised. As bishop he led his priests into service, and changed expectations of Catholics in Buenos Aires. Most importantly he led the Catholic Church out to the periphery of Buenos Aires, a place that he considered the centre of the Kingdom of God. His theology matured to bear personal witness to Argentinean history, the God who creates history, and who accompanies his people through the ages.

Bergoglio developed three theological themes in his homilies, writings and pastoral ministry: the nation, the poor within the nation, and 'others' within the nation – including Christians of other denominations, Jews, Muslims, people of other faiths and those of no religion. His homilies at the yearly Te Deum to mark Argentinean independence, and at the shrine of San Cayetano, still pose theological challenges to the Catholic Church and to other Christian Latin American churches. His efforts to establish inter-faith and inter-religious dialogue were quite unique in an otherwise 'fortress' Latin American Church that had become overly concerned with the advance of Pentecostalism and the secularisation of Latin American society during the 1990s. Bergoglio challenged non-inclusive notions of proselitism, and affirmed that a servant Church that proclaimed love, solidarity and service to the poor, was bound to bring people to Christ without concerning itself solely with its own well-being.

The challenge of Bergoglio's life and theology was a focus on mission above ecclesiology, a focus that he brought with him to the Vatican when elected the first Latin American bishop of Rome. Our ongoing biographical challenge is to continue exploring the dynamic pastoral life of Jorge Mario Bergoglio, in order to better understand the life and theological thought of Pope Francis.

Post Script

Cardinal Bergoglio expected to retire from office as archbishop of Buenos Aires in 2013, following the rule of episcopal retirement at seventy-five years of age. When the conclave was called to elect a new pope, he had already put his papers in order and had left instructions about what to do in his absence; no one knew how long the Conclave to elect a new pope would last. As it turned out, he never returned to his dear Argentina. He remained in Rome, accepting the role of the 'pope from far away', the pope from the margins, the first pope chosen from Latin America. Pope Francis carried his own unique concerns to the Vatican and to the papacy. His Argentinean pastoral concerns, for the primacy of the peripheries and the well-being of the public, the poor and representatives of other faiths in dialogue with the Catholic Church, have become those of his papal ministry.

The first months of Bergoglio's pontificate were marked by his warmth and clear personal commitment to his previous lifestyle. He moved out of the official Vatican apartments to live at the Santa Marta residency in Rome, and he spoke time and again about his need for simplicity of life. He also spoke of the great joy of being a Christian, a joy that must be shared with others. As bishop of Rome he commenced his visits to parishes within his diocese on 26 May 2013, travelling to the parish of Santi Elisabetta e Zaccaria on the occasion of the Solemnity of the Holy Trinity. His first visit outside Rome was on 8 July 2013 to the island of Lampedusa, a point of arrival for thousands of African refugees. Many refugees drown each year when inadequate boats used for the journey sink. Pope Francis' first journey outside Europe took place in July 2013 (22-29) when he attended the world meeting of Catholic youth in Rio de Janeiro, Brazil, and captivated millions with his simple and warm manners, his insistence on breaking protocol and his easy speech with those waiting for him.

I have felt a freshness and newness in my own life after visiting Bergoglio's home in Buenos Aires, the Metropolitan Cathedral and the shrine of San Cayetano in Buenos Aires, as his biographer, and as a Latin American exploring Bergoglio's life. In this work I have examined his life from childhood until his election as the leader of the world's one billion Catholics, leaving an assessment of his pontificate and his life as Pope Francis to future scholars. However, from his first weeks at the Vatican, Pope Francis has shown the world his remarkable identity and personality, consistent with the values and actions of the young Argentinean, Jorge Bergoglio. It would be difficult to understand the unique style of Pope Francis' papacy without dwelling on his previous actions and values as Jesuit, bishop, archbishop and cardinal of Argentina. His enduring simplicity is summarised in the answer he gave to journalists returning with him to Rome after his very successful and moving attendance of the World Youth Meeting in Brazil. In an attempt to penetrate the 'mystery' of the black briefcase he carried with him, the journalists asked: 'what do you have in that black briefcase that you carry with you at all time?' No other pope had carried his own briefcase during his journeys. Pope Francis replied: 'I don't have the key to an atomic bomb. I carried it with me because I always did before. What was inside? The necessary tools to shave, a breviary, my diary, something to read – I brought a book by Saint Teresita, of whom I am a devotee. I always carried my briefcase myself during my journeys: it is a normal occurrence and we must be normal!'[1]

---

1 'Papa Francisco: "¡Fue un viaje hermoso, me hizo muy bien espiritualmente!"', Radio Vaticana 30 July 2013.

Bibliography

Selected Writings by Cardinal Jorge Mario Bergoglio

Bergoglio, Jorge Mario SJ. *Reflexiones en esperanza*. Buenos Aires: Ediciones Universidad del Salvador, 1992.

— *Ponerse la patria al hombro: Memoria y camino de esperanza*. Buenos Aires: Editorial Claretiana, 2004.

— *La nación por construir: Utopía, pensamiento y compromiso*. VIII Jornada de Pastoral Social. Buenos Aires: Editorial Claretiana, 2005.

— *Sobre la acusación de sí mismo*. Buenos Aires: Editorial Claretiana, 2005.

— *Corrupción y pecado: Algunas reflexiones en torno al tema de la corrupción*. Buenos Aires: Editorial Claretiana, 2005.

— *Educar, elegir la vida: Propuestas para tiempos difíciles*. Buenos Aires: Editorial Claretiana, 2005.

— *Educar: Exigencia y pasión. Desafíos para educadores cristianos*. Buenos Aires: Editorial Claretiana, 2006.

— *El verdadero poder es el servicio*. Buenos Aires: Editorial Claretiana, 2007.

— *Nosotros como ciudadanos, nosotros como pueblo. Hacia un Bicentenario en justicia y solidaridad 2010-2016*. Buenos Aires: Editorial Claretiana, 2011.

— *Mente abierta, corazón creyente*. Buenos Aires: Editorial Claretiana, 2012.

— *En Él solo la esperanza: Ejercicios espirituales a los obispos españoles*. Madrid: Biblioteca de Autores Cristianos, 2013.

— *Papa Francisco: Pilares de un pontificado. Las grandes líneas del Magisterio del Cardenal Jorge Mario Bergoglio*. Madrid: San Pablo, 2013.

— and Abraham Skorka, *Sobre el cielo y la tierra*. Buenos Aires and New York: Random House Mondadori, 2010.

Selected Writings about Cardinal Jorge Mario Bergoglio

De Vedia, Mariano. *Francisco el Papa del pueblo: La primera biografía del hombre que quiere cambiar la Iglesia.* Buenos Aires: Planeta, 2013.

Elphick, Winston H. *Francisco repara mi Iglesia: Dios aleteando sobre la Iglesia que camina, construye y confiesa la fe del siglo XXI.* Santiago: Fundación Iglesia Educa and Decamino Editores, 2013.

Fritz, James. *Pope to the Poor: The Life and Times of Pope Francis (Jorge Mario Bergoglio).* BookCaps Study Guides at www.bookcaps.com 2013.

Gaeta, Saverio. *Papa Francisco: Su vida y sus desafíos.* Buenos Aires: San Pablo, 2013.

Himitian, Evangelina. *Francisco: El Papa de la gente.* Buenos Aires: Aguilar, Altea, Taurus, Alfaguara, 2013.

Medina, José. Francisco: *El Papa de todos, vida, semblanza, pensamientos.* Buenos Aires: Editorial Bonum, 2013.

Romero, Antonio. *Biografía del Papa Francisco – No oficial (Jorge Mario Bergoglio).* www.fotolia.com 2013.

Rubin, Sergio and Francesca Ambrogetti. *El jesuita: La historia de Francisco, el Papa argentino.* Buenos Aires: Vergara Grupo Zeta, 2013. Originally published as *El Jesuita*, 2010.

Index